To Lillie —

Best wishes —

Gene Allen

Other books by Steve Allen

Funny People
Bop Fables
Fourteen for Tonight
The Funny Men
Wry on the Rocks
The Girls on the Tenth Floor
The Question Man
Mark It and Strike It
Not All of Your Laughter, Not All Your Tears
Letter to a Conservative
The Ground Is Our Table
Bigger Than a Breadbox
A Flash of Swallows
The Wake
Princess Snip-Snip and the Puppykittens
Curses
What to Say When It Rains
Schmock! Schmock!
Meetings of Minds: Volumes 1 and 2
Chopped-Up Chinese
Ripoff: The Corruption that Plagues America
"Explaining China"
The Talk Show Murders
Beloved Son: A Story of the Jesus Cults

STEVE ALLEN

STEIN AND DAY/*Publishers*/New York

First published in 1982
Copyright © 1982 by Steve Allen
All rights reserved
Designed by Louis A. Ditizio
Printed in the United States of America
STEIN AND DAY/ *Publishers*
Scarborough House
Briarcliff Manor, N.Y. 10510

Library of Congress Cataloging in Publication Date

Allen, Steve, 1921-
  More funny people.

  Continues: Funny people
  1. Comedians—United States.   I. Title.
PN 2285.A43   1982   792.7′028′0922   82-42553
ISBN   0-8128-2884-4

To Jayne, for providing an environment within which I can work

Contents

Acknowledgments

Most of those who helpfully provided information and opinion on the various comedians this book concentrates on are mentioned in the text, usually in the context of quoted material for attribution. Among those who are not, I wish to thank first Jeffry "Flash" Freundlich of my office staff for his valuable assistance with research, for reminding me of gaps in the various narratives, and his insightful editorial suggestions, as well as assistance in typing what must have seemed to him endless drafts of the manuscript.

Ethel Saylor and Loretta Lynn have done yeoman—or yeowoman— service in transcribing the original dictated tapes. Dawn Berry, my personal secretary, has been helpful in overseeing the performance of tasks more directly connected with the manuscript. And in New York, Jill Neimark, and Sol Stein of Stein and Day have rendered important editorial assistance.

Some who provided information did so on the understanding that their names would not be used. I am grateful to them, in any event.

Lastly, I thank the comedians themselves, a number of whom were kind enough to contribute biographical data, examples of their sketches and monologues, and answers to questions put to them.

Before many more years have passed, a number of those written about here will no longer be living. A few are already dead. But each has made truly significant contributions to the art of comedy. By means of this book—among many others—the work of such gifted funnymen and women will perhaps be remembered and understood, longer than might otherwise have been the case.

(There is incidentally, no significance to the order in which the chapters appear; it is simply alphabetical.)

Introduction by Larry Gelbart

In his previous study of comedians, *Funny People,* Steve Allen stated that he does all his writing by dictation. This book, being his twenty-sixth to date, proves he's a great dictator. The jacket further informed us that he has also composed 4,000 songs. Actually, we're a lot alike, Allen and I. To date, I've heard 4,000 songs and read 25 books.

In *Funny People,* which like most of his work appears effortless, Allen gave us an in-depth look at eighteen American comedians, some living, some dead, some a little bit of each, and comments on a score of others. In the fifties, he wrote a book called *The Funny Men,* about a number of then-popular comics. He intended to use the title "More Funny Men," but that was no longer appropriate once he decided to include a chapter on Lily Tomlin, proving that it is only when a woman is added that men become people.

To read both *Funny People* and *More Funny People* is to rediscover that Steve Allen is a one-man meeting of the minds. Who else can quote with such ease such disparate wits and sages as Woody, Groucho, Plato, Da Vinci, and Dr. Johnson? And all in the service of profiling not necessarily those funny people Allen finds the funniest, but those people people think are funny. In the earlier study they ranged from Andy Kaufman and Robin Williams, back to W. C. Fields and Jimmy Durante, with side trips for comments on the work of the Rickleses and Buttonses, the Murrays and the Youngmans—or is it the Youngmen? Allen writes about each with care, with insight and with a perception honed by his own experiences—personal as well as professional—with the people who populate these pages.

Allen writes, "Actors are not particularly generous." (Sorry about that, Mr. President.) Either Allen is mistaken or else he's not really an actor because I find him very generous. This book is filled with his appreciation of the work of his subjects. Allen is a wonderful audience. He is in very good company. So is Milton Berle. So was Jack Benny. If

you should happen to say something truly amusing in Allen's presence—
or witty or even the right kind of silly—his laughter comes free and easy,
ungrudgingly. He is not one of those in our business who will say
"Great," or "Fun-nee," or stamp their feet on hearing a good line—
anything not to laugh out loud and thereby admit that someone has half
a wit more than they do. Steve Allen can be and has been reduced to
helplessness, on-the-floor helplessness, by more than one comic. Sometimes it's hard to know whether to just go on being funny with Steve or to
give him CPR.

But he's not a pushover. Not in person, nor in his book. After a
lifetime spent in the pursuit of laughter, he knows what he doesn't like,
and that he makes very clear. For sure, off is not his favorite color. His
admiration of the new, younger comics is apparent—there is no generation gap where he's concerned—but he is not a fan of the gratuitous
vulgarity, the 4-, 6-, 8-, 10- and 12-letter words that a good many of them
employ. Actually, I like the book best when Allen takes his glove off one
or two fingers and points out what he doesn't particularly admire about
certain performers. He has a sharp critical sense; I wish he'd criticize
more. He has the ability to do so in a constructive manner.

What I do like is that he does not forget to mention a number of
comedy writers who have helped, and continue to help, make a great
many of the people he writes about funny. We don't generally read about
comedy writers unless they become comics themselves or they're lucky
enough to make the obituary column in *Variety*.

Another aspect I found noteworthy in Allen's two new books on
comedy—I mean, besides their existence . . . my God, when does this
man sleep?—was his control, his holding back from punching, being
funny himself, letting his subjects hold center stage, especially admirable
since it would have been so easy to try to upstage them, top them. They
weren't, after all, there to protect themselves.

From his chapter on Groucho—and his words about the great man's
last days are quite sad to read—"To his sort of mind, words are just not
what they were to everyone else. They are rubbery, many-sided globs of
thought that can be knocked about into all sorts of shapes." That's about
as good an analysis and definition of Groucho's gift as we're ever likely to
get. Those same words are true about Allen, but it is to his credit that he
never competes with those he's writing about, although the temptation
must have always been there.

What he does do is offer us the backgrounds, the influences, and motivations as well as samples of material that make the men and women in this work the funny people they are. And he does it with the skill and expertise we've come to expect from a man whose energy, industry, and productivity make an ant colony look like a home for the infirm.

In the present book Allen directs his attention to Bob Hope, Milton Berle, Fred Allen, John Belushi, the often-overlooked Martha Raye, and other leading comics who have helped us all in our pursuit of happiness. Once again, Allen's perceptions and observations are enhanced by his knowledge of these people onstage, offstage, and even at the Stage Delicatessen.

In his earlier studies of humor, Allen has marvelled at the fact that so many funny people are Jewish (males) and suggests it's possibly "because they have more trouble—and trouble is often the heart of fun."

Let me tell you, Steve, as one who is one of them, a Jewish male, who starts life by receiving the unkindest cut of all, expects the worst from then on and is rarely disappointed. If no one else is inclined to give him a bad time, he will do it to himself and then make light of his pain, real and/or imagined. He will find a cloud in every silver lining. He will tell you to have a nice day, knowing with all his heart that that's impossible. If your enemies don't spoil it, your friends will. Jews. It's not that it only hurts when we laugh—we only laugh *when* we hurt. And that's pretty much all the time.

Writing of Groucho (forgive me for harpo-ing on Groucho's chapter—his influence on me is endless), Allen says, "He was a humorist, helpless in the grip of his talent." That is, to me, the sharpest of all Allen's observations. For, in truth, one doesn't have a sense of humor. It has you. And it is a gift you can neither purchase nor refuse. Anyone who is truly funny cannot choose to be otherwise, but only hope to become the best possible medium he can be for his own irrepressible form of expression.

The best of the funny people view life through a highly individual prescription. They tell us what we already know, but illuminate that truth with such wit and color that we see it in an altogether new and entertaining way. Example: David Letterman on the subject of Andy Kaufman: "Sometimes, when you look in Andy's eyes, you get the feeling someone else is driving."

So it's not enough just to be Jewish or gentile or black or even a woman. You need that divine spark. And Steve Allen, comedian, author, composer, lyricist, musician, moderator, producer, director, thinker, actor, critic, philosopher, laugher, speaker, listener, host, confrere, interviewer, interviewee, researcher, scholar, star, and fan, has given us a closer look at those so blessed, even as he himself is.

Larry Gelbart has produced the TV series "M*A*S*H," and written *Oh God!* and *A Funny Thing Happened on the Way to the Forum*. He is the recipient of both the Emmy and Tony awards.

Abbott and
Costello

*W*E NEVER SEEM ABLE TO DECIDE whether we wish to hear truth or legend about heroes. The part of ourselves that is appealingly naive and thirsts for the glamour of leadership, tends to romanticize political officials, military leaders, religious figures, artists, and other celebrities past and present. The part of ourselves that is disrespectful of authority, envious and small-minded, has an appetite for information about the great, whether true or false, that will demean their stature and make them, God help us, more like ourselves.

As regards one type of popular hero, the comedian, there is an odd resistance to perceiving him in his actual three-dimensional form. He— or she—makes us laugh. That is enough. We are made uncomfortable by reports that, in addition to being funny, the popular favorite may also be an alcoholic, a habitual adulterer, emotionally unstable, a drug addict, incredibly stingy, or a petulant egotist.

It doesn't seem to matter much if the comedian is not one of our personal favorites. But if he is, the very fact that we are habituated to laughing at him means we have made an ego investment in him; we have put the stamp of our approval and affection upon him. We therefore may feel personally betrayed if we learn something about him of which we disapprove on moral, political, or other grounds.

Some people were never able to laugh at Charlie Chaplin—the greatest comedian of his time—after they learned of his leftist sympathies. Others were never as amused by W. C. Fields after learning that politically he was a bitter reactionary, a Roosevelt-hater, and shamefully ungenerous.

In the first flush of that truly Golden Age of television comedy, the 1950s, comedians were enormously popular, highly paid, blessed with good ratings: in a word, true cultural heroes. Then writers and producers who knew these entertainers personally began to paint less flattering portraits. The film *A Face in the Crowd*, TV dramatic shows, a host of harsh journalistic assessments signaled that the honeymoon-is-over stage had been reached.

Television itself eventually produced a fully-shaded portrait of Bud Abbott and Lou Costello, one of the most popular comedy teams of the 1940s and '50s, though their chief success was realized in motion pictures rather than TV. It could hardly be a surprise that their reality was not the same as their public image. More so than with any other pair of modern comics, that public image was like that of comic-strip characters. There was Costello—the funny one, the frustrated child who wore silly clothes and seemed incredibly stupid and gullible. There was Abbott—the glib, fast-talking con-man. Neither spoke in a realistic, human way. They were always make-believe characters, almost as removed from reality as mime clowns or Punch and Judy dolls. In most of their films there was never any character development, rational story outline, enlightenment, or change of heart. The plot lines were merely devices that served to justify inclusion of three or four of their standard burlesque routines, which in turn reinforced the cartoon image of the pair.

The truth, of course, was unrelated to this on-screen image. Each man had his full share of tragedy, and, by the time they achieved a measure of success, their eventual break-up was a foregone conclusion. Although personal differences never intruded into their smooth onstage or before-the-camera functioning, in private there were years of bitter in-fighting over billing, the division of the team's earnings, and so forth.

And yet, if a comedian wishes to have full-length biographies written about him it is not enough that he be funny. It is at least as necessary that the details of his personal life be essentially tragic. Otherwise there would be little story. Not only is tragedy concerned with unfortunate doings, obviously enough, but comedy, too, deals with tragic raw material. Even the Bible—although it is officially referred to as Good News—deals with bad news in far more voluminous detail.

So in discussing Abbott and Costello there would be little to say if all there was to write about was how funny they were. In fact, the critical fraternity generally gave them the shortest possible shrift. The insightful James Agee referred to them as "semiskilled laborers at best." It can hardly be expected, after all, that a generation of critics predisposed to appreciate either the physical genius of Charlie Chaplin, Buster Keaton, or Laurel and Hardy, or the word-oriented humor of Robert Benchley, Groucho Marx, or Fred Allen would be particularly impressed by the simplistic, earthy humor of Abbott and Costello's burlesque sketches.

Nevertheless, Bud and Lou became great popular favorites, chiefly with the same audience that loved *Ma and Pa Kettle, The Beverly Hillbillies, Petticoat Junction, Gilligan's Island,* and similar fare.

Incidentally, given the common interpretation of the word *burlesque,* it may surprise some of today's younger generation to learn that Abbott and Costello always did a clean act, even in burlesque's latter days when other components of their shows became markedly raunchier.

William "Bud" Abbott was born in Asbury Park, New Jersey, on October 2, 1895, the son of a bareback rider and an advance man for the Barnum and Bailey circus. After completing the fourth grade, Bud left school to earn money at Coney Island. Working there seems to have had some effect on his later character: One of the jobs he held was that of shill, and there always was a slight flavor of carney huckster to his "straight" character.

After a couple of years of knocking about Coney Island, Bud took a job as assistant treasurer at the Casino burlesque theater in Brooklyn. There he could watch the great comics of the day perform, and study their style, timing, and delivery. One funnyman with whom Bud was particularly impressed was a comic juggler named W. C. Fields.

His career was soon interrupted by an event that might have come from an Abbott and Costello movie script: he was shanghaied. One night after the final show at the Casino, a gentleman bought Bud a drink. He gratefully accepted and woke up aboard a Norwegian steamer already miles out at sea.

After an interim of shoveling coal, cooking, and teaching Norwegian sailors to speak English, Bud returned to New York and his job at the Casino theater.

For the next few years Abbott traveled around the country on the burlesque circuit—as treasurer, manager, director, and in one instance even producer, on money borrowed from an uncle connected with Tammany Hall in New York. But he stayed behind the scenes, watching, absorbing what performers good and bad could teach him.

In the lives of many entertainers there is a particular moment characterized by the realization that "I can do that," which propels them into their career. For Bud Abbott, the moment came while he was managing the National Theater in Detroit. The leading straight man in the show decided he was too funny merely to feed lines to his partner. Unhappily, the audience did not agree. Bud, watching backstage, thought to himself, "I can be a straight man." The would-be comic was fired, and Bud stepped on stage for the first time.

For several years he traveled the circuit teamed with his wife, Betty, and then with several different comics, never finding the ideal partner. But his reputation grew, and word spread through the burlesque world that Bud Abbott was a pro.

In those days a straight man was often more highly regarded than a comic, and generally received both 60 percent of the "split" and top billing (as in "Abbott and Costello"). It's no longer widely recognized how difficult "playing straight" really is. Bud was one of the best at the underrated art. He had a superb ability to pull back the manic Costello from the brink of going overboard and losing the audience, to propel their routines into a smooth and seamless track with impeccable timing, and to always make it look effortless—and consequently make Costello look even funnier. Ultimately the very ease of Abbott's talent made it difficult for many to see how really good he was.

Lou Costello was born Louis Francis Cristillo on March 3, 1906, in Paterson, New Jersey. His father, Sebastian, was an Italian immigrant who worked for Prudential Insurance most of his life. His mother, Helen, was Irish-American.

Early in life Lou had two main interests: athletics and movies. He claimed to have seen Chaplin's *Shoulder Arms* 25 times, until he could perform every scene by rote, and he once won first prize in a Chaplin contest; no small feat considering his stocky build. After he became famous, Lou was more than repaid for his dedication when Chaplin publicly praised him as the best clown in films in his day. Chaplin, as it happens, was mistaken; Red Skelton was Lou's superior.

Because we remember only the fat and helpless middle-aged cherub of the movies, it is difficult to believe that Costello, as a young man, was a formidable athlete, a good basketball player in spite of his 5'4" height, and three times the state champion at foul-shooting. As an amateur boxer, fighting under the name of Lou King, he won 11 out of 12 fights—the twelfth was a draw—before his father convinced him he should retire from the ring.

At the age of 20, Lou decided to try his luck in Hollywood. He wanted nothing so much as to be in pictures, and his preoccupation with getting into movies continued until he did so. He equipped himself with $200 borrowed from his father and the beginnings of an act mostly consisting of a cigar and a new name. Lou's older brother, Pat, had changed from Cristillo to Costello when he began to work as a band leader. Lou followed suit and, with a pal, headed west. Although he got work as a set carpenter and stunt man, Lou remained undiscovered. Eventually, nearly broke and discouraged, he headed for home. As fate would have it, he ran out of money in Kansas and could not continue his journey. Hearing of an opening for a "Dutch" comic at a St. Joseph theater, Lou talked himself into the job.

In the early days of the century, when a great many American immigrants had the accents of their homelands, comic characters who spoke in thick dialect were a staple of vaudeville. Even Americans with accents of their own found it excruciatingly funny to hear other foreign-sounding voices mangle grammar and mispronounce words. Performers who could do a German accent—invariably referred to as "Dutch"—were particularly popular. While Lou was never a dialect specialist, he had heard most of the immigrant accents in his hometown of Paterson, New Jersey, and could do them. He got valuable experience on this first job and a year later was confident enough to apply for work at New York's Orpheum Theater, where he was taken on as a burlesque second banana.

During the next few years Costello built his reputation, steadily working upward in terms of both salary and the class of the houses he played. Soon he was a "Top Banana," or leading comic, working with a straight partner.

One day in 1936, Lou and his partner of the moment, Joe Lyons, were playing the Eltinge Theater in New York. As Lou came offstage a dapper, nattily attired man complimented him on his performance. The man was Bud Abbott, also playing the bill with a partner. According to one version of the story, the two had been watching each other perform for quite a while, each admiring the other.

After a short period of casual friendship, the two arranged to have dinner with each other and their wives after the last show one night. Seated at Reuben's restaurant, they agreed to try a partnership.

Soon after joining forces, Abbott and Costello met two men who would have a tremendous influence on their career. The first was Eddie Sherman, a then small-time booker with large ideas. Sherman became their manager and later won for them the first ever "percentage of future earnings clause" in their contract with Universal Studios. The clause, virtually invented by Sherman, earned Bud and Lou a great deal of money and changed movie-making itself significantly.

Sherman convinced Bud and Lou that burlesque was dying. He was correct about this, too. After a series of successful bookings, Sherman placed them with the William Morris Agency, which got them their first appearance on Kate Smith's radio program. The rest, as the saying goes, is history. Listeners demanded the return of the new team. Soon they were appearing regularly and eventually had their own show, which led to movies and later to television—skillfully guided by Sherman.

The other man Bud and Lou hired at about this time was John Grant, who wrote or refined most of their material—including "Who's On First"—until just before the team broke up in 1956. He left after refusing to sign a loyalty oath for Lou, who—as a political reactionary—was a fervent supporter of Senator Joseph McCarthy.

Sherman had steered the team out of burlesque just in time. The nation was still suffering from the Great Depression and many vaudeville and burlesque houses were going out of business. In an attempt to revive popular interest, burlesque shows were getting dirtier. Far from having the desired effect, the trend produced a perhaps-inevitable reaction. New York City shut down its burlesque houses because of the controversy created by the increased reliance on off-color jokes and near nudity. But by the time the burlesque houses started closing down, Bud and Lou had made inroads into other areas of the entertainment world. Within two years of their first appearance on Kate Smith's radio show they were given the opportunity to do the summer replacement show for the popular Fred Allen. Just as radio success had led to increased stature in films for Bob Hope, Red Skelton, and Burns and Allen, among others, the success of Bud and Lou's own radio comedy series, which started in 1941, led to a film career.

Their first movie was a third-rate production for Universal Pictures titled *One Night In The Tropics*. Generally, even talented performers do not make a strong impression in a weak film. But in this instance Bud and Lou were doing their own material and, consequently, looked good. Feeling that they were worth another try, Universal starred them in a low-budget comedy called *Buck Privates*. Because it became a big hit, it assured their continued film activity. In time they made 38 pictures together.

Although their greatest success involved written and rehearsed material, Abbott and Costello were quite capable of comic inventiveness, as Bob Thomas suggests in his biography, *Bud & Lou*. Early in their career they were in a revue titled *The Streets of Paris,* starring vaudeville great Bobby Clark. Clark was known as a man who had never been topped, and one of the great authorities on comedy. It was said that he knew every joke in the world and was never at a loss for an appropriate gag or comeback. Bud and Lou managed to stump him. As Thomas tells the story:

> During an out-of-town performance, Clark happened to drop his beret. Lou grabbed a hat rack, Bud produced a cane, and together they played the beret like a hockey puck. Clark was temporarily awed.

The ad-libbed bit of business naturally got a big laugh. The boys decided to keep the bit in the show, and at the next performance, when Bud scored the beret, Clark got his own back again by whipping out a whistle and blowing a shrill blast to signal a goal.

After making four films in twelve months Bud and Lou were aware that, if they had not exactly bowled over the critics, they had at least won the hearts of moviegoers. Their films did very well at the box office and, because of their percentage-of-profits arrangement, the boys were well paid for their services.

But success either made Lou aware of his importance or led him to exaggerate it—it is not clear which. In any case, the long-simmering resentment between the two men began to come to the surface. Teams like Abbott and Costello are subject to ill feeling between the partners. The comedian knows that he is, after all, the funny one; yet he is frustrated that he cannot be funny alone. The straight man knows that he, personally, is not funny, but he is also aware that his partner cannot function without him. Each, therefore, tends to think privately, "without me, there's no act."

As they reached the apex of their fame, Lou called Sherman in and told him to tell Abbott that "From now on we split our movie dough 60-40, or I don't work with him." Abbott was, of course, furious, but gave in on the point, perhaps out of guilt that he had previously been getting more than his share. But Costello also demanded that the name of the team be changed to "Costello and Abbott."

Universal flatly refused, but the demand revealed the growing anger between the two men. Gambling also became a major problem. Stud poker was usually the game, and the stakes were high—$10 a card and up. Gambling created a big problem on the film sets because the men wanted to do only one take of their scenes and get right back to the card games.

Another problem emerged when Lou began to take furniture from the studio. Costello never denied that he had the furniture shipped to his house; he simply refused to return it. His attitude seemed like that of the tourist who feels that inasmuch as hotels are taking advantage of him by charging high prices he is therefore entitled to steal ashtrays, towels, sheets, or bedspreads.

The other side of this peculiar coin is that both Bud and Lou were remarkably generous. They often presented lavish gifts to coworkers.

Throughout the early '40s Bud and Lou almost single-handedly kept Universal in business. When World War II began they worked hard on the War Bonds program, too. But in 1943, during a Bond tour, Lou became seriously ill with rheumatic fever. For months he was bedridden, unable to work or even to stand. November 4 of that year, soon after the doctors had said he could return to work, was the worst day of Lou Costello's life. His infant son fell into the family's backyard pool and drowned. Although Lou was scheduled to do a radio show that night, friends and associates felt he would be unable to work. Jimmy Durante, Red Skelton, and Bob Hope, among others, were standing by, ready to fill in. The studio audience was not aware of the tragedy, but co-performers were. Lou insisted that the show must go on.

Never fully recovering from the blow, he became increasingly bitter, in one instance violently berating a producer who had hired comic actor William Bendix to work in a scene with him, "Don't you ever put anybody who's funnier than me in a picture of mine!"

Bob Thomas describes the team's relationship at this stage.

> As their success grew, Bud and Lou no longer lunched together; instead, they gathered their own sycophants separately, each table competing to produce the most laughter. The competition of Bud and Lou spread to other areas. Each seemed intent on building the bigger showplace. After Lou put up his playroom on Longridge, Bud erected on his Woodley property a building the size of a restaurant. It had a bar that stretched the entire length of the room; passersby sometimes dropped in and ordered drinks, believing the place to be a public tavern. And the oblivious Bud served them.
>
> Lou put a large swimming pool in the backyard of his property; Bud built one that was longer. Bud bought a restaurant on Ventura Boulevard, the Backstage, where he could entertain his friends from burlesque. Lou purchased a night club on Fairfax Avenue, the Band Box. Lou invested in a yacht to take his family sailing on weekends. Bud rented a yacht, making sure it was six feet longer that Lou's.

The sort of half-joking rivalry that had always been a part of the team's offstage relationship in time became deadly serious. Lou's ego seemed to grow, making him at times uncontrollable. Bud's drinking got worse, and the team began the slip from peak popularity. The bitterness and distance between the two men intensified. Lou several times threatened to go it alone, but always came back when he cooled down.

In 1956 Abbott and Costello played Las Vegas with a revue called *Miltown Revisited*. It was well received at its opening, but problems developed between the first show and the midnight performance. Bud had been gambling and, as is the custom in Las Vegas, had been plied with drinks while he sat at the gaming tables. By the time the curtain went up, at midnight, he was too intoxicated to know where he was. This, the last appearance Abbott and Costello ever made together, consisted in part of Bud, in a stupor, being slapped by a frantic Lou, who repeated cues over and over. According to biographer Thomas, the two met after the show, agreed to go their separate ways, and never saw each other again.

Lou Costello garnered additional fame by having his Hollywood home lavishly decorated every Christmas for the delight of the neighborhood children, passersby, and tourists. On two occasions I joined the large number of those who drove past the Costello home to marvel at the hundreds of multicolored Christmas lights, the large roof-top Santa Claus with reindeer, the angels, music, and general holiday glamour. George Gobel, who lived across Longridge Avenue from Lou at the time, put an amusing sign on his front lawn which read, "See our display across the street."

Costello's last few years were a nightmare of gambling debts, arguments, outrageous demands and threats, conflicts with studio executives, and total financial irresponsibility. Abbott and Costello had been among the highest paid performers in Hollywood history, but in their last years they were in debt to the government because they had been incredibly careless in paying income taxes. Money, possessions, and health—all were, in time, gone with the wind.

Perhaps somebody ought to open a school for performers in their early twenties, with a course called "Success—Its Rewards and Dangers."

I had the pleasure of visiting Lou on a few occasions in the early 1950s. He was a pleasant man but had a personality unlike that of most professional comedians. There was no wit to him, nor even an antic playfulness. But he was likeable, and had a naive, unpretentious child-ishness that accounted in part for his popularity.

My first professional contact with Lou was in October 1956 when he and Bud formally presented a gold recording of their classic "Who's On First?" routine to the National Baseball Hall of Fame in a special appearance before a national audience on my show over NBC-TV. In 1957-58, after Costello broke up his long partnership with Abbott, he appeared as a solo guest with us several times, doing routines with our regular gang of comics—Louis Nye, Don Knotts, and Tom Poston.

Our shows were presented live and with relatively little rehearsal. Lou fit perfectly into that type of format as his vaudeville and burlesque background had given him the sort of experience that enabled him to create as he went along—to some extent, at least—going outside the boundaries of the prepared script or sketch. I had seen some of the Abbott and Costello films when the team was in its heyday in the 1940s, but in the late 1950s, working in television comedy, I was better able to appreciate Lou's comedy gifts.

When we worked together he was charming, modest, soft-spoken, genial, business-like, not given to the sort of fraternity-house horsing around that the rest of us on the show—Louis Nye, Tom Poston, Don Knotts, Bill Dana, Gabe Dell, Dayton Allen, et al—engaged in.

In late summer of 1982 I agreed to serve as master of ceremonies at a dinner honoring Andy Williams. The producers of the event asked for a copy of one of my old shows on which Andy had worked as a singer, and I happened to see the show that one of my staff people selected. When I noticed that it was one on which Lou Costello was featured as a guest, I sat down and watched it. He did a marvelous hospital sketch, working with Don Knotts, Tom Poston, Louis Nye and the rest of our comedy gang. At one point a tall, bossy, black-haired woman—playing the part of a nurse—came on and brow-beat Lou unmercifully. I suddenly realized that the bit player was the very talented Bea Arthur, who a good many years later would star in her own television series, "Maude." Lou was delightful in the sketch. He worked in a very loose, relaxed manner and did marvelous takes, falls, jumps-with-fear, and other physical schtick in his capacity as the butt of various kinds of abuse. Although it has rarely been commented on in critiques of his work, Lou had a very winning smile, quite unlike the plastic show-biz smiles that are more common.

As for Bud Abbott, there are always difficulties to evaluating a "straight man." Such performers are usually not perceived as funny themselves. The fact is that although comedians are such a rare breed that there are only a few hundred on earth, good straight men—or women—are extremely rare. Lou Costello was not one of those comedians who was funny alone. He had to be in some sort of situation to manifest his funniness and therefore required the services of someone like Bud Abbott.

Some comedians are good at playing straight. Jack Benny was one of the best—so effective, in fact, that through much of his career he made assorted singers, announcers, film stars, band leaders, etc., seem much funnier than they were. Fred Allen, Milton Berle, Dean Martin, Dan Rowan, and Jayne Meadows are among some of the best straight "men" comedy has produced.

Abbott's work was physically quite aggressive. He did not invent the gimmick of physically abusing the comic, nor was he the only one to do it in his time. The origin of this element is lost in the mists of history. Aggressive behavior was an important part of silent screen comedy— witness Laurel and Hardy slapping each other, hitting each other with their hats, and kicking each other in the seat of the pants—not to mention the constant pummeling by Punch and Judy puppets. Such schticks were an important element in burlesque, vaudeville, and minstrel comedy before the turn of the century. Even today one can see traces of such style in Milton Berle's method of playing straight: When the partner he is working with says something particularly outrageous, Milton grabs him by the arm or by the shoulder-pad of his jacket and yanks him around as if to say, "Shape up." It is the job of the comic, of course, to exaggerate the vigor of the movement, to pretend to be even more physically abused than he is. Straight men have also resorted to assorted slaps in the face, yanks on the necktie or jacket, and shoves. A generation of comedians in the 1920s and '30s willingly submitted to such abuse because the physical business always got laughs; being the butt of such attacks made the comic character more sympathetic.

The style is so ingrained, particularly in comedians over 60 with a New York background, that even some ventriloquists work in the same way, slapping their dummies in the face, spinning their heads around, grabbing them by the shoulders, screaming "Now stop that!" Paul Winchell and Jerry Mahoney, for example, perform in this way. By way of contrast, Edgar Bergen always worked gently with Charlie McCarthy. Charlie seemed to be the dominant, aggressive one. So important are such bits of physical business to some performers that the slaps, blows, yanks, and shoves are emphasized by "rim shots," audio punctuation by the drummer.

It may seem pointless to subject "Who's On First?" to analysis. But it is instructive to do so, nevertheless, partly because the routine is (a) eminently successful and considered a classic but (b) one of the dumbest ever written. No one seems to know who created the routine in the first place. Abbott and Costello never claimed to. It seems to be one of those ancient sketches—common in the world of burlesque—that Bud and Lou simply picked up from John Grant and gave their own stamp. If it had never been previously created but were submitted next Tuesday to any professional comedian, he would not only refuse to buy it, but would be so prejudiced against its creator that he would probably be unwilling ever to look at anything else the man or woman presented.

Consider, first, the premise or philosophical rationale of the routine. Abbott says, "You know, strange as it may seem, they give ballplayers nowadays very peculiar names.

Right off the bat, the routine is preposterous. Nobody has ever given ballplayers peculiar surnames. Ballplayers—like other human beings— occasionally have odd nicknames. But this routine is about surnames. As if it sensibly buttressed his case, Abbott proceeds to say, "Now, on the St. Louis team, *Who's* on first, *What's* on second, *I Don't Know's* on third. . . ."

Most routines that are eventually going to escalate a theoretical argument to absurd lengths do so by first stating a point or two that are believable, referring to something that has already happened or could easily happen. But in the case of "Who's On First?" the argument is preposterous at the very outset.

If one tries, as a theoretical exercise, to "make sense" of the routine, it could have been that at some time in the past—perhaps in the last century—there was an exchange between vaudeville comedians based on early American exposure to Chinese names. *Hu* is an actual name in Chinese. So there could have been a realistic conversation which went as follows:

STRAIGHT MAN: You know, there are a lot of Chinese getting off the boats these days in San Francisco. I was down at the docks yesterday and I saw *Hu* get off first, *Hee* get off second, and *How* get off third.

COMIC: Wait a minute. I want you to tell me the names of the Chinamen who got off the boat.

STRAIGHT MAN: I'm telling you. *Hu* got off first—

COMIC: That's what I'm asking you.

STRAIGHT MAN: And that's what I'm telling you.

COMIC: You're telling me what?

STRAIGHT MAN: I'm telling you *Hu* got off first.

COMIC: Who got off first?

STRAIGHT MAN: That's right.

COMIC: What's right?

STRAIGHT MAN: No. *Hua* [What] was still back on the boat.

COMIC: He was?

STRAIGHT MAN: No, not *Hee*.

COMIC: Who's he?

STRAIGHT MAN: No, *Hu* isn't he. Hee is he and Hu is Hu!

COMIC: How do I know who is who?

STRAIGHT MAN: Oh, do you know *How*?

COMIC: Do I know how to *what*?!

(etc.)

I'm assuming it will never be possible to determine if such speculation is related to the origin of "Who's On First?," but the hypothesis suggested is not unreasonable. What *is* utterly unreasonable is the routine as Abbott and Costello did it.

WHO'S ON FIRST?

ABBOTT: You know, strange as it may seem, they give ballplayers nowadays very peculiar names. . . . Now, on the St. Louis team Who's on first, What's on second, I Don't Know is on third—

COSTELLO: That's what I want to find out. I want you to tell me the names of the fellows on the St. Louis team.

ABBOTT: I'm telling you. Who's on first, What's on second, I Don't Know is on third—

COSTELLO: You know the fellows' names?

ABBOTT: Yes.

COSTELLO: Well, then, who's playin' first?

ABBOTT: Yes.

COSTELLO: I mean the fellow's name on first base.

ABBOTT: Who.

COSTELLO: The fellow playin' first base.

ABBOTT: Who.

COSTELLO: The guy on first base.

ABBOTT: Who is on first.

COSTELLO: Well, what are you askin' me for?

ABBOTT: I'm not asking you—I'm telling you. Who is on first.

COSTELLO: I'm asking you—who's on first?

ABBOTT: That's the man's name!

COSTELLO: That's who's name?

ABBOTT: Yes.

COSTELLO: Well, go ahead tell me!

ABBOTT: Who.

COSTELLO: Have you got a first baseman on first?

ABBOTT: Certainly.

COSTELLO: Then who's playing first?

ABBOTT: Absolutely.

COSTELLO: Well, all I'm trying to find out is what's the guy's name on first base.

ABBOTT: Oh, no, no. What is on second base.

COSTELLO: I'm not asking you who's on second.

ABBOTT: Who's on first.

COSTELLO: That's what I'm trying to find out.

ABBOTT: Now, take it easy.

COSTELLO: What's the guy's name on first base?

ABBOTT: What's the guy's name on second base.

COSTELLO: I'm not askin' ya who's on second.

ABBOTT: Who's on first.

COSTELLO: I don't know.

ABBOTT: He's on third.

COSTELLO: If I mentioned the third baseman's name, who did I say is playing third?

ABBOTT: No, Who's playing first.

COSTELLO: Stay offa first, will ya?

ABBOTT: Well, what do you want me to do?

COSTELLO: Now, what's the guy's name on first base?

ABBOTT: What's on second.

COSTELLO: I'm not asking ya who's on second.

ABBOTT: Who's on first.

COSTELLO: I don't know.

ABBOTT: He's on third.

COSTELLO: There I go back to third again.

ABBOTT: Please. Now what is it you want to know?

COSTELLO: What is the fellow's name on third base?

ABBOTT: What is the fellow's name on second base.

COSTELLO: I'm not askin' ya who's on second.

ABBOTT: Who's on first.

COSTELLO: I don't know. (*makes noises*) You got an outfield?

ABBOTT: Oh, sure.

COSTELLO: The left fielder's name?

ABBOTT: Why.

COSTELLO: I just thought I'd ask.

ABBOTT: Well, I just thought I'd tell you.

COSTELLO: Then tell me who's playing left field.

ABBOTT: Who's playing first.

COSTELLO: Stay out of the infield. I want to know what's the fellow's name in left field.

ABBOTT: What is on second.

COSTELLO: I'm not asking you who's on second.

ABBOTT: Now take it easy, take it easy.

COSTELLO: And the left fielder's name?

ABBOTT: Why.

COSTELLO: Because.

ABBOTT: Oh, he's center field.

COSTELLO: Wait a minute. You got a pitcher?

ABBOTT: Wouldn't this be a fine team without a pitcher?

COSTELLO: Tell me the pitcher's name.

ABBOTT: Tomorrow.

COSTELLO: You don't want to tell me today?

ABBOTT: I'm telling you, man.

COSTELLO: Then go ahead.

ABBOTT: Tomorrow.

COSTELLO: What time tomorrow are you gonna tell me who's pitching?

ABBOTT: Now listen. Who is not pitching. Who is on . . .

COSTELLO: I'll break your arm if you say who's on first.

ABBOTT: Then why come up here and ask?

COSTELLO: I want to know what's the pitcher's name.

ABBOTT: What's on second.

COSTELLO: Ya gotta catcher?

ABBOTT: Yes.

COSTELLO: The catcher's name?

ABBOTT: Today.

COSTELLO: Today. And Tomorrow's pitching.

ABBOTT: Yes.

COSTELLO: I'm a good catcher too, you know.

ABBOTT: I know that.

COSTELLO: I would like to catch. Tomorrow's pitching and I'm catching.

ABBOTT: Yes.

COSTELLO: Tomorrow throws the ball and the guy up bunts the ball.

ABBOTT: Yes.

COSTELLO: Now when he bunts the ball—me being a good catcher—I want to throw the guy out at first base, so I pick up the ball and throw it to who?

ABBOTT: Now, that's the first thing you've said right.

COSTELLO: I DON'T EVEN KNOW WHAT I'M TALKING ABOUT.

ABBOTT: Well, that's all you have to do.

COSTELLO: Is to throw it to first base.

ABBOTT: Yes.

COSTELLO: Now who's got it?

ABBOTT: Naturally.

COSTELLO: Who has it?

ABBOTT: Naturally.

COSTELLO: O.K.

ABBOTT: Now you've got it.

COSTELLO: I pick up the ball and I throw it to Naturally.

ABBOTT: No you don't. You throw the ball to first base.

COSTELLO: Then who gets it?

ABBOTT: Naturally.

COSTELLO: I throw the ball to Naturally.

ABBOTT: You don't. You throw it to Who.

COSTELLO: Naturally.

ABBOTT: Well, naturally. Say it that way.

COSTELLO: I said I'd throw the ball to Naturally.

ABBOTT: You don't. You throw it to Who.

COSTELLO: Naturally.

ABBOTT: Yes.

COSTELLO: So I throw the ball to first base and Naturally gets it.

ABBOTT: No. You throw the ball to first base . . .

COSTELLO: Then who gets it?

ABBOTT: Naturally.

COSTELLO: That's what I'm saying.

ABBOTT: You're not saying that.

COSTELLO: I throw the ball to first base.

ABBOTT: Then Who gets it.

COSTELLO: He *better* get it.

ABBOTT: That's it. All right now, don't get excited. Take it easy.

COSTELLO: Now I throw the ball to first base, whoever it is grabs the ball, so the guy runs to second.

ABBOTT: Uh-huh.

COSTELLO: Who picks up the ball and throws it to what. What throws it to I don't know. I don't know throws it back to tomorrow—a triple play.

ABBOTT: Yeah. It could be.

COSTELLO: Another guy gets up and it's a long fly ball to center. Why? I don't know. And I don't care.

ABBOTT: What was that?

COSTELLO: I said, I don't care.

ABBOTT: Oh, that's our shortstop.

COSTELLO: (*Makes noises—steps close to Abbott and they glare at each other*).

Only two very polished, experienced professionals could have gotten such big laughs with such an inane sketch.

Fred Allen

(OPENING OF "WHAT'S MY LINE," MARCH 18, 1956)

JOHN DALY (*standing*): This is a melancholy time for us, as I'm sure it is for you. I'm sure most of you know that during last night Fred Allen passed away.

It was our thought that tonight we would invite some of Fred's old friends here, and we'd talk about Fred and his contribution to American humor and American culture. Or perhaps we would go into the library of films, which we have excerpted, and tell something of the story of Fred Allen and the great contributions he made to our industry.

Mrs. Allen, the beloved Portland, specifically asked us not to do that. It was her feeling that if we wished to pay tribute to Fred, the best tribute we could pay him would be to do this program just as if he were here with us.

Fred was a professional performer and he did a great many shows, I'm sure, when he didn't feel like laughing. But he did them, and we're going to try to do them in that same tradition.

And so, for Arlene Francis, and Steve Allen, an old friend who was kind enough to come and help us tonight, and Dorothy Kilgallen, and Bennett Cerf, we're going to do "What's My Line" the way Fred would have liked to have it done.

ST. PATRICK'S DAY 1956 WAS ONE I have never forgotten. The day before—Friday, March 16—New York was hit by an unseasonal blizzard and on Saturday the city's Irish paraded through snow and bitter cold. One elderly Irishman that night took a stroll from which he never returned. About the time he was putting on his overcoat to go out to walk his dog, I was sitting in a room on the twelfth floor of the Waldorf-Astoria with Sid Caesar, Neil Simon, Shelly Keller, Larry Gelbart, Carl Reiner, and other members of Sid's writing staff. We had just come upstairs after attending the annual award ceremonies of the Academy of Television Arts and Sciences and were enjoying a social drink while discussing that favorite conversational topic of all comedians: comedy.

Sid told a few funny stories about his experiences on a recent trip to Europe, and then somehow the conversation got around to Fred Allen, as it often does when professional humorists get together. Sid recalled how impressed he'd been one day several years before when Fred had dropped into his theater at rehearsal time. "It was really something," he said. "Here was this guy I had listened to on the old Majestic all through my childhood years, this guy who seemed like God or somebody, and all of a sudden there he was hanging around my theater."

"What did you do?" I asked.

"Oh, just talked for a while. It was the day Truman was going through town in some big parade or something. I remember we went outside to watch him go by, and after he'd passed I said, 'Harry looks a little like he's sick,' and Fred said, 'Doesn't surprise me. He probably caught it from the country.'"

When Jayne and I left the Waldorf we drove Carl Reiner and his wife Estelle to their garage, and as we stopped for a red light at the corner of 57th Street and Seventh Avenue we saw columnist Leonard Lyons and his wife Sylvia. Since cabs were at a premium because of the blinding snowfall, we offered them a lift, and as they climbed into the car Jayne noticed that Sylvia seemed shaken. It was then that Leonard told us that Fred Allen had just died. Leonard had identified the body, and to him had fallen the grim task of telling Portland the sad news.

The following day the producers of the 1950's quiz-panel show "What's My Line?" called and asked me to fill in for Fred, who earlier had taken over my duties as resident wit after I began hosting "The Tonight Show."

The next day, Monday, Bennett Cerf, songwriter Howard Deitz, Bob Hope, Kenny Delmar, Peter Donald, critic John Crosby, novelist Herman Wouk, and Jack Benny gathered on my late-night program to pay tribute to Fred, to tell of their love and respect for him and, oddly enough at such a sad time, to laugh heartily at his remembered jokes. I remember thinking during that program what a peculiar thing it was that such a vast talent as Fred's had gone largely unhonored by television. Consider, for a moment, the background.

It is said that the entertainment field is at all times vastly overstocked with talented people and that, therefore, only a select few can get to the top, while the rest must inevitably wend their broken way into obscurity.

Like a great many popular opinions, this one is composed of one part truth and nine parts nonsense. There is only one branch of show business that appears to have more talent than can ever possibly be accommodated: the song-writing field. There are millions of people who can write a fair song in whole or in part, but the market for popular music in this country is so restricted that a stable of a dozen competent tunesmiths could easily satisfy the entire normal demand.

The illusion that there are too many talented performers in the other areas of the entertainment world is created by the great deal of hustle and bustle in agency offices, endless union membership lists, and cutthroat competition for available work. In fact, it is the very paucity of genius that explains why a good many artistically impoverished individuals achieve success anyway. There are simply too many motion pictures to be made, too many plays to be produced, too many orchestras to put together.

This recalls the classic story of an actor who went to his psychiatrist. "Doctor," he said, "you've got to help me. I have no talent, I can't sing on key, I can't dance, I don't tell funny stories, and I'm not handsome. What would you suggest?"

"Why, the solution is simplicity itself," said the doctor. "You've got to get out of show business."

"But I can't," the actor said. "I'm a star!"

Granted, then, that success is not always predicated upon ability. If every big singer in the country retired tomorrow a new crop could fill their shoes within a year. But if all the best funny men and women in the business were taken away from us, it would be a long time before the pain of their loss would be eased. Hollywood can find plenty of pretty faces to throw upon its screens, the record industry will always come up with at least acceptable voices, casting directors can thumb through card indexes for various sorts of talents, but the true comedian is rare. Until the mid-70s, almost the entire job of making America laugh was handled by a small group of about fifty people. Thus it is particularly puzzling that Fred Allen, considered by many to be the group's leading wit, was out of work by 1956, as far as television was concerned. He was retired to the status of grand-old-man of contemporary comedy.

You almost get angry at the whole medium, wondering why it couldn't seem to accommodate a man who could say of California, "It's a great place to live, if you're an orange."

Television needed a man who could say of George Jessel, "Georgie loves after-dinner speaking so much he starts a speech at the mere sight of bread crumbs."

When the price of milk in New York City rose to twenty-two cents a quart, it was Fred who said, "Milk hasn't been so high since the cow jumped over the moon."

In Lindy's one night, Leonard Lyons heard Oscar Levant ask, "Fred, are you an egomaniac?" "No, Oscar," Fred replied. "I've heard that the meek shall inherit the earth and I'm standing by to collect."

Although he may have just been going for a joke in response to Oscar's question, Fred spoke the truth about himself. He was the meekest, the least pretentious of all the famous performers I've met. He never publicly associated himself with any charity, but was one of the most charitable men I've known. Some rich actors, you may be surprised to learn, are tight-wads. A lot of wealthy men give money; Fred gave his time and his talent in addition. Dave Garroway and Henry Morgan found Fred in their corners during the early days of their struggle for recognition. Fred suggested that Herb Shriner replace him when his first heart attack forced him to withdraw from "Two for the Money." Red Skelton has publicly conceded that it was Fred who did Red's famous "Gizzler's Gin" routine. I will always be grateful to Fred for appearing on a special "Tonight" broadcast celebrating the opening of *The Benny Goodman Story* film. We were stuck for a big-name star to open the show. When we told Fred our problem he agreed on the spot to step in, and he was in great form that night. It was to be his last big monologue.

So what about Fred and television? Where did the trouble lie? The fault was neither Fred's nor TV's. Fred's greatest work was behind him, and though he was brilliantly witty to his last day, he was ill at ease before the camera. "What's My Line?" gave him openings for only two or three jokes per broadcast. None of his classically witty prepared material could be brought to the panel table since the show was unrehearsed and ad-libbed. Although he was a master of off-the-cuff chatter, he was always somewhat distracted by the mechanics of the game. Now and then, of course, he would score strongly. But most of the laughs on "What's My Line?" came from the confusion of the panelists and the double meanings that often stemmed from their ignorance of the professions they were trying to identify. The Fred Allen of "What's My Line?" was not the real Fred Allen. As Madison Avenue claimed, he hadn't "found himself" in television.

This search for one's self in the TV jungles can be frightening. When

CBS first brought me from Hollywood to New York there were regular executive sessions devoted to "finding the real Steve Allen." Poor Fred had gone through the same sort of thing for about four years. But he was philosophical about it. Lunching with columnist John Crosby one day at the Plaza, he smiled amiably to a lady who had nodded a greeting from across the room. "I have to be very careful," he said. "My public has shrunk to such an extent that I have to be polite to all of them. I even say hello to people in sewers. You know, I went off the air once before, back in 1944. We got three letters deploring it. This time we're way ahead of that: I think we got fifteen."

From the beginning, oddly enough, even back before he had to work in the medium, Fred had cast a suspicious eye at television. "When you see Kukla, Fran, and Ollie come alive on that little screen, you realize you don't need great big things as we had in radio. They ought to get one of those African fellows over here to shrink all the actors. We're all too big for this medium.

"TV," he said, "gets tiresome. Take 'The Goldbergs,' which has been so well received. It's a good show, but it gets so after you see it four or five times you know what the uncle is going to do and you know what the kids are going to do. The trouble with television is it's too graphic. In radio, a moron could visualize things his way; an intelligent man, his way." Fred's was comedy with a heavily critical content. For some as yet unidentified reason, television is the first medium in history to put a low price on critical humor.

The theater, the press, the lecture platform, radio—all accommodated pungent satire, all were successfully used as bases from which to fire the barbed comic shaft. Television, possibly because of its complete sensual intimacy, possibly because it is a medium wherein a picture may detract from, rather than add to, an idea, has placed the sardonic humorist in an awkward position, although in the late 1970s "Saturday Night Live" revived the format somewhat.

Some thought had been given, therefore, to "softening up" Allen's comedic style. There had been attempts to make him what the trade refers to as "gracious and warm." Such efforts were, naturally, doomed to failure, if only on an old-dog-new-tricks basis. Fred was, after all, the king of radio comedy, and kings are notoriously opposed to change, particularly of a personal nature. Besides, one cannot help feeling that Fred really shouldn't have been asked to modify his professional personality. He had never had to sell "himself" before; he had simply presented amusing ideas. It was audiences, perhaps, who should have been asked to change. How dare they, one is tempted to demand, ignore the work of a man who had brought them so much pleasure on the radio?

Fred's bitterness was essentially a pose and a disguise anyway, a camouflage for his true personality, which *was* gracious and warm. Unlike some performers who are angels to the public and devils to their associates, he exposed his Mephistophelean side to the public and worked his good deeds in the anonymity of his daily routine. While he was an outspoken individualist and a man of many dislikes, he was an eminently enjoyable companion and a top-notch conversationalist. Modest, soft-spoken, without a trace of show-biz front, he was also privately a pushover for anybody in need of a handout. Friends say he had one of the longest "pension" lists in show business. Almost every successful performer has a small and sometimes vocal circle of people who choose to be identified as enemies or critics; I have never heard anyone say a word against Fred Allen.

Mark Goodson, who with his partner Bill Todman produced such shows as "What's My Line?" "I've Got a Secret," "Two for the Money" (which was originally created for Fred), and Fred's "Judge for Yourself," had this to say about Allen's personality: "Fred is a complete paradox. On the air he can't function unless he's holding something of life up by a tweezers and frowning at it. If we had a contestant on the show who had just lost a leg, saved somebody's life, beat out a fire with his bare hands, and joined the Marines, Fred would simply be constitutionally unable to say to the guy, 'Gosh, we certainly are proud and happy to have you with us tonight.' And yet, after the show, when some glad-handing emcee might be brushing the hero off, Fred would probably hand him a personal check for two hundred dollars and walk away fast."

Comedian Sam Levenson had several theories about Allen's difficulties before the camera. "We all love the real Fred Allen," he said at the time, "but I think what is basically wrong is that he doesn't look well on TV. By that I mean he doesn't screen well. Also, on radio the listeners used their imaginations. It helped. Another point is that Fred has worked with a script in his hands for twenty years and it's very difficult for him to get used to this new medium." Although Fred had made a few films, he had never succeeded in pictures either, for the same reason.

Fred himself admitted the problem was a big one. "We all have a great problem—Hope, Benny, all of us. We don't know how to duplicate our success in radio. We found out how to cope with radio, and after seventeen years you know pretty well what effect you're achieving. But the same things won't work in television. Jack Benny's sound effects, Fibber McGee's closet—they just won't be funny in television. We don't know what will be funny, or even whether our looks are acceptable."

Speaking of his ill-fated "Judge for Yourself" program, Allen said, "There are so many things to keep in mind and cues to look out for. No sooner do I get going smoothly on an interview than I get a hand-signal to break it up. A television performer is surrounded by bloody commotion."

In radio the only thing moving on the stage at any given moment was the comedian's mouth. Supporting players have been fired, and with some justification, for crossing their legs or in any other way distracting the attention of the studio audience during a broadcast. A comedian is hired to make people laugh. If there is extraneous movement in the studio, it competes for the attention of the audience. If an audience's attention is divided, it may not laugh.

I shall never forget my first experience on television. Used to the rigid silence of radio studios, the "Quiet, please" or "On the Air" signs, the rapt attention of the visitors in the seats, I was horrified to learn that instead of being separated from the audience by one thin microphone, I was now required to reach them through a jungle of cameras, lights, props, microphone dollies, and scenery inhabited by three cameramen, two men working microphones, numerous stagehands creeping around in the darkness, assorted stage managers, who strode around with headphones muttering audibly while receiving communications from the control booth, and a generous collection of announcers, musicians, actors, and dancers. Trying to make an audience laugh under these circumstances was, in those hectic early days, a little like working at the Palace while between you and the footlights the Harlem Globe-Trotters mapped out a few fast-moving plays.

TV studio audiences were usually so fascinated at being behind the scenes that they could scarcely take their eyes off the cameras to look at the actors. Frequently, I have sat in the living room with friends watching one or another comedian suddenly get four or five seconds of silence after a joke that was obviously of high caliber. The reason may well have been something like a stagehand walking in front of the audience. You don't see him at home. All you see at home is the comic with egg on his face.

This sort of situation was particularly troublesome to a performer like Allen who brought no definite physical punch to the delivery of his lines. Unless an audience was paying strict attention to what he said, his gems sometimes were not picked up. The timing of a joke is a delicate thing; with a comic like Fred it didn't require much to throw that timing off.

Not many people know, incidentally, that, no matter who you are, the laughs you get in a TV studio are not as big as those you'd get in a radio studio. Besides the matter of physical distraction, there is the issue of microphone pickup and studio sound amplification. In radio a comedian's mouth was usually four or five inches away from the mike. That meant the engineers could get a full, close, rich pick-up of his voice, and the public-address system could throw it clearly into all corners of the studio. In TV theaters, mikes are usually kept invisible. That means they are floating around out of the picture two or three feet over the performers' heads. In order to send out sound of the same volume as was maintained in radio, the engineers must crank up the gain very high. This opens the delicate mikes and means the public-address system in the studio tends to play the sound so loud that it floats back into the open microphones, producing that loud, screeching howl you sometimes hear, called "feedback." No self-respecting engineer likes to hear feedback, so he solves the problem simply by turning down the volume of the public-address system. That certainly prevents feedback, but it also sometimes makes it relatively difficult for the people in the theater to hear the comedian. When they have trouble hearing they laugh less. You at home get the impression that the comic isn't very funny. Often he's doing jokes he's been doing successfully for twenty years, but he may not be getting laughs on a particular night because of technical reasons. In the 1950s this was a constant headache for comedy shows.

A comedian of Fred's type is considerably handicapped by the technical exigencies of TV, and he seemed to appreciate the point fully.

"The television set," he said in explanation, "just isn't an instrument of wit. The comedy you see on TV is physical rather than mental and is based largely on old burlesque routines. Take Sid Caesar. He's one of the finest comedians on the air, but if you analyze his comedy you'll find it's the physical type."

True enough. Much TV humor is physical, and such of it as is not is usually worked into a sketch. Even comics such as Bob Hope and Milton Berle, who made their reputations standing up and firing one big joke after another at point-blank range, came to realize that TV audiences wanted to get interested in some sort of story line. The question is: Where did this leave Fred Allen? I'm not sure. But I loved his humor.

The frequently-heard reference to Fred's doleful physiognomy is not a true reason for his television contretemps. When has there ever been a truly handsome comedian anyway? Fred in person made vaudeville, studio, and theater audiences laugh for years and they saw his face, in 3-D and color at that.

Fred, by the way, directed a considerable amount of criticism at people who go to see television comedy programs and sit in their seats and laugh.

"The worst thing that ever happened to radio," he said, "was the studio audience. Somebody like Eddie Cantor brought these hordes of cackling geese in because he couldn't work without a bunch of imbeciles laughing at his jokes."

Every comedian, of course, is just a little afraid of an audience, afraid that people won't laugh. But Fred never let up on the pew-holders. "Would anybody with a brain be caught dead in a studio audience?" he demanded. "Would anybody with a sense of taste stand in line to watch half a dozen people in business suits standing around reading into microphones?"

Allen and a lot of other people who were of the same mind liked to hark back to the days of Stoopnagle and Bud, Amos and Andy, and Easy Aces. "There," they say, "were comedy shows without a live audience. We should never have made a change."

On this point I have always disagreed with Fred.

The old quarter-hour shows were wonderfully funny, but personally I laughed louder at Fred Allen's radio program, the one with the studio audience. And I laughed louder at it than I would have if Fred had broadcast the exact same scripts from an empty room.

It's a simple matter of mass psychology. The appreciation of humor is, at heart, an emotional matter. You won't laugh at the most amusing joke in the world if you're not "in the mood." And when are you more in the mood for laughter; when you're sitting in a room by yourself or when you're with a large group of friends?

Danny Kaye was very funny in the movies. His pictures usually made me laugh so loud I embarrassed my companions. But one time I saw one of his films at a drive-in theater. I didn't laugh aloud once. I didn't hear anybody else laughing.

Fred knew that a joke with which he could make a friend chuckle on the street would make an audience of fifty laugh deeply, and could make an audience of five hundred roar for perhaps half a minute.

But sometimes people say, "Why don't they just *try* a comedy show without an audience?"

They have. Henry Morgan did once: just once. The script was marvelous and Henry was in top form. But at home I didn't crack a smile. Next week Henry performed before his usual crowd and I laughed aloud.

Fred was classic with descriptions, comparisons, and exaggerations. That's why he's still one of the most quoted comedians of our time. One of the funniest jokes ever written was his crack about the scarecrow that "scared the crows so badly they brought back corn they had stolen two years before."

James Thurber said one of his favorite ad-libs was Fred's remark to a bass player whose instrument made such strange sounds that Fred peered down into the pit and said to him, "How much would you charge to haunt a house?"

Another line that broke me up was Fred's answer to a friend who inquired about his destination one time when he was making a trip out of New York. "I'm going to Boston to see my doctor," said Fred. "He's a very sick man." It was Fred who said, in discussing a geometry problem, "Let X equal the signature of my father."

But these are all what the trade calls stand-up jokes, jokes to be flung in an audience's teeth. And therein lies one clue to Fred's TV difficulties. He could function only as an observer, a commentator, a humorist, not as an actor. Fred was an inadequate sketch comic. He had no ability to lose himself in a character. He could put on a costume but you never believed he was the character he was portraying in the way you believe that Sid Caesar, Richard Pryor, or Jonathan Winters have adopted a mystically different personality.

Other comedians can sell you a bad line by giving it a physical push. Jerry Lewis can convulse an audience with a weak gag by mugging as he delivers it. Sid Caesar can do a dialect or emote or make a face and thus make almost any line seem funny. Jackie Gleason could punch a line out with such gusto that you laughed before you knew what you were laughing at. But Fred Allen had to have a good solid joke or you didn't laugh.

Allen's dilemma might have seemed solved when we remember that there were other comedians functioning successfully in TV who did not do sketches. Groucho Marx didn't. Herb Shriner didn't.

The solution, then, seemed simple. Make him a quiz-master. But this solution had been tried and found wanting. Fred's "Judge For Yourself" was called by one critic "a pointless hodgepodge," although it was produced by the same organization that put together Herb Shriner's successful "Two For The Money" and was loosely similar to Groucho's "You Bet Your Life."

At first, the quiz-game format seemed a natural for Allen because he was one of that small minority of comedians able to ad-lib. Like Groucho and Shriner, he was given the additional benefit of interviews that were written out in advance. But though his mind was rapier-quick, he was not used to making small talk with bus drivers and dentists and housewives from Des Moines. He was too honest not to be distracted by the technical froth of "the game," and the result was that he did not develop the ability to relax entirely with his guests. He was impatient and confined and conscious of the pressure on him.

The solution, I think, would have been to give him the sort of program that Arthur Godfrey or Garry Moore or I did. Give him a table and a microphone and a couple of singers to fill in the holes and then just throw him a newspaper headline or a human-interest subject and he'd have done well.

These programs had writers, too, of course. Fred could have had all the help he needed, and he'd have had time to prepare any jokes or stories he wanted. But he'd also have had unlimited freedom. He'd have been under no mechanical restrictions. If he got something going that was funny, he could have let it roll as long as it felt good. If something went wrong, he could have stopped everything and talked about what had gone wrong. If his interest in a subject lagged, he could have called on the orchestra or one of the singers or a guest star. He could at last have been as funny on TV as he was when you talked to him on the sidewalk. Ask any comedian in the business. He'll tell you that Fred Allen was king of the performing humorists.

I ran into Henry Morgan one night on Fifty-second Street. He was chuckling.

"What's funny?" I asked.

"I was just talking to Fred Allen," he said. "Met him coming out of the Waldorf. I asked him what he'd been doing and he said he'd just left a dinner sponsored by the National Conference of Christians and Jews. And then he said, 'You know, Henry, I was just wondering . . . do we really deserve top billing?'"

One thing that fascinated me about Fred's comedy was that it was probably more secure from plagiarism than that of any other performing humorist. Most of Fred's jokes had to be heard coming out of his mouth to sound as funny as they were. If one did not hear him, one had to draw up a mental picture of Allen, to imagine that one heard his nasal, twanging voice, or much of the enjoyment of the humor was lost.

I'll demonstrate.

One night when Milton Berle was doing a warm-up for his radio show somebody turned on a light in the sponsor's booth, revealing to the studio audience that there was no sponsor, no sign of life whatever, in the booth. "Ladies and gentlemen," Milton said, "that booth is a device to belittle the comedian by showing him that the sponsor doesn't care enough for his program to attend it."

At that point a page boy hurried in and switched off the light, which caused Milton to say, "Ah, a boy who has the guts to turn off the lights without a memo from a vice-president will go right to the top of the organization."

Now, regardless of what your reaction was to the above story, I feel quite certain that one thing will be generally admitted: you were not really very amused by it. Milton's comments seem more sarcastic than funny, and they are certainly not jokes. At best, they might get, from the average audience, a sympathetic chuckle.

The point is this: Milton never had any such experience. The thing happened to Fred Allen, and when he responded as indicated above the audience fell into paroxysms of laughter. Believe it or not, if you go back and read the details of the incident over again (this time picturing Fred Allen at the microphone instead of Milton Berle) you will laugh, too.

Debating some point or other with Fred one evening on my late-night TV show I happened to say, "Well, of course there are two sides to this thing." "There are two sides to a Decca record, too," said Fred, and the audience laughed. I laughed, too, for I was genuinely amused. But I do not believe I would have laughed if the remark had been made by Bob Newhart.

Who would laugh to hear Steve Martin say, "A vice-president is a bit of executive fungus that forms on a desk that has been exposed to conference"?

No, much of Fred's material was so uniquely adapted to his delivery that he needed have little fear that it would be stolen. A number of Allen's quips have been lifted, but they constitute a very small percentage of his total output. The old line about starting a fire by rubbing two Boy Scouts together is Fred's.

Fred's old radio warm-ups were wonderful shows in themselves. He used to speak to his studio audience for about ten minutes, saying a lot of things he wouldn't have been allowed to say on the air. "If by any chance," he'd say, "any of you folks are in the wrong place you still have ten minutes to get the heck out of here. Heck, incidentally, is a place invented by the National Broadcasting Company. NBC does not recognize hell or the Columbia Broadcasting System. When a bad person working for NBC dies, he goes to Heck, and when a good person dies, he goes to the Rainbow Room."

There are several things that earmarked Fred's humor as distinctive. One was his sheer playful love of words. He had a poet's regard for peculiarities of sound and expression and seemed never so happy as when he could roll off his tongue some glittering allegory, metaphor, or simile. He was actually much more intrigued by this sort of thing than he was by the simple joke.

Once, in complaining about the fact that he got no help in advance from executives, he said, "While the show was nonexistent . . . the agency men . . . were as quiet as a small boy banging two pussy willows together in a vacuum."

Putting words into the mouth of the Southern windbag character, Senator Claghorn, Allen, to describe how big a dinner was, wrote, "Son, when all the food's on, the four legs of the table is kneelin' down." About a contentious chap, Allen said, "Brother Doe always had a chip on his shoulder that he was ready to use to kindle an argument."

To express as forcefully as possible that the late Mayor La Guardia was a long way from being tall, Allen said, "He's the only man I know that can milk a cow standing up."

This line brings us to another distinctive point of Fred's humor: he loved to conceive what we might call "funny pictures." By way of illustration, consider this exchange from an "Allen's Alley" interview between Fred and Ajax Cassidy:

ALLEN: What is that ladder you have there?

AJAX: I'm going over to Sweeney's house for dinner.

ALLEN: And you have to carry a ladder?

AJAX: The dinin'room table is too high. You can't sit on chairs. Everybody eats on a ladder.

ALLEN: Why is the dining-room table so high?

AJAX: Sweeney is a mounted cop. He always rides in to dinner on his horse.

ALLEN: Oh.

AJAX: Sweeney never uses a napkin. He wipes his hands on the back of his horse so much, he has mice under his saddle.

This is a peculiar, individual type of humor. It is closely related to the humor of the modern, sophisticated cartoon, à la George Price. Certainly it is a far cry from the general level of radio comedy with which it was contemporaneous.

Another earmark of Fred's humor is recognized in its occasional close resemblance to poetry. On the subject of true love he has written: "To me, Sonia was prettier than a peacock backin' into a sunset. I used to dig up the ground she walked on and take it home."

When one of his scripts was cut from sixty minutes to half an hour, Fred said, "The lines looked as though they had been written with a riveting machine dipped in ink."

He has also written of the chinchilla-winged siskin, a tropical bird that bites people to death and feeds on their screams. Note the double-talk work *siskin*. It's also a Jewish surname, and probably got an inside laugh from people who worked on the show. The siskin is evidently closely related to another of his creatures of fantasy, the four-toed gecko, a jungle swine that chases people out into the sun and eats their shadows. These ideas are entirely poetical in concept and are humorous only in a most incidental way.

Fred's habit of using actual names of people and places also identifies his style. Offering to make Orson Welles at home in the field of variety radio, Fred said, "Well, if I could give you some hints, or introduce you to Ma Perkins, I'd be . . ."

To indicate what life would be like in this country if people became extinct, Fred said, "It will be like Philadelphia on a Sunday."

Another example of Fred's closeness to the Abe Martin-Bill Nye-Josh Billings school lay in his practice of naming things poetically. Consider the famous radio interview between Fred and a certain Captain Knight, who owned an eagle. In the course of this chat, Fred referred to the eagle in the following ways: "The gentleman buzzard"; "This bloated sparrow"; "The one we see on the half dollar: the Mint Macaw"; "A bald eagle wearing a toupee"; "These Tenth Avenue canaries"; "The King-

Kong Robin." One is reminded of some of W. C. Field's flights of verbal fancy.

The poetic style of Fred's humor puts him, I believe, closer to the classic American humorists than any of his contemporaries.

"The Shanghai rooster is built on piles like a sandy-hill crane. . . . They often go to sleep standing and sometimes pitch over, and when they do they enter the ground like a pickax."

That's a line from Josh Billings, and it's greatly similar in style to Allen's work.

"Sending men to that army," said Abraham Lincoln, no mean humorist himself, "is like shoveling fleas across a barnyard—they don't get there."

That is not just a word-joke; it's a funny picture and it could have come straight from the lips of Allen's Titus Moody.

Among Fred's other inspired creations was the only armless sculptor in the world. He put the chisel in his mouth and his wife hit him on the back of the head with a mallet. On one occasion Fred claimed that his dear mother in Boston had kept a light burning in the window for him for twenty years. "When I finally came home," he said, "she gave me a royal welcome and an electric bill for $729."

In going through my old files I came across the following jokes Fred did when he appeared on "The Tonight Show" as part of some hoopla for the premiere of *The Benny Goodman Story*.

Good evening, ladies and gentlemen. It's wonderful to be here tonight. Of course, it's a little past my bedtime; I'm the *older* Allen, you know. In fact I'm so old I can remember when The Big Four meant the Benny Goodman Quartet.

But it's great to be standing here tonight. As a matter of fact, I've been sitting on the "What's My Line" panel for so long it's wonderful to be standing anywhere.

To tell you the truth, I'm a little tired from going to the premiere. They used to have these things around Times Square but this one was held way up town. I don't remember exactly how far up town but I do recall having a little trouble getting through Canadian customs.

The picture was very exciting, though. It's one of those new wide-screen productions. At least that's what they tell me. The studios say the screens are getting bigger. Actually the audiences are getting smaller.

And of course the picture is in color. But that's not news. These days *everything* is in color. It's getting so whenever I see a rainbow I look for a title underneath.

It was quite a kick, though, to see Steve in pictures. I enjoyed his performance, but one thing bothered me. I kept waiting for him to do the commercials.

Benny Goodman does the actual playing, but Steve did a good job of pretending to play. Of course in one scene I could have sworn I saw him playing a salami.

I don't know if you folks realize it, but this picture is a New York first. It hasn't been on "The Ed Sullivan Show" yet. Ed has so many film clips on his program that the engineers have installed popcorn machines in the control room.

The music was pretty exciting tonight, what with that stereophonic sound thing. You hear the sound where it comes from, ya know. I was in the balcony and I heard a few sounds that weren't even in the picture.

But it's a great night for Benny and Steve. Steve always surprises me because he proves what a great thing TV is. I mean where else could a guy with my name, Garroway's glasses, Benny Goodman's clarinet, and Jerry Lester's time-slot make good?

Fred Allen made some interesting predictions about television. He always decried the Milton Berle approach to the medium. Milton and the score of funnymen who work like him did not seem, to Fred, to be ideally suited to TV. "All they're doing," he said, "is photographing vaudeville shows."

He once predicted that the eventual big comedy star of television would be a fellow who would just sit in an easy chair and talk to people in a quiet way, as if he were talking to them in person in their living rooms. I think Fred Allen could have learned to function in just that way, and, ah, then what a program we would have seen! He didn't really need television, of course. His reputation is secure; nothing can diminish his stature. But television surely needs people like Fred.

The night we said goodbye to Fred on "What's My Line," I said,

Just a few months ago, sitting in this chair, Fred read a postcard a viewer had sent to "What's My Line" asking, "Is Fred Allen Steve Allen's father?" Fred laughed. The answer, of course, was no. Last night when I heard the sad news, I couldn't have been more depressed if the answer had been yes.

John Belushi

John Belushi

Shortly after New Year's Day, 1951, a woman I knew was staying with a friend who had a small apartment on New York's East 55th Street, just off Sixth Avenue. The friend, who so far as we knew was in good health, went into a hospital for minor surgery. The next day I heard that she had died during the operation. Since the woman's family lived in a distant part of the country, it fell to my friend to attend to the sad task of closing down the apartment, packing the woman's belongings, contributing most of them to the Salvation Army, etc. She asked if I could help her. Accordingly I spent a couple of days at the apartment organizing the dead woman's few belongings. Among them was a collection of books, magazines, scrap books, letters and other documents—all about comedian Will Rogers. The deceased, we learned, had years earlier been the president of a Will Rogers fan club. I wish now that I had retained all this material. One of the items was a book titled *What Great Men Say of Will Rogers*. It had been published not long after Rogers' untimely death in an airplane crash. It was a moving experience, in the context of the death of the woman who had occupied the apartment, to read a series of emotional tributes to the most beloved entertainer in America's history. Various distinguished Americans—political leaders, statesmen, authors, journalists, artists, other entertainers—expressed their sadness about Rogers' passing, their personal affection for him, their admiration for his humor.

I thought of all this recently when reading a collection of comments on the death of John Belushi published in *Rolling Stone* shortly after his tragic death from an overdose of drugs. The contrast between the two collections of tributes and personal reminiscences was striking. In the case of Rogers' it is no exaggeration to say that a nation wept, as if at the death of a beloved president. Rogers was a true cultural hero, admired by both leaders and common people. There is, of course, a sense in which it is unfair to make a flat comparison between Rogers and Belushi, or between the public reactions to news of their equally-shocking deaths.

★ 45

Rogers was the only American entertainer whose affectionate popularity must have involved 99% of the American people. Those who wept at news of Belushi's passing would have constituted a very small percentage. But there is another sense in which it is instructive to compare both the emotional tone and the specific components of the reminiscences about the two comedians. With Rogers the tone was one of grief at the unexpected loss of a major figure in society. People perceived that Rogers was, despite the unusual nature of his gifts, nevertheless—as a person—somehow an archetypal American, a true cowboy, a man of plain speech and manners, a brilliant wit, an individual of remarkable charm. As regards John Belushi, even his closest friends and associates, those who knew and liked him best, contributed to *Rolling Stone* a series of recollections that added up to a strikingly unappealing picture of the man. They respected his talent, energy, ambition, his contribution to the success of "Saturday Night Live" during its early, important period. But beyond that, most of their memories referred to an ugliness of spirit, a self-centeredness, an almost barbaric social irresponsibility.

To the relatively disinterested observer, one of the sadder things about Belushi's death at so early an age was that he was cut off not only in his professional prime but before he had come to terms with himself as a human being, before he had developed the sort of self-insight and growth that, at least in ideal terms, is necessary for the achievement of even a working-degree of maturity. Belushi was 33 when he died, but sometimes he still behaved like a teenage delinquent, driven to defy even minimal standards of civilized social behavior.

I was not among Belushi's detractors. Referring to him in *Funny People,* published in 1981, I had said, "That Belushi is talented cannot be debated. He was marvelous in some of the old "Saturday Night Live" sketches. His Japanese "samurai warrior"—though it would seem largely an imitation of Sid Caesar's samurai—was superbly done." I added a qualifier, however:

> But the one quality that Belushi seems to lack, as a comedian, is charm. There is something overtly aggressive about the image he projects, something that seems hostile, whether or not he is playing a hostile character. He rarely smiles, which strikes me, in some ways, like the attitude of certain jazz musicians of the Bop Era of the 1950s, who chose to merely let audiences witness their performances but to give nothing more of themselves. Whether the musicians were white or black, one was not asking for

either Uncle Tom or any other sort of fawning appeal of the hat-in-hand sort. The Basie band still swings the most, but one never gets emanations of surliness from its players. Some of the '50s types not only were angry, which is certainly forgiveable in the light of their difficult social circumstances, but they took no pains to disguise this during their performances. Belushi gives off this same dark-glasses image. He could probably get away with it and achieve popularity anyway if he were, say, one of the greatest comedians since Chaplin. But he is not. He is simply very good at the sort of thing he does.

While I found John less amusing than Chevy Chase, Dan Ackroyd, and Bill Murray, I nevertheless recognized his ability and energy. Later, I enjoyed most aspects of his performance in *The Blues Brothers.* But, rightly or wrongly, few people of my age-bracket—in fact few over the age of forty-five—were Belushi admirers.

But there was far more behind public reactions to Belushi than a simple generation gap. Most people over forty-five do not find Steve Martin particularly amusing, although personally I think he's very funny. But in the case of Belushi there was far more than insensitivity to his humor. There was a surprising degree of open antagonism.

That Belushi aroused such feelings while he was alive is hardly surprising. He seemed to do so deliberately and appeared to be not only incapable of the element of ingratiation, which is characteristic of the art of entertainment itself, but even contemptuous of the tradition. All of that made inevitable at least some degree of negative reaction to the man and his work. But, generally, criticism of a relatively unpopular figure is respectfully muted for at least a brief time after his death, particularly when his passing is sudden, unexpected, or otherwise shocking. Belushi was accorded no such period of bereaved respect. Almost at once one began to hear contemptuous, sometimes even angry comments about him.

Jeffry Freundlich, a young member of my staff, has an interesting insight into Belushi's personal and professional dilemma. "The two most striking facts about him are (1) he did have talent, and (2) he blew it. He actually seemed to shed his talent like so much snakeskin. As he got increasing kudos *for* being rude and obnoxious, he became more so *off*-screen, and continued to get away with it. I don't mean to sound the old klaxon that 'society is to blame' but his destructive behavior *was* encouraged and applauded. His failure was that he could not fit that reaction from his young fans into any kind of perspective; he could not seem to adjust to the difference between on-camera and off-camera reality. Given all the power and money he had—and remember, he was finally in that enviable Hollywood position of being able to pick his own projects—he chose instead to shove it up his nose and run amok."

As I have earlier observed—in *The Funny Men* (Simon and Schuster) and *Funny People* (Stein and Day)—it was my intention to write analytical essays on various comedy performers who interest me, and not to deal with the gossip-magazine elements of their lives. Full-length biographies provide such details, but my concentration, in this shorter form, is on the simple factor of funniness.

In the case of certain entertainers, however, it is impossible to draw a sharp line of demarcation between the individual and his or her ability to amuse. With Richard Pryor, for example, those who write about his humor invariably refer to certain aspects of his personal experience since, for one thing, Pryor discusses his misadventures publicly and uses them as raw material for some of his monologues. His comedy and his emotional problems are related. Belushi is another entertainer about whom it is impossible to make extended analytical comment without reference to him as a human being. No comedian since the early Lenny Bruce has stirred up so much animosity among people age forty-five and older.

There are a number of successful comedians in the under-40 bracket whose appeal was not readily apparent to mature audiences; for example Steve Martin, Martin Mull, Andy Kaufman and Robin Williams. But I have never encountered the slightest personal dislike for such performers, merely—occasionally—the comment, "He doesn't seem funny to me." The case of Belushi, however, is quite different. Many who were not amused by him actively disliked him. Since this reaction was so common, it naturally must be considered in any analysis of Belushi's comedy. The explanation is self-evident. It was the surly, aggressive quality that John projected which so antagonized his critics.

The nation first became aware of Belushi, of course, from the original "Saturday Night Live." Although I have reservations about the inherent funniness of some members of that production's cast, by and large I thought they were quite a talented and amusing group. Chevy Chase, even when saddled with weak material, always came through as likeable, mischievous, and funny, with just the right amount of natural silliness. Bill Murray had a personable, likeable quality and was an effective naturalistic actor. We had worked together a couple of years earlier in a sketch I'd written for Howard Cosell's variety show. Bill—and later, his brother, Brian Doyle Murray—brought an immediate quality of warmth and charm to the SNL show. Dan Ackroyd had a strong presence, was marvelous at doing impressions and imitations—his Tom Snyder was a classic—and he seemed to enjoy what he was doing. Jane Curtin, too, appealed, with her wonderfully insightful depiction of a typical television newswoman. Indeed within 12 months after she began to perform in the newscast sketches of "Saturday Night Live", it seemed that half the actual female newscasters in the country were sounding like Jane Curtin. And no matter what sort of sketches Curtin worked in she gave the funny impression of being just short of distraction at either her predicament or the antics of those performing with her. It was as if a young Katherine Hepburn had been thrown into the company of the Marx Brothers. John Belushi, although clearly talented, had no such advantage as these charming young entertainers. There was always an element of aggressiveness to what he projected publicly.

A friend with whom I discussed John recalled that the word *gross* was often applied to his characterizations and then, sadly, toward the end of his life, to the man himself. My friend wondered whether Belushi's overweight, beefy quality explained the unfortunate aspect of his image. Absolutely not: Oliver Hardy was far heavier than Belushi but always seemed light-spirited, fey, a loveable victim rather than a threat. Jackie Gleason, too, was frequently overweight, known to be a hard drinker, and worried for the public record about his bouts with gluttony. But he, too, had a peculiarly Irish sort of charm, a genial the-drinks-are-on-the-house quality and, behind his braggadocio, sensitivity and vulnerability.

There was no such luck for John Belushi. When he acted like a boor in certain roles he was convincing because he seemed to *be* a boor. Consequently, when he dealt with vulgar or shocking subjects it struck the viewer more directly, for there was no charm to mediate between the shocking subject and the actor. Steve Martin, Chevy Chase, or Richard Pryor can be sleazy, but their natural cuteness and impish charm often covers a multitude of such sins. It was not so for John Belushi.

Even Belushi's most fervent youthful admirers would not, I think, consider him their personal favorite as regards the simple factor of funniness. They laughed more at Steve Martin, Richard Pryor, or Lily Tomlin, even Rodney Dangerfield. What America's 18-year-olds were responding to in Belushi, I think, was his outrageousness. From the ages of roughly 14 to 21 we all go through a rebellious stage. There is even a degree to which this is psychologically healthy, although it can be carried to pathological or criminal extremes. But that element in young adulthood that tends to the disrespectful, obstinate, irresponsible, violent, suddenly found in Belushi a successful representative. In both *Animal House* and some of his "Saturday Night Live" sketches, as well as in his personal life, Belushi thumbed his nose at mature, responsible society and—in marked contrast to most of those who did so—became enormously successful, sought after by the film industry, praised by those journals that chronicle both the admirable, creative, radical elements of social growth and those which are merely destructive of the social fabric.

If Belushi, at the age of 50, had acted so boorishly, a generation of 20-year-olds would have turned their backs on him. But he seemed one of their own, an anti-hero who was admired because of his defiance of convention, somewhat in the way that in ghettos and slums successful criminals are admired, at least so long as they remain successful.

What created, in the 1970s, the sudden explosion of vulgarity, obscenity, pornography, and Just Plain Bad Taste that, to some extent, "Saturday Night Live" capitalized on? No social critic or philosopher has argued that such a collapse of moral and ethical standards—and the consequent virtual disappearance of behavior informed by those standards—is a sign of healthiness or strength in our society. Critics of the political left and right agree: What we witnessed in the '70s was a true social sickness of mind and spirit.

To draw back a bit, I do not suggest that every four-letter word uttered by a comedian, or every instance of vulgarity on stage or screen, is necessarily wrong. I have elsewhere written in defense of Lenny Bruce— and as early as the 1950s—that when Bruce used vulgar language he invariably did so to make a philosophical point. But that is almost never the case with today's barbarians of the theatrical arts. Some of them are simply people who have (a) a clear gift for the comic combined with (b) a personal ugliness of spirit. At least some of these comic entertainers are not following in Lenny Bruce's footsteps at all; they are simply conveying impudence, defiance, and disrespect. The world has seen such behavior for at least a million years, and there is no shortage of it at present outside the boundaries of the entertainment field. It characterizes the daily mode of discourse, for example, among delinquents and criminals.

What is unprecedented about the current situation is that the delinquents and criminals have not, as a class, been reformed; rather, their sickness has infected the technically law-abiding majority of society so that now one could not tell—simply by listening to a lower-class criminal and a young comedian in social conversation—which was the more socially handicapped and dangerous.

The fact that Belushi attained popularity in the way he did, projecting the image he did, is indicative of a social trend much larger than the simple popular taste of the moment.

But, despite their faults and offenses, were the creators of "Saturday Night Live" performing an important philosophical service?

George Carlin—certainly no defender of the establishment—has said, "The show made me laugh but it didn't really take on a lot of issues. It *seemed* daring, and there were things that were sort of irreverent, but mostly they didn't present any alternate ideas, they just tore down— which is a form of comedy I can live with but don't love."

Carlin's point relates to a more fundamental objection about the present *forms* of vulgarity, expressed by Norman Cousins.

> In our business—books and magazines—we are often astonished to see what passes for triumphant achievement in the cause of freedom. A writer we know exulted because he was able to get a half-dozen four-letter words past an editor who may well have been elated because he was able to get the same words into print past his editorial chief. *At one time in the history of publishing, freedom was connected to things worth saying.* Writers like Ida Tarbell, Lincoln Steffens and Walter Lippmann saw a connection between freedom to print and the need to do battle with predatory forces in our society. *There is nothing wrong with the four-letter word per se; what is wrong is the disfiguration of values that makes the four-letter word a symbol of literary freedom and excellence.* [Italics supplied]

Among the leading practitioners of the comic arts in television, radio, film and the theater—the long-time professionals—the apparently unanimous view regarding the quality of writing on "Saturday Night Live" was that it was remarkably uneven. On each show there would usually be one sketch that was brilliant—well-written and performed—another one or two that were good, and two or three that seemed pointless, weak, or in inexcusable taste. All the rest were embarrassing. It might be thought that inasmuch as the ability to create comedy is a demonstrably rare talent, it therefore follows that the percentage of good-to-lousy was about the best that could be hoped for. But this is simply not the case. On the typical sketch comedy series of the 1950s there were almost never any sketches that were really amateurish, although by no means all were of high quality. Those who wrote many of the sketches of the 1950s were as capable as anyone else of writing a light-weight joke or an ineffectual scene. But generally we ourselves were the first to perceive the inadequacy of the material. Anything that was weak was usually thrown out either the first or second day of rehearsal. On the "Saturday Night Live" show one has the impression that nothing at all has ever been thrown out.

Another reason this is remarkable, compared with the comedy material of the 1950s, is that in those days our shows generally had only five or six writing participants. The credits at the close of "Saturday Night Live" have on some nights listed sixteen or seventeen writers. Another important factor is that in the 1950s we were on the air every week, often for 39 weeks a year. "Saturday Night Live" constantly runs repeats or is pre-empted.

Then, of course, there is the matter of taste, the general level of which on "Saturday Night Live" has distressed mature viewers—and many younger ones as well—since the first night the program went on the air. The program's writers seemed at times unable to distinguish between a *joke* about something and a simple *reference* to it. There were far too many instances where the live studio audience was responding to the mere mention of cocaine, heroin, sado-masochism, vomiting, the excretory functions, and whatever other shock value factors the writers or performers contrived to introduce.

Among those who take a dim view of the doper, goof-off factor that is part of today's comedy world is Woody Allen, who addressed the subject quite directly in his fine film, *Manhattan.* In one case Woody is standing in a television control room, distressed by a weak sketch being presented on the program on which he works. At that point the scene goes as follows:

IKE: (OVERLAPPING) Jesus, this is terrible. This—this is really embarrassing to me. I mean, I—I mean, this is so antiseptic. It's nothing like what we talked about.

DICK: (OVERLAPPING) No, no, wrong, wrong. That's not antiseptic.

IKE: (OVERLAPPING) I mean, this isn't—This has nothing. . . .

DICK: (OVERLAPPING) That's—that's very chancy material. I mean, who fights . . ?

IKE: (OVERLAPPING) How do you see this as chancy?

DICK: . . . who fights more with the censor?

IKE: (OVERLAPPING) It's empty.

MAN: (OFF) M-slide three.

DICK: (OVERLAPPING) That's funny! Funny.

IKE: Why do you think that it's funny?

PAUL: (OVERLAPPING) Look at the audience.

IKE: There's not a. . . .

DICK: Look at—look at the audience there.

INTERVIEWER'S VOICE OVER TV MONITORS (continues indistinct under following dialogue):

IKE: (OVERLAPPING) You're going by the—you're going by *audience reaction* to this? I mean, this is an audience that's *raised* on television. Their—their standards have been systematically lowered over the years. You know, these guys sit in front of their sets and the—the gamma rays eat the white cells of their brains out. Uh, you know, um, ya, I'm—I quit.

DICK: All right. Just relax. Take a lude. Take a lude.

IKE: (OVERLAPPING) No, no, no, no, no, I quit. I can't write this anymore. I can't . . . I don't want a lude.

All you guys do is drop ludes and then take Percodans and angel dust. Naturally, it seems funny.

DICK: You know, just relax, relax.

IKE: (OVERLAPPING) Anything would if you're . . . you know, we, y-y-you should abandon the show and open a pharmaceutical house.

Newsday's Marvin Kitman—like most professional critics—was alternately troubled and pleased by Belushi. Of *Animal House,* he wrote that it "marked the beginning and end of Belushi's career as a major comedian. The movie convinced him that he was a legend in his own mind. Its success led to his determination to escape from "Saturday Night Live," where he had become a household word—like acne. . . . The rats started leaving the ship with Chevy Chase the previous season. But Belushi was the biggest of them, in weight if not talent. Everybody was doing a picture deal. Even Larraine Newman was in demand. . . . Belushi did nothing for his reputation by going to California. . . . His first blockbuster movie after *Animal House* was *1941.* Michael O'Donoghue, who had worked with Belushi on the old original "Saturday Night Live," said it best when, after the picture was released, he gave Belushi a button for his birthday which read: 'John Belushi 1949-1941.'

"Stephen Spielberg's comedy about what might have happened if the

Japanese invaded California . . . cost 30 million and it was totally worthless. Belushi played an aviator ace-slob who grunted and chewed on his cigar damply. It was an example of the kind of humor you get when everybody associated with a comedy is sticking Coke bottles up their noses."

The harshness of Kitman's assessment is surprising since earlier he had highly praised John. Kitman, in any event, has a sensitive ear for comedy and laughs easily; obviously he saw something developing in Belushi that he did not like.

Kitman was far from the only critic to be disappointed by *1941*. Frank Rich of *Time* mentioned that Belushi's "repertoire of eating and belching jokes seemed strained."

If most adults—entertainers or not—exhibit irresponsible behavior patterns it is fairly easy to trace the causes to childhood experience. Such tracing is strangely difficult as one looks at Belushi's background, though there are brief hints and glimpses of a lurking strangeness. John's sister, Marion, has recalled that in their childhood she and John used to play in a wooded area near their home. "He would take out his slingshot and shoot down birds, and I'd cry over them, while he just poked at the dead birds, examining them."

On the whole, though, Belushi's childhood seems remarkably straight-arrow. His parents, apparently decent people, were never divorced. He had the benefits of a religious upbringing. In high school he was a responsible sort, a hall monitor who neither smoked cigarettes nor took drugs. He was a linebacker on the Wheaton Central High School football team, in fact captain of the team for two years. There is a clue of sorts, however, to Belushi's later behavior in something he confessed to a *Newsweek* interviewer in 1978. "I was hoping that the aggression I displayed on the football field, the energy in the rock group and the sensitivity on stage, would make up for what I lacked in looks and charm. It was all motivation to get a girl."

Belushi's conventional behavior, in any event, began to unravel at the end of his high school career. After a coach gave him a dressing-down, Belushi deliberately avoided making even a single tackle in the last game his team played.

After graduating in 1967 he left home with some bitterness and for ten years was not in communication with his parents. In the late '60s he and two friends were living in poverty in Chicago, performing weekends at a Universal Life Church. Eventually came the first break, an audition for Chicago's important improvisational comedy troupe, Second City. By

1972 he was working in *National Lampoon*'s production of *Lemmings*.

No one really seems able to explain the deterioration of Belushi's ability to portray the essential character of human beings. Perhaps it was precipitated by the sudden fame brought on by his involvement with the original "Saturday Night Live" company. Perhaps, as Marvin Kitman believes, it was tied to Belushi's desertion of "SNL" before his talent had fully ripened. Kitman felt Belushi had the potential to be "the superstar comic of our time." But then, according to Kitman, Belushi left for Hollywood too early and lost whatever potential he had. "I wish there were some drug," says Kitman, "some chemical they could put into their elbow or between the right big toe and the next one, that would allow John Belushi to go back to *Animal House* of 1978, and start all over again, and keep doing his career until he gets it right."

Perhaps Kitman is right. A change seems to have occurred in the late '70s. The destructive urge lost part of its comic edge. The impulse to rumple, ruffle, and cause disarray is legitimate in comedy, obviously, or there would never have been, for example, a Harpo Marx. But we all still laugh at Harpo, whereas Belushi began to alienate. Harpo was himself having fun, daring his audience to have fun with him. There was always some straight character, like Margaret Dumont, as a witness to Harpo's acts of desecration. Belushi, on the other hand, seemed to enjoy the destruction itself and to be almost oblivious to his audience. Belushi's Blues Brothers act was, like the man himself, aloof, loud, hostile. We watch Marx playing the harp and are seeing the most intimate thing imaginable—a man performing an act of love. Belushi publicly seemed incapable of such an act.

An illustrative instance is provided by the famous scene in which Harpo frantically smashes a piano. He appears to have gone berserk as he rips a beautiful concert grand into rubble. When all about him is in splinters, he picks up the piano's strings in their frame and plays them as a harp. We see that he had a *reason* to smash the piano—to liberate the harp within.

In the final sequence of *Animal House,* Bluto and his frat-brothers attack the Homecoming Parade simply to wreak revenge. There was no apparent sense of purpose in much of what Belushi thought and did on screen.

Then, too, the madcap gleam seemed to leave his eyes early on in the "Saturday Night Live" years. The great funny-folk all seem to have that other-self that shines out from their eyes. When Jerry Lewis, Red Skelton, or Ed Wynn ran screaming through a room with a seltzer bottle, tripping over furniture or ruining a dowager's gown, there was a special light in their eye that somehow made whatever they did okay. Belushi lost that gleam. It's a bit like James Bond's license to kill: without it you're merely a murderer.

Journalist Lewis Grossberger wrote a complimentary piece on Belushi before John's death. It was published in *Rolling Stone* on January 21, 1982. Grossberger writes in a half-hip, half-breathless-fan style, and captures well the pace of carousing around Chicago with Belushi while trying to pin the comedian down for an interview. He refers to their first meeting in late September, 1981. Belushi was coming out of a men's room. Now all over the planet, every day, millions of men encounter millions of others coming out of, or going into, men's rooms. In very few of these cases do the men look at each other. But Grossberger reports that Belushi cocked an eyebrow "in a scowl of majestic suspicion, as if to say, 'Who the hell is this guy, an assassin?'" Next Grossberger, having been permitted to enter Belushi's office, describes what Belushi does there. He plays records. The category—punk.

For the benefit of older readers I must explain that punk rock, judged purely as a musical form, is quite deliberately an immature, barbaric act of cultural defiance. It is really show-biz nonsense, replete with comedy costumes, absurd hair-dos, bizarre make-up. I know of no serious musician—including a good many in their twenties and thirties—who does not hold punk music in one degree of contempt or another. Grossberger describes the audio of such music in Belushi's office as "at brain-lesion level."

Grossberger next relates that Belushi is on the way to Chicago and that he is allowed to go along. It would appear to be Belushi's chief intention in Chicago—in addition to doing some interviews—to go to a bar and get drunk. On a Chicago news program a journalist asks the inane question: Was Belushi actually wearing underwear under a blanket in what was represented as a nude love scene in the film *Continental Divide*? The reaction: "Belushi is outraged. Belushi is pounding the desk and shouting." A Woody Allen, Mel Brooks—indeed any spontaneously funny comedian—would welcome the inanity of the question. Comedians pray for such marvelous straight-lines. But there was little likelihood of a witty response from Belushi since his style of comedy had no component of wit to it.

Later, when discussing with Grossberger his early experience in

Second City, doing ensemble comedy acting in Chicago, Belushi makes an interesting concession: "I think I've never grown up."

In a private saloon in Chicago, Grossberger reports, Belushi turns the juke box up to extra-super-loud. He tells a friend how pleased he is to be present. "That TV stuff," Belushi explains, by way of contrast, "It's all bullshit." So much for "Saturday Night Live." So much for Belushi's fellow performers. So much for the achievements of dozens of gifted comedians over the past 35 years. To Belushi, it was all bullshit.

Belushi watches a fight on television. "What a fuckin' fight," he repeatedly exclaims, and asks if he can get drunk, "or do I have to do another TV show?"

Understandably enough, Grossberger refers to Belushi's already firmly cemented reputation: "The party monster. Stuffing every imaginable substance into every possible orifice. Running amok."

The only time I ever met Belushi he behaved in a peculiar manner, indeed. I was appearing on a midday New York City television talk show; I'd been told that Belushi would also be a guest and I was looking forward to meeting him. Bill Boggs, the host, explained that I would appear early in the show and Belushi would come on later. Comedian David Brenner and I had been on stage—having fun—for several minutes when suddenly we saw, to Boggs's right, someone crawling on hands and knees toward the area in which the program's interviews were conducted. At first I thought it might be a stagehand, creeping in to make an off-camera adjustment to a chair or microphone wire, in a way that is sometimes necessary on television programs. But the unexpected crawler turned out to be Belushi.

I took no exception whatever to his coming in, unannounced and unexpected, while I was being interviewed. I enjoy that sort of looseness. It's the sort of thing Jerry Lewis used to do so effectively early in his career, walking on "The Tonight Show" unannounced, taking over, and almost invariably being very funny.

Belushi, to my disappointment, did no such thing. He remained on his knees for some time, saying nothing, and making no other attempt to amuse. Boggs was disconcerted and the studio audience puzzled. In any event, nobody laughed.

Belushi was induced to sit in a chair, after which, without the slightest provocation, he threw a glass of water on the neatly dressed Boggs, then pushed his feet forward, placed them against a coffee table—on which there rested a potted plant—and kicked out vigorously. The result was to send the table and plant flying. Earth and gravel from the low ceramic bowl were strewn about the floor. Again—to everyone's embarrassment —there was no laughter, from either the shocked studio audience or the host, by now visibly annoyed.

I had to leave the studio a few minutes later, and never did learn whether Belushi recovered from the awkwardness of his entrance.

Boggs later recalled:

> I remember thinking three things at once: one, this was one of the few times I found myself not knowing how to react. It was difficult to determine if this was John Belushi being crazy, or acting as the iconoclast; two, I felt embarrassed for you and David Brenner; and three, I saw the faithful little plants that had been part of our set for so long, uprooted and sent flying on the floor.
>
> I chose to figure that Belushi thought this was funny, and I tried to play it for laughs. Yet at the same time, I had to cover my anger at the embarrassment to my guests, and the death of the plants . . . Many people have felt that John acted this way as an insult to me. However, I feel that he would not have awakened from his sleep to come on the show if he did not feel like a friend. I learned after the show that one possible reason for this behavior was because he did not like appearing with David Brenner. I told him I thought David was very funny, and I felt pleased to have three such well known celebrities on my show.

Comedy writer Don Novello recalled a typical Belushi story in contributing his thoughts to *Rolling Stone*'s Belushi memorial edition. He and John had been working on a film script called *Noble Rot* in Belushi's office at Paramount Studios. A record player in the room was turned up to extremely high volume. Recalls Novello, "The producer and director of the film we were writing walked into the office. One of them asked John to turn down the music."

As it happens, the phrase "turn down the music"—by some sort of cult-peer-group agreement—has come to be recognized as typical of the reaction of squares to the excesses of hipsters.

Belushi's reaction to the perfectly reasonable request? He walked to the record machine, moved the needle back to the beginning of the disk and turned the volume up to twice as loud as it had been before.

Michael O'Donoghue, of the "Saturday Night Live" show, contributed an interesting recollection to the *Rolling Stone* feature. In following his account, try to envision, not Belushi, but Bob Hope, George Burns, Sid Caesar, Bob Newhart, Bill Cosby, or any other established comedian over 45 years of age.

Candy Bergen and John worked together on the first "SNL" Christmas show. She had never done live television and didn't know most of the people on the show. John had written a sketch that parodied a Sam Peckinpah kind of director, a director who, in order to act out a scene, brutalizes his actresses. John wanted to run this down with Candy, and I was fortunate enough to be sitting in Lorne's office when he did. He grabbed her, threw her against the wall and then threw her to the ground. Ultimately, it got down to them wrestling on the floor. Lorne, who was sitting behind his desk, wouldn't look at them. And I, with an affinity for the Japanese cinematic school, didn't really want to look either. I mean, being on the periphery of this action was the most fun.

Candy was a good sport; she took it. John was ultimately sitting on top of her, banging her head against the floor.

Filmmaker John Landis has told of flying to New York to arrange a meeting with Belushi, who came to his hotel room, immediately ordered ten shrimp cocktails, twenty beers, and ten Perriers, and—a few minutes later—the relevant business having been completed, simply rose and left. The food and drink arrived shortly thereafter. Landis, understandably, referred, in his *Rolling Stone* reminiscence, to "what would be totally unforgivable behavior on the part of anyone else . . ."

The gifted young musician Tom Scott tells a story in the by-now-familiar vein.

The burden of being John's buddy could be fairly exotic. John was in Los Angeles in 1981, finishing up *Continental Divide,* when Judy's birthday rolled around. He called up my wife, Lynn, and me one night to invite us to a party at their rented house in Beverly Hills. He asked if we'd be kind enough to pick up a cake big enough to serve forty-five people. No problem. He hung up and then called back.

"I want it to be a surprise. Could you call most of the people for me?" No problem. He hung up. Called back. "Could you guys come a little bit early to greet the guests? I won't be there and the house will be locked, but you

can crawl in the back window and unlock the front door." Er, no problem.
Goodbye.

Hello again. "And could you entertain the people with some of the
'make-out music' you play on that horn of yours?" No prob—yeah, sure.
See you tomorrow night. Bye.

The phone rang again.

"Tom?"

"Yeah, John."

"I never said it would be easy being my friend."

Not long after John Belushi died I was interviewed by Jack Carney,
the top radio personality in St. Louis. During our conversation Carney
asked if I had seen a feature on Belushi written by San Francisco critic
Terrence O'Flaherty.

"No," I said, "I haven't heard of it."

"Well," Carney said, "I never thought Belushi was funny myself, so I
read O'Flaherty's piece on the air and I must say I was surprised that I
got so many letters and calls *agreeing* with me."

Later that day Carney had the O'Flaherty commentary delivered to
my hotel. What is noteworthy about O'Flaherty's reaction is not simply
that he found Belushi unamusing; no comedian in the world amuses 100
percent of those who see him. But O'Flaherty was saying something
quite separate; that he did not *like* Belushi.

The feverish press and TV coverage of the death of John Belushi is
significant only as additional evidence of today's low standards of performing excellence, and I have looked and listened in vain for an honest
appraisal of the man's talents.

His contribution to the art of television comedy was minimal. There
were occasions on "Saturday Night Live" when his sledge-hammer technique was amusing but largely as a curiosity and often a pathetic one at
that. On a list of television comedians he deserves a place near the bottom,
in my opinion, and he will be totally forgotten in a few years.

On the human scale, he wouldn't weigh even that much. On the occasions when I have had the misfortune to be in his immediate company, he
was a miserable, uncivilized bore who had a sadly inflated opinion of his
own talent. In person, he would have repulsed all but his most blindly
devoted fans.

It is a sad but accurate fact that NBC's "Saturday Night Live" series was designed to attract the mellow, late-night audience composed of the sleepy and the sloppy and it has been remarkably successful in doing so.

The bottom-line truth is sad: It would have been impossible for John Belushi to have survived a sober, unstoned audience—then or now. He went out in style—HIS.

The question still presents itself: if much of Belushi's behavior was so blatantly offensive, how does one account for the loyalty of his legions of fans? There are several factors to the explanation. One is simply his talent. Those who enjoyed his comedy performances did so precisely because something about their own experience has prepared them to prefer barbarous behavior and raunchy humor to more civilized forms.

Secondly, the shock of his death left the emotions of his admirers raw. The sudden death of a young entertainer—strange as it may sound—is the best thing that can possibly happen to him so far as his ultimate reputation is concerned. Orson Welles recently observed that Marilyn Monroe did not achieve true superstar status until her death. James Dean, too, was more popular dead than alive. And the cult of Elvis developed after his death from drugs and general abuse of his body. The third part of the explanation is that Belushi was successful. So infatuated are the American people with success that it dims their eyes. Even successful criminals are sometimes idolized.

Again, it is sad that Belushi died, particularly as a victim of his own tendency to excess. In so doing, he deprived his admirers of what might have been many remarkable achievements.

Jack Benny

*T*HERE IS SOMETHING A BIT ODD about quoting particular jokes from Jack Benny's shows, or Bob Hope's shows, for that matter. The point is simply that neither Bob nor Jack created the joke in question. On the early February 1981 television special, "A Love Letter to Jack Benny," Jack was shown in an old clip, explaining that his show was not really a special. "All it is is two half-hours put together. It's not a special. To me a special is when coffee goes from 85 cents a pound to 74 cents." A marvelous line; I wish I knew the name of the man who wrote it.

Jack was, however, a great editor of scripts. He knew what was right for him. On the other hand, there being no perfection in the universe, Jack was not always right about material. His long-time friend and manager Irving Fein recalls instances when Jack would complain about material that had been written for him. "I don't want to do this crap," he would say. Recalls Fein, "Those shows were always the best."

In 1926, reviewing the Broadway musical "Great Temptations," the *New York World* said, "There are probably more chorus girls, more pink feathers, more high notes on the cornet and more sets of steps than in any two shows ever given." Little was said in the *World*'s review about a comedian new to Broadway, although the *Herald-Tribune* did note his presence, calling him "a pleasant imitation of Phil Baker." The newcomer's name: Jack Benny.

The comparison was valid. Baker was at the time an established star and his manner of speech was much like Benny's—a deep voice, a slow, casual manner—as opposed to the more staccato Bob Hope or Milton Berle style. Baker played the accordion, Benny the violin.

It's interesting that years later, in 1936, when Jack broke up with his long-time writer Harry Conn, Phil Baker—then a top radio star—came to his rescue by permitting him to borrow two of Baker's writers, Sam Perrin and Arthur Phillips.

Unlike Jack, who was unable to write jokes, Baker himself was a writer and was, in fact, hired by Jack in 1957 to create a theme song for the Gisele McKenzie show, which Benny's company produced.

Another vaudevillian of the early 1920s who influenced Benny early in his career was Frank Fay. Fay was an enormously talented but personally troubled comedian-master of ceremonies. I refer at greater length to his influence on Benny in the forthcoming *Funny People, Volume III.*

In the early days, although he had come to use the violin largely as a prop, an excuse to lead into jokes, Jack still needed it to give him a reason to walk onstage.

"Jack," Fred Allen once said, "was one of the last of the funny musicians to come out of vaudeville. Phil Baker, Ben Bernie, Jack—all started out with music and ended up in comedy."

Just when did he stop being a funny musician and become a comedian? By now the reader will not be surprised at the difficulty involved in trying to determine whether Jack was a true natural comedian or one of the best comedy actors of his time. The word *comedian* can be used in many ways. In its broadest sense it describes any performer who makes audiences laugh; hence it would cover a host of entertainers who would possibly be surprised to find themselves so defined. Jimmy Stewart, Robert Cummings, Cary Grant, Fred MacMurray, Ray Milland, Robert Young, and William Powell, for example, during the '30s and early '40s frequently played comedy roles in motion pictures. More recently Jack Lemmon, James Garner, Burt Reynolds, and James Caan have done the same. Are they comedians? We must be wary of dogmatic pronouncements in any field of the arts; in the area of humor only a fool makes rules.

Jack Benny was basically an actor of comic genius rather than a true essential comedian. As a performer who specialized in comedy roles, Jack was one of the best. He was certainly the smoothest of them all, he appealed to high and low brows, was able to rise above his material, and (one is tempted to ask if anything else matters) he always made audiences laugh. He was the one comedian who never seemed to turn in a bad personal performance.

Yet, although the public rarely differentiates between the creative humorist and the polished comedy technician, authorities tend to make a distinction.

"To me," producer Max Liebman has said, "the true comedians are the people like Groucho, Fred Allen, W. C. Fields, Benchley—those who are funny on stage or off. The others, mind you, can be just as funny, but only when in character. Basically, they don't seem to be comedians. . . . Perhaps there ought to be some other word. They are actors, entertainers or mimics."

Jack Benny, in my opinion, was to humor what Artur Rubinstein was to music: a gifted performer.

Others have remarked that Jack was not creatively humorous. TV-radio critic Ben Gross, of the New York *Daily News,* said, "On no occasion that I have been with Jack Benny socially have I heard him say anything that was truly funny."

Of himself, Jack has said, "I may not be the world's greatest comedian, but I am one of its most successful performers. And I have an explanation for this success. In the first place, I work closely with my writers, who are good ones. But the one factor which has been . . . important is that I'm a damned good editor. Most people don't realize that the star of a weekly comedy series is like the editor of a newspaper or magazine. He has to assign writers to produce certain material."

Unlike comedians of the Milton Berle type who are rarely able to stop entertaining and are consequently amusing in a barbershop, living room, or subway, Jack was reserved, almost shy, and a chronic worrier. Forty years at the very top of the heap did not give him a great deal of emotional security.

Comedians of the Fred Allen genre cannot help speaking in a witty way, even when making small talk, but Jack was a straight man for the whole world; he rarely amused actively, only passively. His was the true "sense" of humor. He understood what was funny and reacted perfectly to it. Indeed, one will search through many pages of his scripts before finding Jack taking the punch line of a joke himself. Jack, except in rare instances, did not tell jokes on his programs, nor did he do many of the funny things for which his program was famous. The jokes were "on" him and the funny things were done *to* him.

Why, then, did we all love to laugh at Jack Benny? For perfectly valid reasons, but they are not the same reasons that we laugh at Richard Pryor, Steve Martin, or Lily Tomlin.

The first reason we laugh at Jack's old films and tapes today is, simply enough, that we have been *conditioned* for over 40 years to do so.

The first time this factor was brought forcefully home to me was one evening in, I believe, 1945, when I went to see a broadcast of the Armed Forces Radio Service program, "Command Performance," that was so popular during World War II. The star of the show that evening was Bob Hope. When announcer Wendell Niles introduced him and he walked on stage, I was surprised at the nature of the ovation the audience gave him. As might have been expected, it began with simple applause, but this was soon drowned out by the sound of laughter, which continued for at least a minute and a half while Hope simply stood at the center of the stage bowing and smiling. He had neither done nor said anything funny, but we were laughing. Our reaction could be explained only on the basis of conditioning. The truth involved in the example is not obscure. On the contrary, it is so obvious that it is often overlooked. A thousand-and-one examples of this sort of emotional conditioning come readily to mind. If a motion-picture director wants to terrify us, he need only present an actor we are conditioned to fear, such as Boris Karloff. A composer need only change a major chord to minor to change our mood from pleasant to sad. Jack reaped tremendous rewards from this simple phenomenon.

His bag of tricks had not been filled when he made his radio debut in 1932 on the old Ed Sullivan show, but two years later when he landed his own series for Jell-O he began almost at once to establish the character that his millions of fans came to know so well.

From the first his scripts were of high caliber, and in the '30s, the first Golden Age of radio comedy, one could see early traces of the personality traits (stinginess, conceit, impatience) that are better known today than the emotional characteristics of Abraham Lincoln. In Sam Perrin, Milt Josefsberg, George Balzer, and John Tackaberry, Jack had for two years a quartet of the best situation comedy writers in the business. For that was Benny's great discovery: he realized that although he had done jokes in vaudeville—almost in what later became known as the Henny Youngman manner—the comedian who depended on big single jokes in radio would suffer when either his supply ran low, styles of humor changed, or better joke-tellers emerged. Ed Wynn, Eddie Cantor, Joe Penner, all were jokesmiths; Jack decided to go by another route, the one blazed by the first giants of radio comedy—Amos and Andy. Freeman Gosden and Charles Correll utilized a story line in what we today think of as the situation comedy formula. So did the wonderful Lum and Abner. You wanted to tune in to their next program partly to be amused and partly to find out what was going to happen. While Jack's shows were always complete within themselves (Amos and Andy continued stories from day to day), he nevertheless moved himself and his supporting players around and motivated them like normal people. He kept his approach realistic, as distinguished from the Bob Hope well-here-we-are-on-the-moon technique. His announcer, Don Wilson, played the part of Don Wilson, the announcer. Kenny Baker and, later, Dennis Day played the role of the young singer on the program. Phil Harris was a band leader. Rochester alone did not play himself, but he played a real-life character, and there are probably millions of Americans today who would swear that Eddie Anderson was actually Jack Benny's valet.

The "situation-comedy" aspect of Jack's radio and TV style is important. Over the course of several years his radio program evolved from an initially conventional form (a comedian, in a radio studio, doing jokes with his announcer, his orchestra leader, etc.) into a form in which story-lines were developed. And then, in the final stage, actual story-plot programs that were not recognized as such simply because Jack was not playing a bartender, a bus driver, or any other make-believe character, but—of all things—himself. The story of one broadcast might simply concern the adventure of putting on a 30-minute program, or inviting Ronald and Benita Coleman to Jack's house for dinner. There was almost always a realistic basis. Only occasionally would Jack play make-believe characters—such as his cowboy klutz Buck Benny—but even these programs had the bedrock of reality under them.

He consistently played a half-cynical, half-naive braggart, parsimonious to a pathological degree, constantly frustrated in the face of insults and physically conceited in such a defensive way that he would lie about his age, his social position, anything that threatened his dignity. Jack's characteristics were always clearly spelled out. Characters for his supporting players were also clearly defined. Irish tenor Dennis Day, for example, was portrayed as stupid. The following was a typical exchange from the late 1946 Benny show.

> DENNIS: (*Offering to change a $20 bill.*) Maybe I can help you. I've got an $18 bill.
> JACK: An $18 bill? Where did you get it?
> DENNIS: Oh, I bought it from a friend for $3.
> JACK: But Dennis, that isn't right.
> DENNIS: I know, but I'm not going to tell the jerk.

In *Jack Benny, An Intimate Biography,* Irving Fein describes the relationship between the two men after Fein joined Benny's staff as a young publicist.

> Although at the time I knew it was a forward step for me, I could not realize that it was the beginning of a relationship that would span almost twenty-eight years and that soon I would come to love Jack Benny as I would a father or a son because he always seemed so helpless and dependent in everything but the creation and performance of his program. His helplessness was communicated to everyone else, too, and just as I found myself worrying about him during all my waking hours, I soon discovered that many others were fretting over him, too, even total strangers. I used to become anxious about him when we were at airports waiting at the gate for the plane's departure. Invariably, he'd wander off to buy a newspaper or magazine, and as the time for the takeoff approached, I knew he could never find his way back to the proper gate alone. When I first started to travel with him, I'd scurry all over the airport looking for him, but finally I learned to relax in the certainty that someone would befriend the unprotected star and get him to the plane on time. And to verify my faith, he always showed up with a guard or a pretty girl or some stranger steering him to the right place at the right time.

Fein reveals another side of Jack that only his close friends were aware of.

> One day, after a few weeks, when I thought that things were rolling smoothly and that I had got to know Jack well, I heard his footsteps coming up the stairs to my office. But instead of his usual springy step, he seemed to plod the stairs slowly, one by one. He walked into the office and sat down opposite me without a word of greeting. I offered an opening line of some sort, but he didn't answer and just sat for several minutes, looking glum and not speaking. I couldn't understand what was happening. Was he getting ready to fire me? What had I done that could have displeased him so much? Was there an item in one of the columns that I shouldn't have planted? While those disquieting thoughts were running through my mind, Jack rose, mumbled a brief good-bye, and left.
>
> Immediately I went to Myrt Blum and asked him to clarify my position and to explain Jack's peculiar behavior. To my astonishment, he just laughed. "Jack isn't like you or me," he said. "Jack gets highs that are much

higher than most when he's exuberant and exhilarated—they can last for days and sometimes weeks. But when he hits a low, and it might be for no reason we know of, he is impossible to talk to."

That was my introduction to Jack's low mood, a condition I was often to find him in through the years. We talked about it frequently, and Jack said that he had been that way all his life. I learned with the passing of time not to worry about it if he became sullen and silent.

Another insight that Fein offers suggests that the usually mild-mannered Benny may have been consciously suppressing an anger he was able to let out only in occasional explosions.

Although he was a mild-mannered man on the surface and most people thought he didn't have an angry bone in his body, quite often Jack would explode. Even though it wasn't a frequent happening, when he would become incensed, it was the anger of a person accustomed to keeping the plug over the boiling water—when the plug was pulled, watch out! Knowing this about himself, he warned people close to him how really angry he would become on occasion. The first time I saw it happen was during a Saturday rehearsal when Mr. and Mrs. Ronald Colman were the guests on the program, probably their second or third guesting. It was the routine to read the radio script while sitting around a table on Saturdays at noon, and then Jack and the writers would polish it after hearing it read, giving them all day Sunday to rehearse and perform the show.

Rochester was very often late for rehearsal, but usually not more than five or ten minutes, but on this day we waited about twenty minutes for him. Jack became more and more embarrassed to hold up the reading with such luminaries as the Colmans until he decided that the reading should start without Rochester. They went through the entire program, and by the time it was finished it was one o'clock, and still no Rochester. "Let's write him out of this show," fumed Jack, and the writers agreed and left to go to the script room for the rewrite. Just as they reached the other room, Rochester arrived, explaining that his plane from San Francisco was late. Jack glowered at him and then, in a voice chilled with anger, said, "You're finished on this show, Rochester," and quickly walked away, leaving Rochester openmouthed.

Rochester was written out of the program, but he came to rehearsal the next day and tried to speak to his boss. Jack remained tight-lipped, refusing to talk to him. Finally, Mary took Jack aside and persuaded him that he was breaking poor Rochester's heart, so Jack relented, and Roch was back on the show. By the following week Jack appeared to have forgotten all about it, and the two were again best of friends.

Born in Chicago in 1894, Benny Kubelsky (whose mother had moved down from Waukegan for the event) showed an early interest in the violin. It is probably common knowledge that Jack did not play the instrument as badly as he professed to. By the time he had reached his teens he was proficient enough to get a job in the pit band of a Waukegan theater. After high school he teamed up with a piano player and began playing small-time houses, but this time on the other side of the footlights. World War I and Jack's enlistment in the navy gave him the opportunity to acquire valuable experience entertaining fellow servicemen. When the war was over it was a more suave, polished performer who returned to vaudeville, although he worked as a violinist for six years before he began doing out-and-out comedy.

On the *Love Letters* show George Burns—Jack's life-long friend—offered an interesting explanation for some of the famous Benny hand-gestures. In vaudeville, Burns pointed out, Jack usually held a violin. In radio his left hand held the script and his right hand turned the pages. Apparently when he began television in the early 1950s, Jack was not entirely sure what to do with his hands. According to Burns, Jack devised his famous hand-to-cheek gesture as one way of solving the problem.

By 1926 he had done well enough to be called to Broadway and *Great Temptations*. In 1927, not long after his marriage to Mary Livingstone, Jack began what was a largely unsuccessful attempt to carve out a film career. Fortunately, during the 1930s he became so big that he no longer needed Hollywood to become a star; radio had done the job. He did appear in several pictures, starting with *The Hollywood Revue* in 1927 and reaching a climax of sorts with his much-kidded *The Horn Blows at Midnight*. Jack, ever mindful of the value of playing the fall-guy, adapted his movie career to good advantage; it was one of the stock subjects on which he could always count for a laugh.

One of the reasons Jack's film career was disappointing is that he had limitations as a physical comedian. That also made it impossible for him to achieve on television the phenomenal success he had enjoyed in radio. Some of the Bennyisms worked for him in the visual medium, most notably the long Oliver Hardy-like blank-faced stare into the camera after a straight-line relating to stinginess, the wearing of the toupee, his age, or any of the other dependable subjects. And his slow, easy-going Phil Baker or Frank Fay vaudeville delivery was better suited to the intimate new medium than was the rapid-fire delivery of the Hopes and Skeltons. For all this, however, he and TV were not ideal for each other, even though his television shows were usually well written and produced. But his own stature was such, by the 1950s, that various film stars, most of whom had refused to appear in TV, finally agreed to do so on Jack's show. Jimmy Stewart, Humphrey Bogart, Fred MacMurray, Kirk Douglas, Bing Crosby, Gary Cooper, Gregory Peck, Claudette Colbert, and others placed their faith in Jack's good taste and were, in consequence, well presented.

Jack was not the only comedian to have a "family" of players around him—Sid Caesar had Carl Reiner, Howard Morris, and Imogene Coca; Jackie Gleason had Art Carney, Pert Kelton (later Audrey Meadows), and Joyce Randolph; Fred Allen had Portland Hoffa, the Mighty Allen Art Players, and the characters of Allen's Alley; and I had those wonderful funnymen Louis Nye, Tom Poston, Don Knotts, Gabe Dell, Bill Dana, Dayton Allen, and Pat Harrington, among others. But Jack and his writers got more mileage out of the formula than the rest of us because of the way in which they utilized Mary Benny, Dennis Day, announcer Don Wilson, singer-bandleader Phil Harris, guitarist Frank Remley, Eddie Anderson, Mel Blanc, Frank Nelson, and others. Part of the reason—as I have earlier observed—is that Jack used his characters in a seemingly realistic "situation comedy" way. Gleason did the same thing in "The Honeymooners," but only 39 of those 30-minute shows were ever made, whereas Benny's characters were firmly impressed on the public consciousness during the 1930s, '40s, and '50s, as well as in numerous personal appearances.

Irving Fein, in recalling Jack's great success in London in 1948, refers to the way that Jack used the identification of the hard-drinking, conceited, loose-living public image of Phil Harris.

JACK: You know, folks since Phil made that picture *Wabash Avenue,* I haven't been able to do a thing with him.

PHIL: Thank you, Jackson. You know I was really great in that picture, wasn't I? What a lover!

JACK: Lover! Phil, if you're such a great leading man, how come at the end of the picture, Victor Mature wins out?

PHIL: He didn't win, Jackson. He lost.
JACK: What are you talking about. He got Betty Grable.
PHIL: I know . . . but he wanted me!

After the Benny-Harris routine, Phil would sing three songs and invariably would finish to tremendous applause as Jack would come out clapping his hands halfheartedly. This jealous reaction would lead to more applause until Phil would raise his hands for silence and then say, "Don't worry, folks, I'll be back . . . because this old man needs me."

And as he made a slow exit with some grinds and kicks, with sound effects from the drums, the laughs would be tremendous as Jack would look with feigned irritation at the spot where Phil had exited. Then Jack would turn and stare at the audience, and, as long as he wanted to continue this maneuver, he could keep the audience laughing. I think the longest laugh I ever heard in a theater happened one night when Jack was in a particularly good mood and kept that laugh going for a very long time, and just as it was dying down, a voice from the second balcony called out, "For God's sykes, Mr. Benny, sye something."

Jack also got more mileage than any other comedian in history playing on the character-failing of conceit. The quality is simply irrelevant to the humor of most comedians. Phil Silvers and Phil Harris played make-believe conceit to an outrageous degree. Jackie Gleason, Danny Thomas, and Bob Hope convey a degree of actual conceit but the factor is a difficult one to work with for the obvious reason that in reality it is an unlikable characteristic.

Irving Fein feels that Jack's penchant for self-deprecating jokes had a negative effect on his film career. "When he began to make movies he continued that line of humor concerning his acting career until unintentionally he gave the kiss of death to offers for more acting jobs in film. Although his motion picture career wasn't particularly distinguished, it was not as bad as his radio gags made it."

Although I share Fein's admiration for Jack, I differ with him on this point. One reason that Jack had no serious prospects as a film actor, was that, like most comedians, he was not a good actor except in comic roles. He could not be believable saying anything the least bit serious. A second problem was that he did not have the physical appearance of a leading man, as did Bob Hope, Red Skelton, and Danny Kaye—and, later, Chevy Chase and Steve Martin.

A third factor was that Jack never *did* anything funny; he merely said funny things, or reacted in a facially amusing way to the funny things said by other characters. This limitation rules out the possibility of his performing in the kinds of scenes that were the stock-in-trade of Chaplin, Laurel and Hardy, Buster Keaton, Harold Lloyd, and other physical comedians.

It might well be asked why, if Jack was so poorly cast for film roles, he had a motion picture career at all. The question is unlikely to be posed by anyone in the entertainment industry. The Peter Principal is relevant. If a performer is successful in one field it is inevitable that attempts will be made to market him in other entertainment areas, whether he is qualified or not. In the 1930s there was something of a vogue for what were generally low-budget films featuring comedians who were successful on radio. Fred Allen, Harold Peary, "The Great Gildersleeve," Fibber McGee and Molly, Eddie Cantor, and a number of other radio personalities appeared in a succession of undistinguished films.

The one good picture in which Jack starred was *To Be or Not to Be,* in which he played opposite Carole Lombard. In this Ernst Lubitsch film Jack played a Polish Shakespearian actor who happened to be doing *Hamlet* with a touring company in 1941 in Warsaw when the city was overrun by the Nazis. We all look better, of course, in a good film and yet something about the natural hamminess of the Shakespearean character harmonized perfectly with the public image that Jack's writers had already established for him on his radio series.

After *The Horn Blows At Midnight,* made in 1946, Jack never did another picture, except for a few cameo appearances.

Perhaps the single most effective element of Jack's style was his ease and relaxation. His slow, naturalistic delivery and apparent confidence put audiences at ease. Many comedians—even including some who are quite funny, such as Don Rickles, Jack Carter, Milton Berle, and Jerry Lewis—make audiences experience moments of discomfort. Jack Benny, by way of contrast, could relax an audience more effectively than any of his peers.

Above all, Jack was comedy's master of timing. You might think a joke in the hands of any proficient professional would stand or fall largely on its own merits, but such is not the case. A split-second delay here, a rushed word there, can make a joke misfire. Benny never missed. Sure-footed as a cat, he walked his confident way through a monologue or a sketch, feeling with the delicate sensibility of the true craftsman just what was the best possible moment to speak, what the most advantageous time to remain silent, regarding the audience with a large, baleful eye.

Timing was extremely important to Jack's comedy, which involved chiefly the humor of reaction. A gifted entertainer can get just as big a laugh from his response to a joke or action as the average comic can with the joke or action itself. The reaction comic is also a superb straight man in that he is able to multiply the value of a laugh.

Jack's usual method was to build to a joke by setting up a straight line, taking it between the eyes with almost effeminate petulance, and then to regard either his adversary or his audience with that distinctive and solemn appraisal that said so much. Technically, he might vary the looking bit by saying, "Well!" or "Hmmmm!" but the dramatic effect was the same.

Arthur Marx has suggested that Jack also used the staring-at-the-audience business as a means of making certain that no supporting radio player would come in too soon and step on the laugh. When Jack had decided he'd milked the reaction to the proper extent, Marx says Don Wilson told him, "he turns away from the audience and faces the person who had the next line. Until then that person isn't allowed to speak."

Jack had an alternative reaction too, the openly angry "Oh, cut that out!" take.

That Jack could go on year after year getting laughs with those two readings was the ultimate tribute to his sense of timing and script judgment. He knew just when to throw the proper punch.

Another fascinating point about Jack's humor is that he made himself consistently inferior in a limited and familiar number of ways. Here was the formula: Jack Benny is ridiculous because he is a *liar,* a *penny pincher,* and a *conceited ham.* He is a liar because he claims to be only thirty-nine years old, when we know he is in his sixties or seventies. He also lies about his toupée.

Jokes on his stinginess filled every script. Jack's appropriation of the humor involved in all the ancient Scottish jokes was, in my opinion, the most consistently successful single comedy gimmick in the history of humor. For 40 years we laughed at the same sort of jokes. Finally, a phase was reached where it didn't even have to *be* a joke; any passing reference to Jack's close-fistedness would make you laugh. The conditioning had been perfect, and the personal identification ironclad.

Consider, by way of proof, this example, which I first quoted in *The Funny Men,* a book on comedy published in 1956: Bob Hope, in one of his films, is walking down a dark street. Suddenly a hold-up man appears from out of the darkness and shoves a gun in his ribs, saying, "Your money or your life."

Bob pauses momentarily and then says, "I'm thinking it over."

Good joke? Yes, fair enough, although not up to Hope's usual standards.

But the incident, if you are not a million miles ahead of me, is *not* from a Bob Hope movie. It's from a Benny radio script. Go over the scene again now and notice the difference in your reaction.

On the air the laughter started after the *straight* line! The very *idea* of someone holding up Jack Benny was amusing. Jack let the audience relish the simple prospect for at least half a minute. Then, at just the proper split second, when the audience had squeezed every last drop of enjoyment out of the situation, he read the "I'm thinking it over" line in his spoiled-child sort of way. The laugh probably set a record for length and volume.

Jack had a better, clearer understanding of himself in his professional capacity than I have found in any other comedian. He was at all times aware of what was best for his character and had an uncanny knack for predicting what would be funny. When I functioned as master of ceremonies for the television "Emmy" Awards in 1955, it happened that Jack and I were on the same plane going out to Hollywood for the show. Later, sitting in the hotel lounge talking before we retired, I asked him if he had seen his part of the script. He told me he had not. Next day he telephoned and said, "Steve, I've just seen the script. These jokes are no good in a spot like this. They're just the usual penny-pinching, tightwad stuff that everybody always tries to write for me. I think I'll kick something else around and bring it in to rehearsal."

What Jack brought in the next day was just a page and a half of dialogue, but it was right. It was suitable for the occasion. It was simply relaxed conversation that built to one big laugh, then picked up the pieces and headed slowly but surely after another.

After I introduced him, Jack said:

JACK: Thank you, Steve. . . . It's nice to see you again, and I want to congratulate you on all the fine shows you've done from New York.

STEVE: Thank *you*, Jack. You've been doing a swell job too. By the way, are you one of the nominees for an award tonight?

JACK: Yes, Steve. I'm in the category of the Variety Musical Shows.

STEVE: Well . . . do you think you'll win?

JACK: Well, Steve, you know me. . . . You know I'm a pretty modest fellow.

STEVE: That's right, Jack. Modesty has always been your nature.

JACK: You've never heard me brag in my life.

STEVE: No, that's right, Jack. I never have.

JACK: You've never heard me talk about my shows or how good I am, have you?

STEVE: No, I must admit, I haven't. That's why I ask you—do you think you'll win an Emmy tonight?

JACK: Well, Steve, let me put it this way, I can't see *how* I can possibly lose.

STEVE: But, Jack, what about the other shows in your category— "Disneyland," George Gobel, Jackie Gleason, Ed Sullivan, "Hit Parade"? They're all good television shows too.

JACK: What?

STEVE: They're all good *television* shows too.

JACK: Oh, television! . . . I thought this was for *radio*. Well, let's see . . . "Disneyland," George Gobel, Jackie Gleason, Ed Sullivan, and "Hit Parade." There's five votes against me right there. Gobel's so young, too. . . . Oh, well.

STEVE: Well, anyway, best of luck, Jack. *(Steve walks off.)*

JACK: It's hard to believe he's Fred Allen's son.

The long build-up to a laugh was another distinctive thing about Jack's style. Most other comedians cram a volume of jokes down the throats of the audience; Jack got a more realistic feeling by using great stretches of what seemed to be true-to-life dialogue and then scored strongly with an isolated powerful line.

At the rehearsal for the "Emmy" show, Jack said to the director, "Now, when I get to the line where I say I don't see how I can possibly lose, give me a good close-up and I'll look right into the camera. I mean, that's such a *terrible* thing to say that I'll just have to stand there alone and let the audience hate me. You know what I mean?"

A few minutes later, when we were going over the lines, Jack said, "Steve, I hope you don't mind playing straight to me here. After all, I've been a straight man for twenty-five years."

Here is seen again Jack's complete understanding of his comedy character.

Benny's personal character was as warm and generous as his make-believe character was despicable. Lunching at the Brown Derby the afternoon of the Emmy show, I asked his advice as to what sort of material would be suitable for an address I had to make the following week at a testimonial dinner for Dean Martin and Jerry Lewis. Jack talked for fifteen minutes, telling me what I wanted to know, advising me wisely and well. Our luncheon finally broke up because he had to go to Cedars of Lebanon Hospital to visit his director Ralph Levy. If he hadn't felt the need to visit Ralph, Jack could have spent the afternoon at the golf course. Many other actors would have gone to the country club and *called* Levy. Some wouldn't have done that much.

Benny was always a good audience for other comedians, unlike some of his peers who seem determined to remain grim-lipped rather than acknowledge that someone else is being funny. One night Jayne and I were having dinner with him, Mary, and some others at a Beverly Hills restaurant. In the close quarters of our corner table a waiter, passing behind me with a silver pot of hot coffee, accidentally spilled some of the liquid on my head. Naturally I was startled, yelped a soft "ow!" and dabbed at my head with a napkin.

"I'm terribly sorry, sir," the waiter said. "Is there anything I can do?"

"Yes," I said. "Would you please drop a little cream and sugar up there, too?"

Jack not only laughed hysterically but insisted on interrupting other conversations going on at the table and quoting the line. Most other comedians, I'm afraid, wouldn't have done that.

Jack was always willing to take the time to help and advise younger comedians. Tom Dreesen reminisced about this for me.

Jack was one of my idols and I was told early in my career to study the masters. Before he passed away I was able to meet him, several times, with the help of Irv Kupcinet in Chicago, a columnist who put me on his TV show with Jack. After the show we were going to have something to eat. We walked down the hall and Jack held on to my arm like a father would do, this gentle old man. He started talking about what acceptance was. He gave me some advice I used on my first "Tonight Show." He said, "Tom, when you first walk out on a national television show, don't tell the people what you don't like about the airlines, what you don't like about the federal government. They don't know who you are yet. Tell them about *you*. Tell them Tom Dreesen and where you're from—Harvey, Illinois—and tell them where Harvey is—it's a suburb on the South side of Chicago—so that they now know where your accent is coming from. Then tell them about your eight brothers and sisters, getting laughs with all of this. Tell them about your Catholic school background. You know, whatever it was about your childhood.

So that after six minutes of laughter, you walk off and they'll say, 'Gee, wasn't that boy funny? And you know, he's from Harvey, Illinois. And do you know that he had eight brothers and sisters? And do you know that he went to Catholic school?' And now what you've done is you've introduced yourself to America with laughter."

I took his advice.

Jack told me something else very interesting. He said, "Tom, comedians have been saying for years, 'I'm from New York, I'm from Chicago.' You're from Harvey, Illinois. There's never been a comedian, ever in the history of show business, from Harvey, Illinois. So that's going to set you apart from all the others immediately." Then he began to talk about what acceptance was. He told me the most interesting story, about how through the years all these mannerisms of his became nationally known, and so consequently they received great acceptance. He said that one time in Las Vegas one of the stagehands said to him, "Jack, how long could you be on stage without saying a word and still get laughs?" Jack said, "That's an interesting thought. Let's try it."

That night they played "Love In Bloom," and the audience began to titter, anticipating Jack's entrance. When Jack walked on, he took two steps on stage and the spotlight hit him. He froze. He looked up at the spotlight as if to say, "Where did that come from?" And the audience started to laugh at that. When they began to laugh, he looked out at them with his deadpan look, as if to say, "What are you laughing at?" And they laughed some more. But when they laughed a little louder he looked into the wings with that puzzled look on his face, like "I don't know what they're laughing at." He then started to walk slowly toward the microphone, with that duck-walk that he had, and they began to roar. Well, when they started to roar and applaud, he stopped again. And he looked at them again, then looked in the wings, and, of course, more laughter followed. And finally, when he got to the microphone, he stopped and deadpanned the audience from stage right to stage left, with the audience hysterical. He hadn't said a word. Now he began to take his time and look at his watch. Well, they began to roar at him looking at his watch. When they started laughing again he looked into the wings, as if to say, "What's *wrong* with these people?" He started to tape his foot, as if just passing time. They began to laugh at that. He put his hands on his hips and, of course, that got more laughter—his famous pose. For seven minutes he did not utter a sound. They timed it backstage. And he finally opened with, "Well . . ." Of course, more laughter.

I've always been impressed by that story. Jack said, "That's what acceptance is. And Tom, that won't come to you in your first year of comedy. That might not come in your first 25 years. But eventually America will know you and you'll have that sort of acceptance. And how wonderful it is to go out to an audience. At this stage of your career you're walking out in front of a group of strangers every night who do not know who you are. That's why you must introduce yourself to them. You must tell them who you are and where you're from. So now they know a little bit about you, they're willing to laugh at you."

Jack Benny was on top for a long time by playing "himself"; maybe the fact that he himself was the exact opposite of this public character had a lot to do with his success.

Milton Berle

THERE USED TO BE AN OLD SAYING in show business that "nobody likes Milton Berle except his mother and the public." Well, Milton's mother is no longer around to cheer him on. But, happily, almost all of Milton's former critics have departed as well. In the 1980s Milton has achieved a stature like that of George Burns—something of a grand old man of comedy. The word *old,* however, must be modified when referring to Milton, for although he is in his seventies he is amazingly youthful in appearance, attitude and energy. And he is, too, a dear fellow, warm and generous with his time and talent.

Some of his earlier critics were Milton's fellow comedians. He had not so much talent, they said, as energy. He had carefully memorized, according to their theory, almost every joke ever written; he was a scene-stealer and a ham; he lacked taste and sublety. In responding to these charges, I once said in print, "At the risk of seeming controversial I should like to state that I think Milton Berle is a very funny man."

That is not to deny that some of the things his detractors have said about him are true. Milton is a ham. He does—if rarely—use other people's jokes (so do most comedians). He will do anything for a laugh. But the important thing, to my mind, is that he gets the laugh.

Woody Allen agrees that Milton has a continuing ability to amuse. "I find Berle hysterically funny," he has said. "He's one of the few people I've gone to see in years. There is a certain kind of broadness one associates with television show presentations like the old "Milton Berle Show," as opposed to, say, a much tighter kind of thing like Nichols and May or Sid Caesar. Caesar does a sketch about a Japanese movie, it looks like a Japanese movie. It's very realistic and consequently it's funny. Milton belongs to that school of comedy that's very broad, and of course he's the best of that school. If he does a Japanese movie he comes in with the two teeth hanging down and it's hysterical, but for Milton exclusively. Most of the TV shows had all the stupid broadness of the

Berle shows without the genius that Milton had. At least when Milton's in women's clothes he's hysterical. He's a guy whose delight in dressing up in women's clothes and blacking teeth out is so spectacular that you're overwhelmed by it."

It is not correct to say that he has more energy than talent. Part of his talent *is* his energy. Another part is his consummate technical mastery of his craft. His comedy timing is superb. He is, mechanically speaking, a marvelous clown. Berle is a top-notch buffoon, and buffoonery, despite its apparent slapdashery, is a delicate art. It isn't enough to walk on a stage and simply make faces and repeat jokes, as any bank clerk who has ever tried to entertain can attest. You must know at precisely which fraction of a second a grimace will add to the power of a joke and not weaken it. You must know exactly what to do with your hands, how to stand, how loudly to speak, how to spar with an audience. You must know how to recover from the shock of getting no laugh where one was expected, and how to turn the momentary defeat into a greater triumph. If these things were talents in the public domain then you and your Aunt Fanny would have been known, in the 1950s, as Mr. or Mrs. Television and Milton Berle would be running a meat market.

Berle is an excellent mimic and a smooth dialectician. His face is a rubber mask that in the twinkling of an eye can mirror whatever emotion he believes will augment his delivery of a line.

The amusing combination of gestures with which Milton has for years responded to applause—holding one hand up as if to stop the applause while, with the lower hand, half-surreptitiously signalling that more will be acceptable—is reminiscent of the ancient words of the great teacher Hillel, addressing the question of the conversion of gentiles to Jewish faith: "Let thy right hand ever repel, and thy left hand invite." (*Sanhedrin* 107B. and *Sotah* 47A)

Any critic who feels that Milton is nothing more than a walking gag file underestimates the dimensions of even that capacity. I don't see why a man should be criticized for memorizing thousands of jokes, as have Milton, Morey Amsterdam, and Henny Youngman. To me it seems a tremendous feat. I wish I could do it.

A few years ago when Berle was Mr. Television in fact as well as in name, his critics offered a peculiar reason to explain his success. "It's not surprising," they said, "that Milton is number one man in TV right now, because so far it's been a field day for amateurs. What competition has he got?"

There was something to that argument, but not much. When the big-name entertainers did deign to take the TV plunge nothing serious happened to Milton's popularity. Eventually he was no longer king of the hill, but no performer has ever long remained number one. The American public can never sustain feverish enthusiasm for any entertainer for more than a few years. The cry for new faces and new shows is forever loud.

A thousand examples, in every field of entertainment, could be supplied. Bing Crosby was not only a big name, but practically an American institution; it is probable that no other singer will ever match his over-all long-time popularity. Yet try to find one story about Bing in the fan magazines of the 1950s. It was all Eddie Fisher, Julius La Rosa, and later Elvis Presley. The mood of the people is ever-changing. When Berle finally slipped from the pinnacle of popularity it had very little to do, I think, with the matter of competition.

Berle's success as a nightclub and vaudeville entertainer stood him in good stead on TV stages. His monologue technique—and it is one imitated by many of his 1940s and '50s competitors—is to engage in a sort of running battle with his audience. Stock lines like "What is this, an audience or a jury?" are his specialty. He doesn't just tell jokes *for* his audience, in the way that Bob Hope does; he tells jokes *at* his audience.

"Say, mister," he says to a bald-headed man at a ringside table, "would you mind moving? Your head is shining right into my eyes." After the laugh he sneaks in with "For a minute I thought you were sitting upside down." That's a peculiarity of Berle's style, too. Hit 'em with a laugh when they think they're through laughing. Berle does jokes about jokes, about the audience. "I just got wonderful news from my real estate broker down in Florida," he will say, chuckling. "They found land on my property down there." Then, before the laughter dies: "You think I'm a fool, eh? Don't forget, you paid!"

Most of Milton's traditional monologues sound less than exciting in cold print. The reason, paradoxically enough, is that second-rate comics have done the same kinds of jokes for years, sometimes picking up the lines from Milton. The gags have been overworked in every night club in the country. But Berle can still make you laugh with them, even if you've heard them before.

Good evening, ladies and gentlemen. (But why should I call you ladies and gentlemen? You know what you are.) But folks, on behalf of the

Copacabana (and believe me, I'd *like* to be half of the Copacabana) I just want to *(slight belch)*—I don't remember eating that. But mind you . . . mind you . . . (Adolph Mindyou) I just got back into town from Florida. I flew up. Boy, are my arms tired. They surely do gamble down there, though. You know that white flag above the Hialeah race track? That's my shirt. I had a wonderful compartment on the train on the way down. But the conductor kept locking me in at every station. And now, folks, I'd like to bring out a wonderful little dancer. You've all heard masters of ceremonies say, 'I now bring you a boy who needs no introduction.' Well, folks, this kid needs plenty of introduction.

But first, ladies and germs—I mean gentlemen—Don't mind me, folks. It's all in fun. I'm just kidding. It all goes in one head and out the other. But I feel good tonight. I just came over from Lindy's. I always go over there for a cup of coffee and an overcoat. (I'll dig 'em up if you'll remember 'em.) But as I was saying—this next boy needs no introduction. He just needs an act. No, I'm only kidding. I want to bring him out here right now. Our worst act—I'm sorry, I mean our *first* act. *(Woman laughs.)* Say, are you laughing longer or am I telling 'em better? Say, lady, are you sitting on a feather? *(More laughter.)* Look, madam, if you want to lay an egg don't do it here! I just want you to know that I'm going to play the piano with this first act, and I want you to notice that at no time while I'm playing do any of my fingers leave my hands. *(Frowns at audience.)* All right, these are the jokes! What is this, an audience or an oil painting? Looks like a staring contest out there. I don't have to do this for a living, you know . . . I can always sell sleeping pills to Senator Hayakawa. Now folks, I'd like to prevent, I mean *present* our first act . . .

The above gives a good idea of the style of the old Berle, the pre-Goodman-Ace Berle. Machine-gun gagging of this sort kept Milton on top for several years, but when at last audiences began to tire of the sameness he was wise enough to restyle his program. No longer did he simply emcee a vaudeville show. He became aware that a story line was important.

Ace and Milton worked out an arrangement whereby the "new" Berle would become more sympathetic by occasionally playing straight for other comics, by being the target of jokes rather than firing them. Jokes about Milton's actual (or popularly supposed to be actual) faults were heavily interlarded into his scripts. His gag thievery, his hamminess, his desire to run the whole show, became the basis for countless put-downs.

Consider the following portion of the script from the broadcast on which prizefighter Ezzard Charles, actress Janet Blair, and I were Milton's guests.

> MILTON: Hello, Janet. Long time no see.
>
> JANET: Well, Milton, I've been on the road for three years in *South Pacific*.
>
> MILTON: Oh, long time plenty of sea, huh. I got that joke from Maria Riva. Clever joke?
>
> JANET *(Coldly)*: You ought to wash that joke right out of your files.
>
> MILTON: Say, Janet, you look wonderful. How about being a guest on the Buick show?
>
> JANET: Wonderful. Do you know anybody connected with the show?
>
> MILTON: Are you kidding? Do you know who the star of the show is?
>
> JANET: Yes, but I can never get in to see Jack Lescoulie.
>
> MILTON: Listen, you'd be pretty lucky to come on my show. After all, forty million people will catch you.
>
> JANET: Yeah? How come they haven't caught you?

Or, for another example, consider the part of the script where, while wandering through the audience interviewing people (supposedly on my own program), I come across Milton. I have just found a man who didn't respond at all to my questions and after lifting one of his closed eyelids I have reported, "Usher, this man is dead!"

> MILTON: *(Smiles goofily as Steve turns to him)*
>
> STEVE: Usher, here's another one!
>
> MILTON: What program is this: "This Was My Life"? What is this, a ghost-to-ghost network? So you're the M.C., Master of Cemeteries, huh?
>
> STEVE: Folks, the views expressed by this gentleman are not necessary.
>
> MILTON: Oh, that's good. I wish I'd said that.
>
> STEVE: You will.* But Milton, I'm glad you came over to my show. I must say I think you're one of the great stars of television.
>
> MILTON: Thank you.
>
> STEVE: I must say it because you said you wouldn't come on the program unless I did.

---

*This joke may have been done on every Berle show of the past 30 years.

The story-line approach and the appeal to sympathy were perhaps a necessary concession to public taste, but to me Milton is still funniest alone, off the cuff, battling an audience, or reacting to a real-life situation. Countless times I have seen him on night-club floors, at banquets, at telethons, on bare stages, creating humor spontaneously, striking fire by combining his two great assets: a prodigious memory and a lightning-quick sense of the ridiculous. There is nothing dignified about Milton's work. He is not the stately humorist dropping pearls. He is the bad-boy extrovert, the wisecracking, punning, iconoclastic clown who even now, in his 70s, can make any audience laugh, whether they want to or not.

Now and then people who do not clearly appreciate the power of a talent like Milton's have said to me, "Boy, I'd have liked to see a real ad-libber like Groucho Marx or Fred Allen up against Berle sometime." Well, do you know what would have happened if Groucho, Fred (or I) actually had attempted to compete with Milton? We'd have been slaughtered. While we were creating and delivering one good quotable new joke, Milton would be doing five old ones.

Berle is fast on his feet but is more creative than his critics realize. Perhaps the next day, if you had a transcript of everything Milton and his adversary said in the exchange, you might find that the humorist's two or three jokes were, judged individually, more amusing than Berle's two or three dozen, but that's not the way the game is played. You don't play it on paper; your instrument is the audience. And Milton would have the audience so distracted and amused that, at the time, they'd scarcely be noticing what the other fellow was saying. This actually happened to the very clever Henry Morgan one night and when Henry was at the height of his popularity at that. Berle had just finished speaking at a dinner at the Waldorf; as he was leaving the room Morgan, at the microphone, threw a barb about his ad-libbing ability. Hearing the laugh, Milton turned and walked back to Henry. "So you want to ad-lib, eh?" he said. What followed was painful to watch, but the audience watched—and laughed. With insults, old jokes, new twists, mugging, voice volume, arm-waving, interrupting, and every trick in the book, Milton succeeded in making Henry look like an inept newcomer. He accomplished it not by being funnier than Henry but just by overpowering him. Interestingly enough, there are comics in the business who can top Milton by the same methods. I have seen Jack E. Leonard, Morey Amsterdam, and Henny Youngman top Milton, as the phrase goes, by simply outshouting and outinsulting him. Pure distilled humor has little to do with it.

But Milton succeeded in television where most comedians of the steam-roller type are too unsympathetic to secure regular employment on TV. One reason is that for all his rough-and-tumble exterior, for all his super-confidence, there is something genuinely warm and likable at the heart of him. Milton personally is friendly, outgoing, and generous. He is a tireless worker for charitable causes and always willing to give a friend or an acquaintance a helping hand. Speaking of his character, columnist Bob Sylvester has said, "As brash and confident as he is while working, Berle is paradoxically a sensitive man, and he can be almost overwhelmingly kind. He rarely brushes off a down-and-outer. He has time to stop and converse with anybody in the world who will stop him for advice. He is openhanded with everyone who comes within his orbit, with one exception—Milton Berle. He spends very little money on himself and dresses no better than many an out-of-work imitator."

Sylvester also tells the story of a girl named Jean Kurowsky, who was president of one of Milton's fan clubs. Somewhat shy because she had an oversized nose, Jean was thrilled one Christmas when Milton gave her a present that he knew she'd especially appreciate: a nose operation.

The Berle story began on the twelfth of July 1908 in the home of Moe and Sarah Berlinger on New York's West 118th Street. When Milton was seven years old he polished up an imitation of Charlie Chaplin, his mother entered him in an amateur contest, and he won. Milton's father was ill, his mother had to work as a department store detective, his three older brothers were not yet old enough to win the bread, and for several years Milton knocked around the semiamateur circuit. Then one day E. W. Wolf, a Philadelphia agent who booked kid shows for small vaudeville circuits, offered Mom Berle forty-five dollars a week for Milton's services. Since this was fifteen dollars more than she was making catching shoplifters, she quit her job and became a fulltime stage mother, thereby setting up a professional relationship that became one of the most legendary in show-business history.

Not long after that Milton and the other Berle children got into motion pictures on the real ground floor: at the Fort Lee, New Jersey, studios across the Hudson River. Sarah Berlinger had learned that children were paid a dollar-fifty an hour as walk-ons, and since she had a brood of five it wasn't long before the pioneer moguls had accepted her as a sort of unofficial casting agency for youngsters. Soon Milton was earning seven-fifty a day playing small parts with Pearl White, Lloyd Hamilton, Milton Sills, Marion Davies, and other stars of the early silent days. During all this period, of course, there was the matter of education to attend to, and Milton was enrolled in the Professional Children's School, from which he was eventually graduated with honors.

Believe it or not, at this stage of his career, Milton earned a few extra dollars one week by working as my baby-sitter. He and my mother (who was in vaudeville) were on the same bill, and, apparently, backstage arrangements for my care were in a somewhat confused state. I was about two years old at the time. (Years later, when my mother died, in her late seventies, Milton returned the favor. He had once described my mother—whose professional name was Belle Montrose—as "the funniest woman in vaudeville." In any event, when he heard of her death he called me and said that he would be happy to serve as one of the pall-bearers. And serve he did. As he helped carry the casket out of the Blessed Sacrament Catholic Church on Sunset Boulevard in Hollywood, he was muttering jokes to me—I wish I could remember what they were—and all-in-all helping to make a painful moment easier to bear.)

When Milton was eleven years old, a boy named Ben Grauer, later familiar to radio and television audience, had left the act of a young entertainer named Elizabeth Kennedy on the big-time Keith-Albee circuit. Milton replaced Grauer, and the team of Berle and Kennedy was an immediate hit, at last playing the Palace Theater, the mecca of all vaudevillians.

After several years Elizabeth Kennedy left show business to get married, and Milton found himself working alone. It was during this period that he got the reputation of being a material thief. Milton makes no bones about the matter, however, and insists that he is the only comedian honest enough to admit that he has borrowed other people's jokes, whereas many others do it under the table. He feels that almost all jokes are in the public domain.

Another point which should be made, of course, is that the matter of Milton's joke pilferage had been exaggerated. He contends today that his reputation as the Thief of Bad-gags was largely the result of a planned feud between himself and a monologist named Richie Craig. "It's like Benny's tightness or Hope's nose," he says. "I go along with the gag now because the public expects it. But the man on the street wouldn't be able to tell you one joke I ever stole." True.

Ironically enough, Milton had such an effect on the style of young comedians who followed in the 1940s and '50s that he is probably more sinned against than sinning. As Richie Craig said, before his death, "I'm still not sure whether Milton Berle sounds like all comedians or all comedians sound like Milton Berle."

To anyone who remembers Milton Berle as merely a file of one-line jokes and a gag-man, I submit the following account. In the late 1930s, Milton had just opened in Chicago, to great critical acclaim. "The audiences loved me," he has recalled. "I ran wild on the stage, and almost everything got a big laugh." Then the shocking recollection:

One evening I was on stage doing my act. I was standing out on the runway ripping through my one-liners. I always got a big laugh on the line "My idea of moving fast is to see Hitler running down Maxwell Street," which was the Jewish section of Chicago. I got the laugh, which Mama built by adding her high-pitched giggle, but just as it was dying down I heard someone say, "Kike!"

Maybe I heard wrong, maybe I didn't. I went on, and a moment later I got "Jew bastard." I spotted the guy, an ox with a bald head and a neck like a wrestler. He was in the first row, which was maybe a foot away from me because of the runway I was on, and his face was red with anger. I looked at him. He looked right back and muttered, "Hitler's right."

I started steaming, but I tried to go on with the show. A minute later I heard "Kike!" again. Danny Russo, the pit-band leader, also heard it. He signaled me to ignore it, but I couldn't. I took a flying leap from the front ramp over to the aisle and grabbed for the guy, who was in the second seat off the center aisle. I dragged him out into the aisle. "Leave me alone, you dirty Jew!" he screamed, and the theater suddenly went dead quiet. Now, everyone had heard him.

I tried to make it a big joke to keep the audience in line. I started waltzing the guy, as if we were doing a routine together. I was in close to him and I spun him so his back was to most of the audience. "Shall we dance?" I shouted, and there was some laughter. It covered the groan as I kneed him in the groin. As he sagged, I gave him a short chop in his belly. I don't know where that guy got his strength from, but he managed to get in one good punch at me. It sent me into a blind rage. The last thing I saw was the guy falling into the aisle. I wanted to kill him. I slammed my foot into his face and then I fell on him, punching away. I could hear screaming all around me, and over it my mother's scream, louder than all the rest. Then there were hands all over me, pulling me off him. The next thing I really knew, we were both in the manager's office, with at least three ushers still hanging on to me. The guy's face was a mess, and I could feel my own blood running down my chin. Then the police were there and I was arrested. I missed the last show that night, but I was out in time for the first show the next day. So were the newspapers, with headlines that read: "Berle Flattens Nazi Sympathizer."

Few people realize, incidentally, that because of Milton's wide variety of experience in the many phases of show business he is equally at home whether he is pitching or catching. Arnold Stang says, "In twelve years I haven't seen anyone to compare with Milton Berle as the finest straight man in the business. Watch him when he works with me, or with Ruthie Gilbert. He makes us seem lots funnier than we are." This ability, to make supporting performers seem vastly amusing, is a very specialized one.

In early March of 1981 I had the pleasure of performing on a three-hour PBS comedy-variety special with the embarrassing title of "Something Spectacular with Steve Allen." We performed Milton's classic "That's Not Funny" routine, in which the two participants get into a seemingly serious argument over what is or is not funny. The sketch opens with Berle starting to sing, in all seriousness, "September Song." At that point the master of ceremonies walks on, interrupts the vocal and demands to know what is going on.

Milton explains that he is singing, at which I—or whoever might play straight in the sketch—protest, saying that it is absurd for one of the great comedians to sing a dull ballad "in the middle of a swinging comedy show."

Milton responds by saying that he appreciates the compliment but thinks it might be worthwhile to demonstrate his versatility.

I answer that when people see Milton Berle advertised they expect to see him do the schtick and routines for which he is famous. Milton explains that that sort of thing is now old hat; "that's not funny" anymore. At this point I remind Milton of the wonderful things he used to do—the things that people like Laurel and Hardy had also done—such as Oliver Hardy taking a pair of scissors and cutting Stan Laurel's tie with it. From that point on the sketch is physical mayhem. The straight man acts out every old sight gag that he claims to want to see.

Milton nevertheless steadfastly refuses to see the humor in any of it, despite the fact that within a few minutes his tie has been cut, his suspenders have been cut, his pants have fallen down around his ankles, revealing bright comedy underwear, his face is covered with powder from a large puff, and his body is drenched with water from a seltzer bottle. I will not reveal the "surprise ending" of the sketch but simply point out that it is a classic of its kind and that probably no other comedian could perform it in the marvelously broad, old-fashioned, and perfectly proper way that Milton does.

Milton stressed, when we were rehearsing (he always takes charge of rehearsals, whoever he is performing with) that in conducting my argument with him I must do so in all seriousness and not deviate, for even a split-second, by any sort of word-play or physical mannerism that could be construed as out of character. Needless to say he was absolutely right about this, nor was there any difference of opinion between us on the point. To be amusing the sketch must be played in deadly earnest. I later heard from a good many people, including some in their twenties, that they thought this was one of the funniest routines they'd ever seen. Indeed it is.

For all his night club, theater, and television success, Milton did not achieve stardom in radio or motion pictures. The reasons are obvious. On a movie lot Milton was not working in front of an audience and although he could still be amusing he was not the complete Berle, the catch-as-catch-can madman who plays an audience as if it were a musical instrument and can adapt his material to suit the exigencies of a given situation. In radio he was an invisible voice; his unsympathetic characterization and flagrant mugging combined to make him essentially as unsuited to the medium as were Dean Martin and Jerry Lewis at a later time. In television, of course, he was in his element because it allowed him the closest approach to his nightclub technique. Even so, TV, with its technical frustrations, proved to be more of a nervous strain on Milton than any other medium. Berle's reaction to the strain was simple and straightforward: he spent most of his rehearsal week growling at his director, conductor, writers, and technicians. As air time approached he got even more touchy. His rehearsals were interrupted every few seconds by emotional pleas for quiet in the studio, for more volume from the public-address system, for changes in camera moves, or for faster entrances on the part of supporting players. Milton perspired freely and carried a towel wrapped, scarflike, around his neck. He used to carry a police whistle, too. Even when the show was on the air he was still worrying, sweating. I have stood waiting for an entrance cue and seen him come charging offstage for split-second costume changes, making demands in angry whispers in the wings, cursing a blue streak at what, if anything, had gone wrong on stage. It is small wonder that he cannot go home to bed immediately after a show but must spend hours on the town or visiting friends to relieve his tension. "It's like a race horse after a mile-and-an-eighth," he explains. "You have to cool off and get unwound."

In the process of getting unwound Milton becomes once again the considerate, if occasionally rambunctiously funny man his friends know. Ruth Berle, his wife, told me that on their first date Milton took her to the then-famous Lindy's restaurant in midtown Manhattan. On their table was a serving bowl of cold sauerkraut.

At one point, Milton grabbed a handful of it, held it to his chin as if it were a beard, looked her in the eye, pointed a finger and said, "Uncle Sam wants *you!*"

Milton makes pleasant small talk at the table. He is a check-grabber, delights in reminiscing and telling old show-business stories. And, significantly, I think, he seems eternally young. Comedians in general retain their youth better than, say, bankers, clergymen or truck drivers. Milton particularly will seem for many years to come a young man. He has the energy of a child, and a child's desire to please, to be laughed at, accepted. Audiences will continue to accept him. A comedian has, after all, only one function; to make you laugh.

Milton always does.

George Carlin

George
Carlin

*L*IKE MOST OF THOSE WHO EVENTUALLY become professionals at the art of comedy, George realized by the age of 7 that he had the ability to amuse. At first, in keeping with the traditional pattern, his audience consisted of friends and members of his family. Seeing comedian Danny Kaye in a film provided him with a goal toward which to aim. Most of us, looking back, cannot recall even the general time period when we first knew what we wanted to do with our lives. In Carlin's fifth grade yearbook, under the question, "What about your future?" George had written, "When I grow up, I would like to be either an actor, a radio announcer, an impersonator or a comedian."

George was born in 1937. His social background is New York upper West Side's Morningside Heights. Contrary to what is sometimes assumed—that his present anti-Catholic monologues grow out of the traditional soil of a too-strict disciplinarian approach to grade school education—George in fact attended what even he refers to as a progressive Catholic school. In my own childhood I was accustomed to having the hell beat out of me by assorted nuns, brothers, and priests, by no means always deservedly so. The nuns that taught Carlin, he reports, were reasonable. "There was no Sister Mary Discipline with a steel ruler—Whack!"

Carlin's high school experiences were, to some degree, par-for-the-course. He attended Cardinal Hayes, which he describes as "a big league Catholic high school, big jock, big band."

Although it is sometimes argued that Lenny Bruce and George Carlin have done more or less the same kinds of jokes about the Catholic Church, there are important differences in their approaches to the subject matter. Lenny took a lot of heat simply because he did *any* jokes about the Church. In the '50s and '60s that Just Wasn't Done. His joke, for example, about the Dodge Company planning to raffle off a 1964 Catholic Church was, while funny, actually quite innocuous. There probably isn't an over-45 Las Vegas comic in the business who doesn't do Catholic raffle or bingo jokes of the same sort.

Carlin, however, is a former Catholic, and a joke from one who has Abandoned the Faith always carries a certain weight that the same line from an outsider would not. Carlin's Catholic material is usually more hard-hitting and bitter than Lenny's, despite the fact that he said to journalist Mark Goodman in 1978, "There's more gentleness in my comedy than there was in his."

It is difficult to find the gentleness in the following Carlin monologue:

> I used to be an Irish Catholic . . . I was worried about sin, especially the sin of "wanna" . . . "Wanna" was a sin all by itself . . . It was a sin to wanna feel up Ellen, a sin to *plan* to feel up Ellen, a sin to figure out a *place* to feel up Ellen, a sin to *take* Ellen to the place to feel her up, a sin to *try* to feel up Ellen and a sin to, you know, feel up Ellen. Six sins in one. . . .
>
> And then confession. In my diocese in New York, when Puerto Ricans started moving in, they made a rare display of tokenism for the Fifties—they brought in Father Rivera. All the Irish guys heavily into puberty went to him for confession because he didn't seem to take the sins personally. It was three Hail Mary's and back on the street with Father Rivera—he was known as a light penance.
>
> But he wasn't ready for the way Irish boys confessed. "Bless me, Fodder, for I have sinned. I have touched myself in an impure manner. I was impure, impurity, impureness. Thought, word and deed, body, touch, impure; sex, dirty, impure legs, impureness, touch, impure, dirty, bodies, sex, rub. And covet, Fodder, heavy on the covet."
>
> "Das okay, mane. Tres Santa Marias."

Because his partly-Irish neighborhood bordered on Puerto Rican and black enclaves, Carlin had become familiar, during his teenage years, with the attitudes and speech of these two groups. This was eventually to prove important as his comedy style developed.

> We called our neighborhood White Harlem, because that sounded bad. Morningside Heights was the real name, but that sounded faggy . . . *Fag* didn't mean the same thing in those days; fag meant sissy. A fag wouldn't stay out late or go steal off trucks . . . "Go home, fag, it's ten o'clock. Hey, look, the fag's going home . . ." We knew what a queer was. That was the word after homo, remember? So there was a big difference between a fag

and a queer. A fag was a guy who wouldn't go downtown and beat up queers."

Carlin's eventual method of getting away was to go into the air force, which trained him in the operation of B-47 bomber navigation systems. At Barksdale Air Force Base in the Shreveport, Louisiana, area, George immediately became a discipline problem. On two occasions he was court-martialed but was not required to serve time.

An interesting factor of Carlin's experience at that time was that in his off-base social contacts he felt more at home with the local urban blacks than the red-neck whites. At this time, he began working as a disc jockey at a local radio station. The experience enabled him to move, after his military service, to station WEZE in Boston. He was eventually fired for impertinence, after which he moved to Fort Worth, Texas, and became an all-night record spinner on KXOL.

An important turn in his fortunes occurred when comedian Jack Burns—who later became nationally known as part of Burns and Schreiber—showed up in Fort Worth and got in touch with Carlin, who had known him earlier in Boston. Carlin helped Burns get a job on KXOL and the two began to construct some comedy routines. Emboldened by their early success, they moved to Los Angeles where they began doing local good-morning-folks comedy on station KDAY. While doing some coffeehouse dates, they were fortunate enough to be seen by Lenny Bruce, who brought them to the attention of the GAC talent agency. Not long thereafter they had graduated to the Playboy Club circuit.

In October 1961 they got their first national break with an appearance on the "Tonight Show," during Jack Paar's tenure of office.

Not long thereafter, Carlin and Burns went their separate and successful ways.

Carlin, who had by now married a young woman named Brenda Hosbrook, returned to New York. It was at this point that he wrote one of his first truly brilliant comedy monologues: the Indian Drill Sergeant.

I'm a fan of Westerns. I don't like just any Western though; I like the ones that involve Indians. I like the Indian movies because they're predictable. You *know* what the big scene is going to be, right? It's going to be the attack the Indians finally make on the cowboys. You wait for it to happen for an hour and a half. You can see the clowns standing on the hill. Finally, "Yeeahhh!" It's over.

Now they show us, for 90 minutes, how the *cowboys* get ready for this attack. "Pull the wagons around the circle, get them old ladies up there, load up the weapons, tab their petticoats, give 'em a bang, get 'em the salt bags and sand bags and *(double-talk)* out a here!" It's a big hassle.

But they never show us how the *Indians* prepare. And it's their attack, right?

Well, the Indians were good fighters. Just because they started in Massachusetts and wound up defending Santa Monica doesn't mean they were bad.

They were good fighters. And if they were, they must have been well organized. They must have had a way to divide their manpower. They couldn't have been as chaotic as it looks in the movies with one old chief, "Many moon come chakta" and a lot of guys running around naked. There had to be intermediate authority. There must have been Indian *sergeants*. No army can make it without that tough, veteran, battle-hardened sergeant, and the Indians were no exception.

Carlin now speaks with a lower class New Jersey or New York workman's accent, as if he were a modern U.S. Army non-commissioned officer.

All right, all the tall guys over by the trees. Fat guys down behind the rocks. You with the beads, out of line, come on! Well, there's one in every village.

All right, knock off the horseplay! Come on, knock off the horseplay. You guys over there playin' with the horse, will you knock it off?

Now youse have all been given a piece of birch bark and a feather dipped in eagle's blood. We want youse to write *on* the birch bark with the feather, in the upper right-hand corner. That's the upper right-hand corner. Dat's your arrow hand. You write your name, last name first, first name last. If your name is Running Bear, you write Bear, Running. You got a middle initial please include that, such as Wolf, Howling, W.

A lot of you guys have been askin' me about promotion. You'd like to make Brave, Second Class. Get another scar up on your arm. Well, I'm happy to say the results of your early tests have come tru. Youse are doin' beautifully. Burning settlers' homes, everybody passed. Imitating a coyote, everybody passed. Sneaking quietly through the woods. Everybody passed except Limping Ox. However, Limping Ox is being fitted with a pair of corrective moccasins, and he'll be up and dancing in no time at all.

Now there are two other areas on which you will be tested: running down the hill and yelling like a nut; and leaping off the cliff—which is considered to be the tougher of the two.

A lot of fellas like to save leaping off the cliff for last.

Couple other announcements for you here. The fertility rites have been called off due to the recent cold wave. *(Horse-laugh)* There'll be a rain dance Friday night, weather permitting.

Got a great band: Leapin' Lizard and the All-Stars.

They'll be playing all your favorite tunes, "Pass That Peace Pipe," "Indian Love Call," "Sweet Sioux," all them tunes you've come to know and love through these many moons.

Okay, one other thing. There's another item that goes on your clothing list. And that is your loirn cloth. Now that goes down on your list as one each, cloth, loirn-type.

That there is your *loirn* cloth. You'll want to get to know, and love, your loirn cloth. Someday it may save your life.

There'll be a massacre tonight at 9 o'clock.

We'll meet down by the bonfire, dance around a little bit, and move out. This will be the fourth straight night we've attacked the fort. However, tonight it will not be as easy. Tonight there will be *soldiers* in the fort.

Happy to say I'll be leading the massacre. I'll be running down front. You'll see me. I'm the one that's on fire.

And the uniform of the day, it's a *formal* massacre. You want your class-A summer loirn cloth, two green stripes over the eye, no feather, arms are blue, legs are red, chest is optional.

You might throw a little yellow on the bellies.

What? No, you *can't* put any purple on your eyelids. Is that the guy with the beads? Get outta line, would you please, now!

Oddly enough, my own opinion of the Indian monologue seems to be much higher than George's. In a July 1, 1982, letter to me, in which he enclosed an audio cassette of the routine, he said, "I would wish to remind you, however, that it represents a very early stage in my career. It was recorded in 1966, on RCA records, fully six years before my real breakthrough. . . ." Perhaps George has come to feel that, as was the case with most of Lenny Bruce's better material, everything he does must have a moral or make some sort of point about society. The Indian Drill Sergeant does not. I consider it hysterically funny nevertheless. Some comedy routines, even those that are quite successful, are not particularly amusing to read but depend largely upon the performance to achieve their full impact. This is not the case with the Indian monologue. It reads as funny as vintage Robert Benchley.

In *Funny People* I explained the unfortunate misunderstanding whereby when Woody Allen applied for a job in my writing staff, in the 1950s, he was turned down simply because of a mix-up between his name and that of another writer whose name was either the same or close to it. There was also unfortunate confusion about the name of Shecky Greene, the result of which was that Shecky was denied a booking on my program, even though once I was familiar with his work he became one of my favorite comedians. Something of the sort, I learned from Carlin's letter, had happened to him, too, although I had never before heard about it. "In December, 1963 I auditioned for your staff in a theater on Vine Street for your then-current syndicated TV show. I did the 'Indian Sergeant' and was turned down. It wasn't a case of the staff missing out on something; I simply wasn't ready. Another year and a half went by before I began my first important TV exposure; Merv Griffin's Westinghouse show from New York."

Oddly enough I used to attend a good many of our open auditions during the early 1960s, but obviously was not present when Carlin tried out for the show. Since I have always been able to detect true funniness at a range of at least a thousand yards, George's career might have been accelerated, without the year-and-a-half delay, if only I had been present when he came to our theater. All show business personal histories are full of such sad little stories.

Another early Carlin classic:

> This is Scott Lame with the boss sounds from the boss station in the boss town that my boss told me to play. . . .
>
> Here's a hot new sound from Crosby, Stills, Nash, Young, Merrill Lynch, Pierce, Sacco, and Vanzetti . . . It's moving fast, I say fast. It was recorded at nine this morning, number three by noon, number one by three and now it's a . . . Golden Oldie! Super Gold to make you feel old!
>
> And now WINO news 'round the world from Bill Bleeper . . . Saigon! Bleep-bleep-bleep-bleep-bleep . . . Bangkok! Bleep-bleep-bleep-bleep-bleep . . . Paris! Bleep-bleep-bleep-bleep-bleep. . . .
>
> And now the late sports with Biff Barf. . . ! This is Biff Barf with the Sportlight Spotlight, spotlighting sports, pickin' 'em up and barfin' 'em back at you. Now some scores from the Far West . . . Guam Prep 45,

Marshall Islands 14 ... Mindanao A and M 27, Molokai 10 ... Cal Tech 14 point 5, M.I.T. 3 to the fourth power . . . And a partial score—Stanford 29.

Now over to Al Sleet, your Hippy-Dippy Weatherman . . . Hey, man, que pasa? . . . The present temperature is 68 degrees at the airport, which is pretty stupid, man, 'cause I don't know anybody who lives at the airport. . . . Tomorrow's forecast: dark, continued mostly dark, with scattered light by mid-morning.

It is interesting to note that these extremely funny monologues are from Carlin's "square" period. The word is put into quotation marks, of course, because George was always essentially hip. But this was before he had abandoned his attempt to conform to straight society.

Since Carlin is one of our more original comics, it is probable that he simply did not recall, when he named his sports-announcer Biff Barf, that for some years theretofore the delightful comedy team of Bob and Ray had occasionally presented a sportscaster named Biff Burns. I suspect that what appears to be blatant plagiarism on the part of various comedians usually takes place on the unconscious level. Often they have been strongly influenced early in their careers by entertainers who preceded them. The influences are usually absorbed unconsciously.

In discussing those whose work he likes George refers to an odd assortment. "The first people that attracted me to comedy as a kid would be Abbott and Costello, Danny Kaye, Spike Jones and the Marx Brothers. And then, as a young man, Jonathan Winters, Lenny Bruce, Mort Sahl and Ernie Kovacs.

"In my act there's a bit of everyone I saw. I can't separate them. Danny Kaye was very influential in terms of physical humor—face and hands."

The odd thing about this is that the only influences which are discernible are those of Lenny Bruce and Mort Sahl.

My agent, Irvin Arthur, who represented Carlin in the late 1960s, reminisced for me about once booking George into New York's Copacabana. "This was in 1967 or '68. I was on my way to Israel. But just before I left I had a meeting with the guy who ran the Copa, Julie Podell. He was the only guy I knew on the east coast that read the trade papers—the *Daily Variety* or the *Hollywood Reporter*. We never read them while we were back east. We read *Weekly Variety*. Anyway, he read where Carlin was kicked out of Vegas for using the word "ass" onstage. So I came in to say good-bye to Julie, wish him happy New Year and everything, have a good trip. He says, 'Now I read where this kid used a doity word.' I said, 'Well, I'll talk to him. I'll tell him not to.' He says, 'You know, you don't do anything about the fags, you don't do anything dirty, no swearing, and nothing about religion. Those are the three basic rules when you work the Copa.' Well, on the opening night—now I'm in Israel, remember—Carlin has this nice tuxedo on and everything, and he says, 'Ladies and gentlemen, I've been advised by the management of the Copa I may not use the word *ass*. I don't know *why* I can't use the word *ass*.' And he proceeded to go on like that all night long.

"I was with the GAC at that time and I've got all kinds of agency people covering Carlin for me. But Podell never said a word to any of them. When I came down to the Copa after my trip Podell waited for me. I said, 'Hi, Julie, how are you?' He grabbed me by the neck. 'You p——k! If you weren't a cripple, I'd kill you! Get out!' Next day he apologized to me."

One of the more dramatic episodes of Carlin's career occurred in September of 1970 at the Frontier Hotel in Las Vegas. George had worked at the Frontier on several earlier occasions as an opening act. The fact that he was so often rehired establishes that he had been successful in his earlier appearances. But on this particular occasion he not only performed a monologue on the various ways one might say the word "shit" but opened with it. Needless to say, there were no laughs. The fact that Robert Benchley had, in the 1930s, done routines about the number of ways to say certain words—all of Benchley's words innocuous, of course—had nothing to do with the instant consternation of Carlin's audience on this occasion; there probably weren't five people in the room who remembered Benchley. Even today some people would walk out of a theater after hearing such material. In 1970 there were many more. Within a fairly short time, half of Carlin's audience had left. Few, if any, of those who remained were sympathetic. There was a good deal of hostile heckling.

Whatever else he might have had in mind, Carlin was aware that he was ending his career as a Las Vegas comedian and, once word got around, his career in a number of other conventional nightclubs as well. But, apparently undaunted, he returned to performing in small clubs, coffee houses, and on college campuses.

Carlin's timing—oddly enough—was good in that when he finally busted loose and began to incorporate vulgarity and blasphemy into his act, there was a ready-made audience waiting for him. This was before the Richard Pryor-Steve Martin-Martin Mull-"Saturday Night Live" generation had established itself; consequently, Carlin got in on the ground floor with the Talking Dirty bit.

George has taken a bum rap in being accused of simply deciding, after years of doing conventional comedy, to do Lenny Bruce. What audiences have gotten since he made the switchover, in 1969, is the original, essential Carlin more than the on-good-behavior, three-button-suit Carlin they had seen performing theretofore. "I was always a street person," he said to Mark Goodman in 1978. "The record of my life shows a pattern of rebellion, and that attitude carried over when I got started in the Greenwich Village coffeehouses . . . I went straight for television because I had decided that I wanted to be an actor. But, among other things, I came to realize that what I really am is a writer, a writer who can perform his own work."

George feels strongly about his right to use blunt Anglo-Saxon words. He indeed has that right, although it can not be exercised on television and radio. He is correct, too, in some of the philosophical uses to which he puts such words—as distinguished from the for-shock-value-only approach of many other comedians. In using the hard language to instruct society Carlin follows Bruce.

One of the odd things about Carlin's style is that he has never seemed totally at ease "as himself." Carlin seems unable to say anything to an audience in a simple, straightforward fashion. The words come easily enough, but they are usually accompanied by a slight bit of facial schtick at the end of a sentence or phrase, occasionally by sliding momentarily into another character or voice. This is odd, considering Carlin's early experience in radio, a medium that usually provides ample opportunity for speaking in a direct, natural, person-to-person manner. It's significant, in this connection, that most of those who have become established as major talk show hosts—Jack Paar, Mike Douglas, Merv Griffin, Johnny Carson, myself—had a radio background. Nightclub entertainers who have attempted to host talk shows—Joey Bishop, Sammy Davis, Jr., Donald O'Connor, Jerry Lewis—were ultimately not successful because of their relative inability to speak in a completely naturalistic, non-show-biz manner.

In 1976 Carlin's career suddenly took another detour. After reestablishing himself on his own terms, he simply stopped performing and remained largely inactive for five years, although he was seen occasionally as guest-host of "The Tonight Show." Behind Carson's desk, according to a *Playboy* article, Carlin appeared "competent but uncomfortable."

Describing this phase of George's career, the anonymous *Playboy* editor said, ". . . there were problems, most of them stemming from Carlin's obsessive involvement with cocaine. Finally, in 1976, with his 15-year marriage, his 13-year-old daughter, and his own 25-year history of drug abuse closing in on him, Carlin—for the second time in his life—reined in a galloping career that had somehow gotten away from him. Years of therapy followed. Then a heart attack. Finally, at the age of 44, Carlin emerged straight and sober, with his health and family intact."

Here is Carlin's description of what he suffered as an abuser of the drug. "I'd go on runs, four and five days without sleep. Then I'd crash and sleep about 18 hours a day for seven to ten days. Then it would take a few more weeks to get over a vague sort of depression. Then I'd be off on another run."

As for the effect of the cocaine abuse on his marriage, Carlin has conceded, "the effect of the coke on our relationship was very sick."

Narcotic drugs are not, of course, a recent invention or discovery. Since they occur in nature they have been known for thousands of years. But—to restrict our analysis to Western culture of the last two centuries—we find that the mainstream of society has always viewed with detestation, horror, and a general sense of scandal, the abuse of or addiction to such drugs. Even in the arts in America during the last half-century there were practitioners who used drugs. But they always attempted to keep knowledge of their addiction out of the public consciousness. In the case of some artists, even when such information might have become public, there was a sort of benign conspiracy to maintain secrecy. It has never become public knowledge, for example, that one of America's leading songwriters was, for most of his adult lifetime, hopelessly addicted to an opiate. Since the gentleman in question has been otherwise law-abiding he has simply been medically maintained and otherwise honored for his professional achievements.

It is only within the last two decades that abuse of drugs seems to have lost a large part of its social onus. Indeed, among the under-35 generation it is almost considered a badge of honor to be addicted to drugs. There are several reasons for this morally peculiar state of affairs. One is that modern America worships the god *Success* with a fierce dedication. There is evidence, in the case of various mostly-poor immigrant groups, that if a member of one's own ethnic category becomes financially successful, he is to be forgiven almost any social misbehavior, however criminal or outrageous. Witness, for example, the social respect accorded, among even law-abiding Italian-Americans, the most monstrous Mafia murderers, extortionists, arsonists, sadistic bullies and thugs. The fact that any even reasonably rational and moral society would recognize such criminals as the scum-of-the-earth they are seems to have no relevance. They are "our own" and they are eminently successful; that seems to be enough.

Precisely the same process has long been observable in black slums and ghettos, where the most depraved pimps, drug dealers and murderers enjoy a natural social prestige as long as they are rich and successful. It is true that such honors fall away when criminals are arrested, convicted and imprisoned—at least to some extent—but that they exist at all before such misfortunes is the important fact.

As for those who are the subject of my on-going study—American comedians—it is no longer considered disgraceful, scandalous, or even particularly important, that a number of prominent entertainers have had a long-continued addiction to narcotics. As recently as the time of Lenny Bruce, Lenny denied or down-played his abuse of drugs. In the 1980s, by way of contrast, successful and talented comedians make apparently no attempt to disguise their use of drugs. On television interview shows and in magazine articles they respond to questions on the subject openly.

Another reason for the unprecedented degree of tolerance is that there are millions of Americans in the same boat. Since I do not wish to have my own bias on such questions misinterpreted, perhaps I should spell out here that such entertainers are welcome in my own home; I retain my capacity to laugh at them. I consider their addiction unfortunate but my attitude toward them is sympathetic.

As of mid-1978, George displayed, in his living room, a news-photo of himself being arrested by four policemen in Milwaukee.

One of Carlin's recent albums, *A Place for My Stuff,* is almost consistently brilliant and entirely funny. Just as cigarettes carry the warning that "smoking may be dangerous to your health," Carlin's album is clearly marked "adult listening only." I doubt that George himself would consider it suitable for an audience of seven-year-old girls. As mentioned earlier, although I take a dim view of the increasingly common use of vulgar language by entertainers I always made an exception in the case of Lenny Bruce since he did not use such terms for shock value but as incidental to making a philosophical point. It must be said that most of Carlin's use of shocking language has the same justification. Because he is so strongly identified with blunt language, he is unfairly thought to be doing almost no other sort of comedy. Fortunately some of his routines show that he is still wonderfully funny even when he does not try for shock laughs. Witness, for example, the following portion of his "Rice Krispies" monologue from *A Place for My Stuff.*

Got into an argument this morning with my Rice Krispies. I distinctly heard, "Snap, crackle, f— him."

I don't know which one of them said it, you know. I was reaching for the artificial sweetener at the time and was not looking directly into the bowl.

But I told them, I said, "Well, you can all just *sit* right there in the milk. As far as I'm concerned you can just sit in the milk. Until I find out which one of you said that."

A little mass punishment for my breakfast food. The idea is to turn them against one another. "Just sit in the milk."

Of course—dopey me—big punishment; that's what they do *anyway!* That's their job: sitting in the milk.

You've seen those Rice Krispies floating along, little beige blisters of air, riding proudly in the milk. You can't sink them. They ought to use them in life jackets, that's where they need them. You can't sink Rice Krispies; they float for a long, long time. Rice Krispies would float for a week if you'd leave the dishes out.

I do.

Rice Krispies would float until you've got to knock them off the side of the bowl. *Clunk, clunk, clunk.* "What are you doing?" "Washing the dishes."

Did you ever notice that the Rice Krispies highest on the bowl dry first? It's because they're closer to the sun. Isn't that interesting? Yes, there's a little science in the show each and every evening.

But those Rice Krispies will float forever. Well, you know what they do; they gather together in little groups. Little groups of eight, ten, twelve, sometimes fourteen. But always an even number.

Little *colonies* of Rice Krispies.

You can't sink them. You try to sink them with a spoon, they come up over the side. That's what the *fruit* is for—sinking the Rice Krispies! A good sized peach will take down eighty or ninety of them every time. Kabloom.

If I'm really pissed I'll drop a watermelon on them.

Carlin has demonstrated a fatalistic courage in the face of his recurring health problems. His heart attacks were serious, but even when he was facing surgery, he continued to make jokes about his condition and keep his chin up.

The day after I got George's letter of July 1, 1982, I happened to be in the offices of agents Irvin Arthur and Roy Gerber. "Even though George just had another massive heart attack and will be undergoing open-heart surgery in a few days, he's going ahead with his concert at Universal," Gerber said. "In fact, he's planning to show slides and films of his heart as part of the show."

I suppose we're lucky George wasn't suffering from a hernia.

Tim Conway

Tim Conway

THE BEST SKETCH COMEDY SHOWS are those in which there is an extra factor above and beyond the obviously-required good jokes, strong sketches and funny people to act in them. The extra factor is simply the star's ability to communicate with the at-home audience in a personal way. The communication may be accomplished by either a straightforward non-comic tone, a comic tone, or a combination of the two. The factor is not always something that can be induced by simply willing it to be so.

Tim Conway is one of my favorite comedians, but he's so gifted at playing various kinds of jerks, so wonderfully funny at being stupid, fearful, embarrassed, puzzled, non-plussed, that he rarely attempts to speak to an audience directly.

If judged strictly on the factor of funniness in a sketch, Carol Burnett would no doubt rate herself a few percentage points lower than Tim. But her program enjoyed years of success whereas with Tim the situation has always been touch-and-go. I believe the difference was that Carol was always comfortable (in a formula that originally was one of my own modest contributions to television comedy) simply standing on a stage and producing amusing answers to questions from the studio audience.

With Tim, by way of contrast, the absence of *real* contact makes almost all the rest of his show, however funny, somewhat impersonal.

The one partial exception involves the routines where Tim gets people out of the studio audience to read cue-cards and play roles in simple sketches. He has been kind enough to concede that he and producer Joe Hamilton borrowed the idea from me since it used to be an occasional feature on our Westinghouse program.

Tim was born December 15, 1933, the only child of a middle-class family in Willoughby, Ohio. His father was a professional horse trainer, and Tim learned to ride while still young. He also became proficient at athletics, chiefly tumbling. Consequently, when he entered Chagrin Falls High School he had his sights set on becoming a teacher of physical education.

Like most truly funny entertainers, Conway was amusing as a child. In school, he recalls, "Like when the teacher would ask 'Who was the twenty-fourth president?' rather than admit I didn't know, I'd say 'It wasn't anybody in *my* family.' The grade would still be the same, but I'd score pretty good with my classmates."

Oddly, Conway never wanted to be an entertainer. "In the eleventh grade I weighed 97 pounds and wanted to be a jockey. My dad was a polo player and trained horses when he first came from Ireland, and that seemed more interesting than his work with the gas company. By the time I was fourteen, I weighed 120 pounds and the horses acted as if they would go on strike when I looked like I was about to mount up—and that was the end of my Willie Shoemaker period."

Tim rarely talks about his mother but on one occasion he said to a journalist, "My mother should have been locked up. Sometimes when I'd come home from school she would think that she was an elephant. Just to humor her we'd play along."

At the college level, he realized that a career in radio or TV was easier than an athletic career and began to study speech and drama at Ohio's Bowling Green State University. His natural sense of humor developed even further during a two-year stint in the army, after which he and a friend put together a comedy act. After failing to make a dent as a performer, however, Conway gave up dreams of making a living by his wit and accepted a job at Cleveland's station KWY-TV. Although he had originally been hired at KWY to answer fan mail, his abilities soon elevated him to assignments as a writer and, in time, a director. "I never wanted to be performing in show business," Tim told me recently. "Actually, I was a director in Cleveland, and I wanted to continue being a television director. It seemed that that was the most creative job in television."

One of his duties at KWY was working on a two-hour late-night program hosted by Cleveland television personality Ernie Anderson. "We had a movie and guests, but some of the guests didn't show up, so I began filling the holes."

The following sketch is an early one, written by Conway, and performed with Anderson. It is easy to see, looking back, that Tim's basic style, since it grew out of him naturally, was already essentially formed at that early date, 1961.

ERNIE: You know, in college football if a head-coach doesn't come up with a winning team the alumni are the first to let him know about it. Tonight we're going to be talking to a coach who not only has the alumni booing him, but also seems to be having a little trouble with the players.

Let's go to the locker room and meet Coach Dag Herferd.

Coach Herferd?

TIM: We had a lot of injuries this season. You can't blame me.

ERNIE: Coach, I just want to talk to you.

TIM: Are you from the alumni?

ERNIE: No.

TIM: Are you sure?

ERNIE: Yes.

TIM: Say you don't care if we win or lose.

ERNIE: I don't care if you win or lose.

TIM: You can't be too careful.

ERNIE: I guess when you've had a losing season the alumni can be pretty rough on you.

TIM: You're not kidding. Last night at a pep rally they decided to give me a car.

ERNIE: What's so bad about that?

TIM: It was doing 80 at the time.

Missed by inches.

ERNIE: I think you're letting your imagination run away with you. Where were you when they presented it to you?

TIM: In my office.

ERNIE: It still could have been an accident.

TIM: On the twelfth floor?

ERNIE: I understand since you've been coaching here you've lost eighteen games in a row.

TIM: That's a rumor.

ERNIE: Well, that's what it says in the official score book.

TIM: Then it's not a rumor. Gee, I was hoping it was.

ERNIE: If a coach loses eighteen games in a row, I imagine he stands a pretty good chance of being fired.

TIM: Boy, I bet he does.

ERNIE: Don't you have *any* outstanding players?

TIM: Well, we have this kid McIntyre. He takes the ball and runs with it, passes it, and kicks it.

ERNIE: Really great, huh?

TIM: No, it's his ball.

ERNIE: How long have you been coach here?

TIM: Three years. I took over after they retired Coach Pop Woody. He was 87.

ERNIE: Got too old for the game, huh?

TIM: Yeah. Last homecoming game they won and threw old Pop Woody into the showers. He laid in there 'til mid-term.

Plugged up the drain and everything.

ERNIE: I heard he had the ability to inspire a team to do anything, with his famous half-time speeches.

TIM: He did. But towards the end he couldn't remember what he wanted to say so he'd write them on a piece of paper.

His last game he got the papers mixed up and read the team his grocery list.

ERNIE: That's a shame.

TIM: Yeah, the second half he's out there yelling, "Get this one for old Pop Woody," and half the guys are out getting milk, butter, and eggs.

ERNIE: I can see why they let him go.

TIM: He did the same thing at his retirement banquet.

ERNIE: I guess it's been a pretty rough season for you.

TIM: It sure has. We don't even have a band this year. All we have is a five piece combo.

ERNIE: Well, it's the spirit that counts.

TIM: Maybe, but it looks silly. They're out there trying to spell out "Welcome Alums" and all they got is W, E, and part of an L.

ERNIE: I know it might be interesting for the folks to see how you handle your team in action. Suppose your team is on the one-yard line. You're losing by one touchdown, and there are ten seconds to go. What would you do?

TIM: I'm doing it.

ERNIE: Why are you just staring?

TIM: I've never seen them play so well.

ERNIE: No, look; you need a time-out. Blow your whistle.

TIM: It's no use.

ERNIE: Sure, it is. There's always a chance.

TIM: I lost the little ball out of it.

ERNIE: Well, do *something*. Yell at the ref.

TIM: Hey, ref. You seen the little ball that goes in my whistle?

ERNIE: No, yell for a time-out. Like this. "Time out!"
Now what do you do?

TIM: I go out and tell the team you got a play for them to run.

ERNIE: Why me?

TIM: *You* yelled for the time out.

ERNIE: No, look; you're on the field with the team. Who's the captain?

TIM: Wilson.

ERNIE: Okay. Tell Wilson your best play.

TIM: Got a dime?

ERNIE: Why?

TIM: I want to call Wilson.

ERNIE: Call him? Why?

TIM: He's home.

ERNIE: Home?

TIM: He broke his leg in the second game.

ERNIE: Look, say you tell them to run T-48. They score, and you win by a point. The game is over. What do you do?

TIM: I get carried off the field, I get my hat and coat, call my wife, and tell her we lost another game.

ERNIE: Why would you tell her you lost?

TIM: 'Cause she said if we ever *won* a game, she'd pass out. And I haven't eaten yet.

I first heard about Tim in 1961. After doing comedy for seven years on NBC, I had moved over to ABC and was doing essentially the same sort of show, but with the addition of a few new faces. Jim Nabors, for instance, made his television debut on that series. Marty Ingles was a regular member of our cast. Joey Forman and Buck Henry worked with us. So did a young comic named Don Penny, who apparently gave up the funny business not long thereafter and—the last I heard of him— actually had an office in the White House where he functioned as public speaking advisor to Gerald Ford. I have always thought there was the nucleus of a comedy, perhaps even a Broadway musical, in that bit of historical reality.

But Tim Conway, too, was introduced to a national audience on the 1961 series because entertainer Rose Marie had called me a couple of weeks earlier. "I just got back from Cleveland," she said, "and I know that you're always willing to give a chance to good new funny people."

"Sure," I said. "Who have you found?"

"Well," she said, "I was on this station in Cleveland and I met a crazy guy who—I think—was working there as a director or producer or something. But he just struck me as very funny, and that's why I'm telling you about him."

I thanked Rose Marie and had one of our production people arrange to view the video tape she had brought us. To this day I've never seen more than the first two minutes of it because it took me only about 30 seconds to realize that Rose Marie had been absolutely right. Tim—his name then was Tom—was richly, hysterically funny, before he even opened his mouth. I told the people in the viewing room that there was no need to see any more tape but that we should arrange to have the fellow added to our staff of comedy players at the earliest possible moment.

Not only did Conway soon show up, but we made the happy discovery that he was capable of creating material for himself. The following is one of the first sketches Tim and I did together. It was in the context of one of our "Report To The Nation" routines in which I would do a series of documentarylike analyses of one social problem or another.

INSIDE YOUR GOVERNMENT—"Secret Service Man"
(*Camera:* ART CARD: "INSIDE YOUR GOVERNMENT")
(*Music:* "THE MIRACLE OF AMERICA")

JOEY FORMAN (*voice over*): Inside Your Government.

(*Camera: Film of various office buildings and landmarks of Washington, D.C.*)

JOEY (*V.O.*): This is Washington, D.C., the seat of our federal government. Tonight we take you inside the National Security Bureau.

JOEY: Good evening. We're about to turn our spotlight on one of the most important men in the federal government, the man who trains Washington's plainclothes sentries—the man who sees that the security of our nation's high officials is maintained: the Special Security Officer. Steve Allen, at this moment, is on the scene to bring you an on-the-spot interview with this valiant watchdog. Let's switch over to Steve now.

(*Camera: Cut to an official Washington-type office . . . bunting, pictures of presidents. Tim Conway, as Doug Herford, is seated behind desk, calmly reading papers.*)

STEVE: Here I am in the office of this brave, alert sentry—Doug Herferd. *(Touches Tim on shoulder)*

Mr. Herferd.

(Tim, extremely frightened, falls into protective karate position down behind desk.)

Oh, I'm sorry, Mr. Herferd. I didn't mean to surprise you.

TIM: Oh, you didn't surprise me. It's just that you can't be too cautious nowadays.

STEVE: Mr. Herferd, the job of training men for this job must involve a great deal of responsibility for one man. Being responsible for the protection of our high-ranking officials—I bet that's a big job.

TIM: Gee, I bet that would be.

STEVE: Since you are solely responsible for the selection and training of the members of this group, I wonder if you could tell us some of the interesting facts about our men in plainclothes.

TIM: Well, they're a select group. Each one has to have two important prerequisites. First, they must realize that in a situation where one of our officials is in danger, they must be prepared to lay down their life for his safety.

STEVE: That's a great deal to ask of a man. What is the *second* thing they must have?

TIM: A suit of plain clothes. And of course, they have to be extremely alert, with the ability to make quick decisions in times of danger, able to coordinate the mind and the body.

STEVE: *(Drops his pencil. While Conway talks, Steve picks it up.)*

TIM: They have to make catlike decisions. Let me get that. . . . *(Referring to the pencil Steve has retrieved. Searches floor.)*

STEVE: I've got it, Doug.

TIM: Oh. *(Searches again to make sure.)*

STEVE: Do you personally select these men?

TIM: Oh, yes. I wouldn't leave that to an incompetent.

STEVE: I hear you've made an interesting contribution to this service, some sort of invention. Could you give us an idea of what it is?

TIM: Right, Steve. See this? *(Holds up fifty-cent piece.)*

(Camera: C.U. of coin in Tim's hand.)

TIM: What does this look like?

STEVE: An ordinary fifty-cent piece.

TIM: Ah, that's where you're wrong! This is a secret camera! An exact *duplicate* of a fifty-cent piece.

STEVE: Wow! A camera! That's amazing. Could you take my picture?

TIM· Sure. *(He tries to take a picture. It doesn't work.)* Ah, nuts!

STEVE: What's wrong?

TIM: Oh, I was in a restaurant and I must have given the waitress a camera for a tip.

This is just a fifty-cent piece.

Boy, is the chief going to be mad about this!

STEVE: You have a chief? What's his name?

TIM: Running Bear.

STEVE: Chief Running Bear.

Well, uh, Mr. Herferd, I wonder if you could show us how you train your men?

TIM: Well, first I give them a basic course in karate, so they can learn the fundamentals of physical protection. Would you like me to demonstrate the effectiveness of karate?

STEVE: Yes.

TIM: Well, first of all, if you'll just step over here, I'll show you the power that can be developed. See this board? It's ¾-inch ply. Now, I want you to hold that. Now, I'm going to attempt to break it in half with the bare hand. Just hold that. . . . *(Hits it. It doesn't break.)* Ah, boy. Let me see that a minute.

I'll be right back. *(He goes off.)*

STEVE: Doug Herferd, ladies and gentlemen, is going to show us how he can break a ¾-inch ply board with his bare . . . *(Sound: Sawing offstage and dropping saw on floor.)*

TIM: *(Returning):* There, try that. Hold it. *(He hits it again. It doesn't break.)* Ah, boy. *(Puts it down, as though nothing happened.)* *(Sound: Board breaking)*

STEVE: Do you have anything else?

TIM: Well, I could show you a little physical contact. Try and hit me in the face. *(Falls into crouch)*

STEVE: OK, I'll try. *(Hits Tim in face.)*

TIM: Oh—gosh! Oh, wait. I had the protection for the *mid*-section. I'm sorry. Try and hit me in the stomach.

STEVE: OK. *(Tries to hit Tim in stomach. Tim grabs his hand. Tries to toss him but just brings Steve's arm over his shoulder.)* Say, that's good. Would you normally throw me?

TIM: Oh, no, you're too heavy. But if I got you over my shoulder a little closer, maybe I could talk you out of it.

STEVE: Do you have anything else?

TIM: Well, this is a true test in karate. It really tests the alertness of a man. I'm going to blindfold myself and have you sneak up on me.

Now I want you to touch me anywhere and I'll swing and throw you. *(He puts blindfold on.)*

STEVE: Well, OK, Doug. I just sneak up on you and you'll throw me. *(Sneaks up on Tim, touches him.)* Doug. Doug!

TIM *(Asleep): (Snores. Lets head fall on Steve's shoulder.)*

STEVE: Well, a man who has the job of defending our security *needs* his sleep. *(To Tim.)* Doug . . . Fella . . .

As mentioned earlier, ABC had picked up our program after a seven-year run on NBC. The show itself, as watching the old videotapes makes clear, was every bit as funny as the award-winning NBC Sunday night series had been—and small wonder, when, in addition to the already-established members of our comedy troupe, we had the help of so many funny new performers. The only negative aspect of the situation was that ABC had put us in the worst time slot in their schedule. That, and a combination of poor publicity and promotion before our premiere, resulted in abysmally low ratings for the opening night's show. We were not personally dismayed since the show itself was funny and strong. Also, since we had a 26-week guarantee we were confident that before long the ratings picture would begin to improve. And improve it did, as TV viewers across the country began to find out what night and hour we were on. Unfortunately, the dramatic improvement in our ratings, when it finally occurred, didn't matter. The network had already made one of the classically stupid decisions it was then known for: they cancelled the series after our second show.

When my business manager first told me the news, I literally thought he was joking.

"No," he said, "it's true. They've already decided to drop the show."

"Do you mean," I said, "that we all just go home today and they pay us off for the rest of the 26 shows?"

"No," he said. "They want us to do a total of 13."

"What about the rest of the guarantee?"

"They don't want to pay us for that."

"I see," I said. "Well then, would you be good enough to remind them that they are contractually obligated to pay us?"

The network was naturally not happy to be so reminded, but they did indeed have to pay me for 13 shows we never did. As a result, a degree of ill-feeling developed that rendered me unemployable at ABC for some time thereafter.

The next eleven shows were just as funny as the first two and by the time we went off, to the great lamentation of critics, our ratings were a good deal higher.

Tim's appearance on the series had at least made a strong impression on the professional Hollywood comedy community. He was soon signed as a regular on "McHale's Navy," starring Ernest Borgnine, which ran for four seasons Tim played the role of Ensign Charles Parker, a typical Conway goof-off. The series proved so popular that Universal studios eventually did two films based on it, *McHale's Navy* and *McHale's Navy Joins the Air Force.*

Because of Conway's lavish comic gifts it was inevitable that it would eventually occur to producers to star him in his own series. The results were somewhat peculiar. The first attempt, titled "Rango," was a situation comedy in which Tim played an inept Texas Ranger, working with another very funny gentleman, Guy Marx. "Rango" ran 13 weeks, collected a few bad reviews, and was cancelled. There followed a one-night experiment for ABC called "Turn On." Although the program would be unexceptionable today, it was considered too vulgar in 1969.

Next came "The Tim Conway Show" in which Conway and his partner from "McHale's Navy," Joe Flynn, played the pilot and owner, respectively, of a struggling charter airline. The ratings were low, and the show lasted only half of one season.

The following season Tim did "The Tim Conway Comedy Hour," which also lasted 13 weeks. At this point he got the idea of having special license plates made up for his car. They read, "13 WKS."

After four seasons of making occasional guest appearances on other people's programs, Tim became a regular on "The Carol Burnett Show" on which he, Carol, and Harvey Korman performed in countless sketches of superior quality.

Because of his strong showing on the Burnett show, Tim was given yet another opportunity—this time by CBS. His new show was, for the most part, quite clever, and Tim was as wonderfully funny as always. But critic Marvin Kitman, like me a rabid Conway fan, considered Tim "a prisoner" of producer Joe Hamilton. "Every time he does a variety series for Tim or Harvey [Korman] it's always 'The Carol Burnett Show Without Carol.'" Despite glowing reviews, the network cut the program from an hour to thirty minutes. "It's a new kind of cancellation plan," Tim explained. "Next year we'll do fifteen minutes, then seven and a half, etc."

Fortunately, by this time Tim was no longer dependent on the success of a television series. He had established himself as an important film comedian, not only in critical terms but—far more meaningful to the industry—at the box office. With such pictures as *The World's Greatest Athlete, The Apple Dumpling Gang, The Apple Dumpling Gang Rides Again, The Billion Dollar Hobo, They Went That-a-way and That-a-way,* in some of which Tim costarred with Don Knotts, Conway achieved full recognition of his talents.

It is interesting that, like Tim, a number of popular comedians of the 1970s and '80s have depended chiefly on films for the establishment of their reputations, instead of relying on television. Richard Pryor and Steve Martin are two eminently successful and talented performers. Despite this, their essential security comes from success in motion pictures. The fact that their ratings on television have not sometimes been as high as their great popularity would have led one to predict is simply a fact of little or no importance.

I was surprised when, in response to my question about his influences, Tim told me that I was one. Our styles are extremely different. We do, however, have one factor in common—a certain relaxed amusement with life itself. We tend to laugh at the same sorts of things. The literal transcript of Tim's reply to my question runs as follows:

> As far as what influenced me in comedy—and not because I'm sending this to you but this is the God-awful truth; I'll speak of you as though you were another person—the person who most influenced me in comedy was Steve Allen. "Steve" had an uncanny way of constructing a sentence with every word in the correct order, to get the maximum comedic benefit from the sentence. When you spoke, you drew word-pictures. I actually used to audio tape your shows and listen to them and try to reconstruct a sentence you had said in another way to get more comedy from it, and there would be no other way. You are, and always have been, the master of that aspect of comedy—of drawing the perfect comedic word picture.
>
> I was influenced by the old "Tonight" show to the extent that if I ever stole from anybody in my life, it would be you. And also from Don Knotts.

You could hold Don and me up to the light and we are the same guy. Don will leave with us a character. He has surfaced, as did Charlie Chaplin, Laurel and Hardy. He has given us the *character* of Don Knotts, a truly memorable character in the history of comedy.

If I was influenced by anybody else in the comedy area, I would have to say it was Laurel and Hardy, for their physical comedy.

I owe a great deal of my success also to Carol and Joe [Carol Burnett and Joe Hamilton]. So the people who have influenced me in my life of comedy would have to be: Steve Allen, Laurel and Hardy, Don Knotts and Carol and Joe.

As you study another of Tim's marvelous interview sketches, visualize other comedians doing the funny lines. Think, for example, of Bob Hope, Johnny Carson, Danny Thomas, Don Rickles, Bill Cosby. You'll perceive that none of these other funnymen could have gotten nearly the laughs, with this sort of material, that Conway does. The reason is his natural air of extreme befuddlement. Now it is not all that difficult to *look* befuddled and confused. Many of us are so by nature, I'm afraid. But what makes Tim's bewilderment so funny, in a theatrical context, is that he attempts to cover it over with a glib I'm-in-control-here attitude. It was Tim who first made the already existent cliché, "Moving right along" part of the national comic language. People who, in real social contexts, say, "Moving right along—," are disc jockeys, masters of ceremonies, school teachers, coaches—anybody who is in some position of authority but is having trouble keeping it all together and tries to extricate himself from the impasse of the moment by "Moving right along—" to some new subject matter that, he hopes, will distract our attention. Well, Tim Conway is the "Moving right along—" champion of the world.

Introduction: A warden of a state prison never knows when the prisoners are liable to cause a riot. He has to be able to handle such a crisis, even though the incident may come at the most inconvenient time.

To demonstrate, here's how the situation looked when the prisoners decided to riot and the warden had to be called in from a New Year's Eve party.

(Harvey Korman is dressed in a guard's uniform. He is standing behind the wall talking into a stationary megaphone to the men below. There are riot noises in the background.)

HARVEY: All right you men, keep it down! The warden is on his way here now. He was at the Governor's house for New Year's Eve so both of them are aware of the problem.

He'll—Here's the warden now!

(Tim's hand comes up to the top of the wall and he tries to pull himself up. The hand goes back down. He finally pulls himself up. He has on a party hat and a big lipstick mark on his lips.)

TIM: Happy New Year, Bull!

HARVEY: Happy New Year, sir.

TIM: I hear the men are rioting.

HARVEY: That's right. I was the one who called you.

TIM: Oh. *That's* where I heard it.

HARVEY: It looks bad, sir. I don't know how much longer we can control them.

TIM: Is that right? Well, they aren't getting away with anything. I'll handle this.

(He turns to the back wall, which would be the wall to the outside street.)

TIM: All right, men. This is your warden speaking. I want you to get back to your cells. . . .

HARVEY: Warden, sir—The men are over *here*. That's the street.

TIM: Oh. I wondered where they got all the cars.

HARVEY: Over here, sir.

TIM: *(Startled)* They're rioting!

HARVEY: That's what I told you.

TIM: We've got a situation here. Have you called anybody?

HARVEY: Just you, sir.

TIM: What did I say?

HARVEY: You'd better talk to the men, sir.

TIM: Right, I'll handle this.

(Sticks his head in the large end of the megaphone.) Men, this is your Warden speaking. I want—I want—air—air, I want air! *(Harvey helps him out.)*

Did you see that? They tried to megaphone me!

(He spins the megaphone around. It knocks him out of the picture.)

HARVEY: You'll have to do something to quiet them down.

TIM: I'll handle this. Men, this is the Warden speaking.

(Boos, hisses, jeers, shouts of "Kill him!")

Now what's so hard about that?

HARVEY: I don't think they're quite happy yet.

TIM: What are they unhappy about?

HARVEY: They've been complaining about the food. That might be the problem.

TIM: You think that's it? We'll see. Men, I understand you're not happy with the food here.

(Boos, hisses. Tim gets hit in the head with a pail.)

Well, that's not it.

HARVEY: Maybe you ought to try to find out what they want.

TIM: Right, I'll handle this. Men . . . in order to get along here we've got to understand each other. Now there are some regulations here to be done here and to get order for them to be done we've got to be able to get privileges to earn them before you can have them.

They don't understand me.

HARVEY: Sir, this might help. I found it in one of the cells. *(Hands him a piece of paper.)*

TIM: The warden is a rotten—he's a dirty—a no-good—Ha, I laugh. You know what Warden Riley used to say when he found stuff like this? I'll show you.

Men, I just read your pamphlet. In the words of Warden Riley, "Sticks and stones may break my bones."

(They throw sticks and stones at him.)

You know, they did the same thing to Warden Riley. Broke every bone in his body. He was a dumb warden.

These men ought to be thrown in prison.

HARVEY: They *are* in prison.

TIM: Serves them right.

(To men) You guys aren't pulling anything over on me. Your stool pigeon told me all about the tunnel you're digging under the tennis courts.

HARVEY: Sir, we don't *have* any tennis courts.

TIM: We don't? Well, why did they tell me that? I already told the news reporters.

Now we're going to have to put in tennis courts.

They did the same thing last year. Remember we put in the horse-shoe pits. They never *did* dig under them!

Even though I've known Tim for over 20 years, I was surprised by what he told me about his reaction to professional criticism.

I haven't read a review of myself since 1961, when a gentleman wrote that Tim Conway has made the same impression on show business as the Super Chief going through Elkhart, which is, as we all know, *zzzwert! [brief train noise].* That angered me so much that I decided never to read another review of myself, good or bad. So I cannot tell you how I'm doing review-wise nowadays. I seem to be doing okay.

Such an attitude would perhaps be understandable coming from a comedian of average or slight ability. But I have never met a true expert on the subject of professional comedy who did not feel that Conway ranks high indeed when judged simply on the basis of funniness. Many comedians—including some who are very successful—are not inherently funny and do not amuse Just Standing There. Their success at a given moment depends to a great extent on the quality of their material. Conway is one of the group of funny men who amuse whether or not the material is top-notch. This obviously is not to say that the quality of the material is irrelevant. We are all funnier in proportion to the value of the joke, sketch, play, or film in which we are working.

But certain rare comedians—Conway, Stan Laurel, Buster Keaton, Jonathan Winters, Robin Williams, Dom de Luise, Professor Irwin Corey, Joe E. Brown, Louis Nye, Dayton Allen, Groucho, and a few others—seem to walk in an aura of zaniness separate from their structural context.

"You have six children?" columnist Earl Wilson once asked Tim.

"To the best of my knowledge," Conway replied.

"What do you do with all the money you make?" Wilson asked. "Do you invest it?"

"I count it," Conway said, "to make sure it's all there."

Conway has an interesting theory about the degree to which political leaders can set a social tone in which comedians find it easier, or more difficult, to function. "When Kennedy was in, it was really most enjoyable. He had a sense of humor, and he surrounded himself with people who also had a sense of humor. The most difficult time to get a laugh was when Nixon was in. With Carter we became a G-rated country. We were all carrying our own luggage."

For all his lavish gift of funniness Tim accepts the fact that few comedians attain the stature of a Bob Hope, Jack Benny, or Richard Pryor.

I have never tried to be Number One in this business and so far have been extremely successful in staying right in the middle. I think it's dangerous to actually be Number One, because obviously there's no place to go but down. Besides, just making the climb to Number One—well, I don't think I'd want to make the effort. I enjoy it too much being where I am. I've seen, as you have, too many people destroy themselves. They start to believe their publicity and begin to believe that they should be someplace beyond where they are. The next thing you know, things begin to take their toll—whether it's drugs or whatever. The worst thing is the destruction of the person. I don't ever want to get into that category.

I have what I want. I have six beautiful children who amaze me. I enjoy being here by the pool with myself. I've just spent a few moments with myself and I am very happy. And I'm very happy that you'll be listening to this tape. If you don't listen to it, please erase it and send it back. I'm not doing *that* well.

Jackie Gleason

TO AMERICANS UNDER FORTY, JACKIE Gleason is known in two
ways: (a) as Ralph Kramden, the boastful, bombastic bus driver
seen in the old black-and-white reruns of the 39 "The Honeymooners" shows, and (b) as the heavyset, older gentleman who plays
Southern sheriffs—albeit with a remarkably north-eastern version of a
Southern accent—in funny movies with Burt Reynolds. But such scanty
knowledge hardly does justice to Gleason's important contribution to
the history of television comedy.

The American public, for whatever reasons, seems unable to sustain
enthusiastic respect for any entertainer, perhaps for anything at all, for
very long. In the limited context of television comedy in the 1950s,
Milton Berle was the first funny performer to enjoy great acclaim. In
time, concentration was focused on a succession of others—the team of
Dean Martin and Jerry Lewis, George Gobel, Red Buttons, Sid Caesar,
Phil Silvers, etc.

But during the late 1950's the comedian who, because of his popularity, received most media attention was Gleason. His success was well-
deserved. The scripts of his programs were well-constructed—although
sometimes almost over Gleason's dead body—he had the vitally-
important benefit of performing with the gifted Art Carney, and—in
"The Honeymooners" sketches—he had the support of Pert Kelton, who
created the role of the long-suffering wife, Alice Kramden and then—
after Ms. Kelton ran afoul of the political blacklist, Audrey Meadows.

In the late 50s, Gleason seemed more than just a funny and successful
comedian. He was a powerful, influential force not only on the spoken
language and manner of many of his fellow entertainers, but on the
national consciousness itself. All over the country parlor and office wits
began to use lines like "And away we go," "How sweet it is," "You're a
gooooood group," "One o' dese days, Alice . . .", "Mmmmmm, *boy!*"
etc. Jackie seemed a sort of Diamond Jim Brady of comedy. He also

appeared egomaniacal at times but never in such a way as to alienate either friends or audiences. Gleason seemed so open, so innocent in his conceit, that the public took his posturing and bombast as a calculated gimmick simply designed to make us laugh, like comedy eyeglasses, a rubber cigar, or a fake-arrow-through-the-head. The flourishing of Jackie's ego, during the years of his greatest success, was something like that of Mohammed Ali. Each man said "I am the greatest," and apparently meant it. It is, of course, a matter of fact for a champion fighter to proclaim that he is the greatest because his title establishes that that is precisely what he is at the time. In the case of the comedy arts, there is no such thing as the greatest comedian. Funniness—like beauty—is partly in the eye of the beholder, and audiences vary widely in their appreciation of the various forms of the art. But that Gleason was an important and gifted comedian cannot be doubted.

That Jackie's early personal background was morbidly tragic explains much about his later life. He has recalled, "My father disappeared when I was about seven years old, never to show up again. And my mother died when I was quite young. I didn't start school until I was eight because I had a brother who died when he was fourteen. And then, with my father leaving, I was the only thing left that my mother had. She was overly attentive to me. She didn't even want me to go to school. I was never allowed out in the street to play with other kids. I would sit in the window and watch all the kids playing." The origin of The Poor Soul.

Gleason knew poverty, too, as a child.

"There was never enough to eat. As a matter of fact, I had to go to a shop where they gave you food; my mother would send me twice a week to go and pick up some bread or some spaghetti or something, and they always had big labels on it that said, 'free food.' So the first thing I did when I got out of the store was tear that label off. I was so embarrassed by it.

"So, naturally, when in later years I could afford to get food, I got a *lot* of it. But it certainly started from the fact that I didn't have things as a child, and I was determined to get them, which I think is a good thing. It gave me ambition, anyway."

Almost all of Jackie's childhood recollections are sad. "The day she [Gleason's mother] died—the day we buried her—I had 36 cents, and we came back from the funeral and we were sitting on the stoop, and the

Dunnahys said to me, 'Well, what're you gonna do?' I said, 'I guess I'll go to New York.'

"When you first begin to make money and become a success, you say to yourself, 'I better get all these things I wanted,' because how fruitless it would be if you *could* afford these things and *didn't* get them.

"So you accumulate everything. And then finally you realize that the materialistic things aren't of great value. The big thing is getting them. Once you've *got* them, they lose all their greatness."

I first met Jackie—first heard of him, in fact—in a quiet Hollywood restaurant late one night in 1949. I was doing a late-night comedy-talk show in Los Angeles at the time. I'm not sure how Gleason was occupying himself; probably by working in small nightclubs. Anyway, I was Minding My Own Business when suddenly this warm, good-natured drunk began to address me from a nearby table.

"Hey, Steve Allen. How ah ya, pal?"

I naturally thought that he was one of those well-meaning fans whose overtures can freeze the heart of any celebrity in a trapped position, which is to say, just starting dinner, seated on an airplane, or lined up to vote.

I smiled back, thanked him for the compliments he expressed but had no idea he was an entertainer himself. But he gave me his name and in due course it rang a bell, when, not long thereafter, he began to enjoy a degree of success.

I have never known a successful comedian who was not somewhat neurotic. The unsuccessful ones must be in even worse condition.

The humorist is basically a complainer, but his complaint is the only universally acceptable sort. A difficult early life seems to be an essential requirement for admission to the ranks of the eminent clowns, and the ability to surmount obstacles by hook or crook, to laugh off troubles if they cannot be denied, is one of the things that in the last analysis makes a man or woman funny.

Gleason was one of the most neurotic of the top-flight comedians. Alternating between excesses of the flesh and torments of the soul he seemed, in the 1950s, a driven figure who laughed in spite of himself. A compulsive eater, he is frank to admit that his prodigious appetite is basically a psychological problem. Television made him worry. When he worries, he eats. Putting away a big meal gives him a sense of security in an insecure profession. When a man exposes himself professionally to an audience of millions once a week and regularly feels the slings of criticism, it is not always enough to receive lavish public praise as an antidote. One must constantly build up one's ego in small, personal ways. So Gleason eats. He used to eat himself literally into the hospital. Several times a year, in the 1950s, after one last fit of gastronomic excess, he retired to Doctors Hospital in New York City, where the staff enforced a strict weight-reducing diet. Regularly after these in-town vacations he returned to the wars, his system purged, his mind clear and wary, his will full of eager and erratic resolutions.

Writer Leonard Stern recalled a funny incident. "There's a terribly funny thing that happened to me the first day. I was brought on the show after they started at CBS. I had an idea for a one-hour 'Honeymooners' that I felt could set a precedent. When I reported to the office Jackie wasn't there. The producer kept saying, 'Why don't you go to work with the other writers?' I said, 'No, I'd like to talk to Jackie.' They insisted I go start with the other writers. 'No,' I said, 'I'll come back when Jackie's here.' So they figured, because I was so persistent, 'to hell with him; let him get his come-uppance directly.'

"Now Gleason was at Doctor's Hospital, the place he went every so often to lose weight. I went across town to the hospital, got off at the third floor and started toward his room. A nurse stopped me and said, 'Where are you going?' I said, 'I'm going to see Mr. Gleason.' She said, 'He went home. He wasn't feeling well.'"

Many observers of the TV scene in the 1950s professed to be surprised by Jackie's astounding ambition, his desire to run the whole show, his prodigious energy, his willingness to leap into fields where he seemed ill-equipped to succeed. I think that this flowering of the Gleason ego was not a late development but something that can be traced back to Jack's childhood.

"In school," he says, "I was irritating. Why, I don't know. I know what I did but I'm puzzled as to why I did it. I would sit back until Miss Pappen or Miss Caulfield or Miss Miller would make a point to the class, then I would get on my feet and argue with them. I would tell them that, by coincidence, I had just been reading up on that subject and that the authorities did not agree with them. They would try to shut me up and I would tell them that they were losing their tempers because they were wrong."

Jack's good friend and most charitable critic Toots Shor agreed that success had not changed Gleason. "He was always crazy," said Toots. "The only difference is he can afford it now. He used to come to my place yelling and screaming and dead broke.... One New Year's Eve when he hardly knew where he was going to sleep that night, he came in here and ordered champagne for everybody in the joint. What the heck, it was New Year's Eve. I was going to give everybody champagne anyway, so what's the difference whether I did it or Gleason did it. I kind of admired his nerve."

Jack's Diamond-Jim style of the '50s was the result not only of his tragic childhood but also of his many years of professional struggle, during which time he worked as a carnival barker, nightclub emcee, actor, Broadway-revue comic, and motion-picture bit player. Almost twenty years of relative failure would collapse the ego of the average entertainer, but the years of poverty and rebuff only cemented Jack's determination to come out on top, to justify before the world his almost fanatic insistence on his professional self as "the greatest."

It is my belief that the wide popular acceptance of Gleason's comedy talent was based on his talent, his driving determination, and his genius for showmanship.

Gleason's ability to amuse was based on two factors: his dramatic talent and his warm, likable personality. He is not, at heart, I think, a true creative comedian. He is rather an exceptionally talented extrovert, a gifted actor who can deliver funny lines with polish and vigor. He has few peers as a realistic sketch comic.

Fortunately, Gleason and his advisors had the good sense to realize what his strong points were; his shows therefore were composed almost exclusively of sketches based on make-believe characters. Gleason, though charming and likable, was not at his best when playing himself, alone on the stage in front of a curtain. But let him step back into a set, put on a funny costume and assume the personality of Ralph Kramden or The Poor Soul and he could guarantee that every laugh-line written into the script would get its full measure of audience reaction.

Television was the perfect medium for Jack's talents. He was never professionally happy in nightclubs or vaudeville theaters; his work in Broadway revues was not exceptional, and he was unable to win popular favor in his few brief radio appearances. But with an hour of television time at his command each week for three years he had ample opportunity to introduce and popularize characters like Joe the Bartender and Reginald Van Gleason, the Third. With the aid of the TV cameras he had a chance to turn to advantage his practiced physical timing, his dramatic prowess and his big, good-natured Irish face.

Jackie's face is a tremendous asset. It is an open, honest, happy face, although it can express great sadness. It is the kind of face you cannot help liking, and in television it is by now obvious that a likable face is more valuable than money in the bank. Indeed, as mentioned in an earlier chapter, the dour expression of Fred Allen might have explained in some part the reason for his inability to master the new medium with the ease with which he controlled the old.

Even those who didn't think Gleason particularly amusing the first time they saw him, found that they still liked him personally. A capable entertainer can turn this ability to be liked into a magic key that opens the door to acceptance of his artistry.

Gleason has, of course, other qualities that make him a star—tremendous vitality on stage, a crashing physical warmth. He had only to come bouncing out in front of the cameras, flashing his magnetic smile, exuding confidence and shouting, "Saaaay, you're a dan-dan-dandy bunch tonight!" to win an audience completely.

His ability to convulse a thousand people simply by smiling at them and saying, "Mmmmm-boy!" was something of a puzzle to other comedians, who said, "I don't get that big a laugh with my best jokes." Such competitors did not realize that the people in the audience were not laughing because they were amused by what Gleason was saying; they laughed because of the way he said it, because he seemed to be having such a good time.

If Gleason were not an exceptional sketch comic he would still be an excellent master of ceremonies. He knows how to get people excited, how to put them in a receptive frame of mind for what is to follow. That, in fact, is how he hit his followers with a one-two punch. First he warmed them up without especially amusing them, then when they were ready he stepped back, went into a sketch, and the battle was over.

And in a sketch, too, he exuded warmth and naturalness. It is this ability to seem like a real flesh-and-blood human being that made it possible for Jackie to make a quick switch from humor to pathos. Not many viewers can watch the finish of one of his "Honeymooners" scenes without feeling an unexpected tug at the heartstrings. At its best, a husband-and-wife playlet between Sid Caesar and Nanette Fabray was funnier, but the same sort of scene enacted by Gleason and Pert Kelton (later Audrey Meadows, then Sheila MacCrae) had more emotional impact. Indeed, it is Jackie's ability to engender sympathy that is one of his most powerful assets. At the finish of each "Honeymooners" sketch, by the way, an interesting thing occurs. Jackie ceases to be Ralph Kramden and becomes instead The Poor Soul. He drops the mask of anger and is no longer an aggressive adult. He is suddenly revealed as a defenseless, baby-faced incompetent.

My son, David, when he was four, got into some mischief one day and in reprimanding him I said, "What do you think you are anyway, a little baby?" "No," he shouted, eyes blazing defiance, "I'm *not* a little baby. I'm a *big* baby."

There is a peculiar appeal to a big baby, and in his pathetic moments Gleason expresses it. He is not, at such times, a *little* baby, like the young Jerry Lewis, whose weapon was the ridiculous; he was the big blustering man suddenly exposed. Your heart went out to him.

Some people professed to be surprised when Jack appeared from time to time in a straight dramatic role on the *Philco Playhouse, Studio One* or in films. These appearances were noteworthy, in my opinion, not for their novelty but for the excellence of the job that Jack did at such times, proving that he is a brilliant actor, equally at home in comedy or tragedy. By the 1970s his reputation as an actor in noncomic roles was secure.

On the set the real Gleason was, like Milton Berle, an autocrat. Usually unwilling to rehearse at all until the day of the broadcast, he was a fiery dictator once rehearsal was under way. He supervised the music, suggested numbers, ordered tempo changes. He has been known to take chorus dancers through a step ten times. His views on dancing, music or the technicalities of TV production are like those of the amateur art enthusiast. "I don't know what to call it," he says, "but I know what I like."

His writers feared him, particularly on the day of the show, for they knew that, with his mind on a thousand-and-one details he might not be in the proper mood to see the amusing side of material they presented to him. Gleason's writing staff changed more than any other in the field of television comedy, with the exception of Red Buttons, and because of their own insecurity his writers never felt completely at home with him.

Leonard Stern says, "On the writing staff there were originally five of us—Howard Harris, Walter Stone, Marvin Marx, Sid Zelenka, and myself. Working for Jackie was sort of rough duty for writers. Like most comedians who can't write themselves he had a love-hate relationship with the writers he depended upon. He liked us but also resented his need for us. I remember that when Howard Harris quit after one year he said, 'I quit. I can't stand this Humiliation Festival any more.'

"The scripts usually weren't finished until Friday night and the show was done live, Saturday. Jackie had total recall and the lateness didn't bother him, but Audrey Meadows and Art Carney would grab the pages as soon as we finished them because they needed more time to memorize. Saturdays we either went into the theater or would stay in the office trying to write the self-contained monologue jokes that Jackie liked to open with.

"Gleason was always bringing in other writers that would report directly to him. We never knew what they were doing. The men would be around, then they'd leave and we never saw the material. Gleason handled that part of it personally."

"I can't figure that guy out," one former staff member said to me. "I worked for him for several months and he hardly ever spoke to me. When he had to talk to us he'd come to the room we all worked in and knock on the door. He'd ask one or another of us to step out in the hall; he didn't want to come in and sit down and mingle with us."

"That's right," added another member of Gleason's staff. "The guy's great as a performer, but he's not the judge of material some people think he is. Time and time again I've seen him cut some sharp, new line out of a script and replace it at the last minute with some tired gag that even Berle wouldn't use that late in the game."

"I'll say this," said the first writer, "He's a better judge of sketch material than he is of stand-up jokes." This viewpoint—that Gleason is strongest in sketch, weakest as "himself"—seems to parallel Jack's own evaluation of his work.

Oddly enough, Gleason is one of the few comedians ever to reach the top without establishing a basic character. When you tuned in to a Jack Benny program you knew what to expect. Groucho was characteristically consistent. Ed Wynn was Ed Wynn. Jimmy Durante had one personality to sell. But of himself as an entertainer Gleason has said, "I'd really like to do 'me' on the show, but me, I could never sustain an hour-long program. So I play a dozen other guys. I really do several programs in one." This is in line with the critical judgment of Gleason as, at the very core, a gifted comedy actor. "In spite of all this," one comedy writer has pointed out, "the guy is a natural-born *star*. It's a separate thing in itself. It almost has nothing to do with talent. It's a flair, maybe it's a touch of the ham if you will, but without it you rarely become big."

Gleason's power made it easy for him to successfully employ such devices as the running gag or stock-reference line. To a comedian there can be few things more valuable—especially early in his career—than a line that catches the public's fancy. Although a stock catch-phrase may eventually become tiresome, while it is popular it works tremendously to the advantage of the comic fortunate enough to stumble across it. The history of radio and television comedy is full of famous stock phrases. Jerry Colonna's "Who's Yehudi?" was on everyone's lips during the early days of the old Bob Hope radio show; Jerry Lester's "George" enjoyed national popularity when he was featured on *Broadway Open House*; and Baron Munchausen's "Vas you dere, Charlie?" will never be forgotten by fans of Jack Pearl and Graham MacNamee. Red Skelton owed a certain small measure of his early radio popularity to the innocuous phrase, "I dood it," which in his role as the Mean Wittle Kid he used to deliver each Tuesday night on NBC. Even such old-timers as Ed Wynn, with his "Sooo-oo-ooooo!" and Bert Lahr with his "Ngah-nnagah-nnngah-nnngah!" illustrate the value of a word or phrase the public may use as a means of identification. The line is repeated in partial context until a habitual response is built up. From that point, the comedian has only to stop everything, look the audience in the eye, and plunge the needle into his helpless subjects; their response is inevitable.

As for influences on his comedy style, Gleason owes a debt to several of his predecessors. He was most himself when he was "in one" or when he was doing the "Honeymooners" sketch. When he did The Poor Soul he exhibited mannerisms of Buster Keaton and Harry Langdon, two clowns who did similar sad-faced pantomimes. The soulful expression, the childish clasping and unclasping of hands, the bumbling inability to cope with mechanical props, the approach to comedy through pathos, were not original with Gleason, but he employed these devices more adroitly than any of his contemporaries.

Jack's Reggie Van Gleason characterization was more original, although here too there was some evidence that the role is generic. In his early 1950s performance of Newton, the mustachioed doorman and/or waiter, Art Carney may have contributed discernible influence to the Van Gleason portrayals, and the ghosts of a host of burlesque clowns hovered about the stage when Gleason waved his arms and slithered about the stage in his familiar baggy-pants way.

Red Buttons, after carefully explaining to me that he is an admirer of Gleason's, made the observation that Jackie owes more than a small debt to a comedian Buttons refers to as "the original Jackie Gleason," Jack Oakie. "Jackie works a lot like Oakie," says Red. "He looks like him, he does a lot of the same takes, he has the same wise-guy loudmouth approach, and he does Oakie's bit with the elbows that the public thinks Gleason invented."

The late Jack E. Leonard, the rotund comic known to 1950s TV audiences chiefly for his many appearances on *This Is Show Business,* and a close friend of Gleason's, agreed with Red. "It's simple," he said, "Jackie was always a good mimic and Oakie was one of his idols. Gleason thinks Oakie was one of the great comedy talents of all time. And another thing; the other day I saw an old Mack Sennett movie with the Keystone Kops and Ben Turpin. What do I see Turpin doing all of a sudden but Gleason's 'Away-We-Go' business with the elbows. So I call him up and say, 'Hey, Jackie, Ben Turpin is stealing your bit!'"

Gleason, to his credit, has publicly acknowledged Oakie's influence. Yet despite my admiration for both comedians, I had no idea of the extent of Gleason's indebtedness until, in 1982, I happened to come across a copy of a half-tribute, half-autobiography called *Jack Oakie's Doubletakes* (Strawberry Hill Press). In addition to being an important resource for any serious or even casual student of the history of comedy, the book contains a great many pictures of Oakie—in vaudeville, radio, TV, films, and private life. In some of them one can hardly tell if the subject is Oakie or Gleason, so similar are the facial expressions and physical attitudes; the good-natured, cocky smile, the hiya-folks attitude, the angles of the comedy hats. The resemblance is truly striking. Part of it, of course, is that Gleason and Oakie have the same round-faced, loveable con-man look. Gleason must have noticed the resemblance early in life. Oakie was his man.

Peculiarly enough for such a hurly-burly comic, Jackie likes to go into lengthy "psychological" explanations of the various characters he does. "I insist on doing characters," he says, "because frankly I don't think there's any personality who can sustain himself on television just by being himself week in and week out. There's just no one that brilliant or precious."

"All the characters I do on television," continues Jackie, "are psychologically constructed. I insist that they be always consistent, that each have a touch of sympathy, and that they be to some extent actual. That way the people in the audience see themselves as characters, and this takes the heat and embarrassment off them."

One of the odd things about Gleason—considering how gifted he is at his craft—is that even as of 1981 he did not seem to have any particular insight into his standard characters (Reggie van Gleason, the Poor Soul, etc.), at least so far as one could judge from his answers to questions on the *20-20* show.

Concerning the formally-attired swinger Reginald van Gleason, Jackie says, "He was always dressed in tails, which he associated with having a good time. He was ready for a good time at all times. So he was psychologically constructed."

I have shown this quotation to several people. None has been able to make any sense out of it. The more important truth, in any event, is that Reggie was a wonderfully funny character, in the tradition of silent screen comedians, although he did speak. His tight, constricted comedy voice is occasionally copied by Johnny Carson to the present day and has found its way into the national language of humor.

"All the other characters," Gleason said on the "20-20" show, "were more or less constructed from what I considered to be what they would do in real life." This, too, I'm afraid, is close to meaningless. Joe, the Bartender—perhaps the least amusing of Gleason's various delightful characterizations—was nothing much more than himself in a bartender's outfit. Warm-hearted, gregarious, a bit of a con-man, but likable. Real bartenders, by way of contrast, are usually introverted and exhibit signs of the *MASH* syndrome, without which protection they would no doubt be driven to distraction by the combined boorishness, surliness, drunkenness or other tragic emanations of many of their customers.

As for The Poor Soul, such characters in real life are almost never caught up in comic activity since they are so markedly tragic that only sadistic observers could possibly laugh at them.

The dominant image of Gleason—happily for us all—is that of Ralph Kramden, the loud-mouthed, conceited, opinionated, but basically loveable bus driver. If there were such an individual in real life he would, of course, live through much simpler and less amusing plot lines than Gleason's writers concocted for him every week.

Another comment of Gleason's that is not related to reality was his observation about the utter necessity for the pathetic element in comedy. "There *has* to be pathos," he said on "20-20." "It is difficult for people to appreciate their own laughter unless you show them some pathos along the way. Because without that it's a one-dimensional effort."

This, as I say, is simply not the case. If we pick our way through the irrelevancies of the statement, however, we come to the wisdom that the best, most affecting humor, often does have a pathetic element. There's nothing particularly mysterious about this. It simply involves two things instead of one; in addition to rich funniness you are adding an emotional tug at the heart-strings. Two good things are always better than one. What Jackie means by people appreciating their own laughter I have no idea. Most people are content to laugh but rarely interested in analyzing either the laughter or the factors that have given rise to it.

I suspect Gleason is really often talking, when he analyzes his characters, about aspects of himself. For it is undeniable that, more than in the case of any other entertainer, his characters are drawn from one facet of his personality or another. There is nothing of the German double-talking professor, for instance, in Sid Caesar; nothing of the brash cowboy in Larry Storch, nothing of the boring jerk in Steve Martin, nothing of the baggy-pants Senator Philip Buster in me, but there is a lot of the Reggie Van Gleason in Jackie Gleason. It is not difficult, either, to find The Poor Soul, Ralph Kramden, or Charlie "Loudmouth" Bratton tucked away in the ample Gleason character.

Gleason, perhaps more than any other successful clown, always seemed to be engaged in a great race to get out of himself. His energy is prodigous and for years he lived hard. He is the most ambitious of men. He once planned to build a TV city in the Arizona desert; he directed and produced his own show (a chore that no other comedian but Milton Berle found necessary); he owned a bright-red Cadillac convertible; he buys expensive suits the way an average man buys hankerchiefs; conducts orchestras when the whim is upon him; and, although he has no technical knowledge of music, confers with arranger-composer Dudley "Pete" King and composes melodies. He cannot make up his mind whether he is shy or blustering. He is, in an almost professional sense, a saint and a sinner.

In 1955 Jackie saw fit to scrap all of his show except the "Honeymooners" sketch and to present his program as a filmed rather than live feature. Although initial reaction to the filming of the show was largely negative, I think this was due to the public's natural aversion to change and to the loss of excitement that results when the present-tenseness of live TV is taken away. I predicted at the time, "In a few weeks, I believe people will have forgotten about this inconsequential matter and gotten back to concentrating on the fact that "The Honeymooners" is as wonderfully funny as ever—in fact, even more so, since Gleason films a few more moments of entertainment than he needs and can therefore edit out the portions that do not come up to expectations."

"The Honeymooners" turned out to be the part of Gleason's bag of tricks most destined to succeed over the long pull. It is good, old-fashioned, family situation comedy.

The humor of the Kramden sketches was of a sure-fire type described by Henri Bergson as derisive. There isn't a quotably noteworthy joke in a bushel of "Honeymooners" scripts; the punch lines are almost all pure ego-deflaters with which the audience can easily identify emotionally: "You . . . are a mental case!"; "One of these days, Alice—POW! Right in the kisser!"; "Aw, shaddap!"

Some show-business historians have claimed that Gleason's "The Honeymooners" was based directly on "The Bickersons," the delightful 1940s husband-and-wife series created by Phill Rapp and portrayed on radio by Don Ameche and Frances Langford. Although there are obvious similarities between the two the differences are fundamental. The Bickersons were highly quotable. Rapp created unrealistic comic gems and put them into the mouths of the shrewish wife and her long-suffering and epigram-spouting husband. The jokes were like some Bob Hope jokes: flashy, witty. Gleason's lines were scarcely jokes at all—they derived too logically out of the story line to be amusing out of context. But audiences were even more amused by "The Honeymooners" because of the psychological truism that what involves your emotions is more effective than that which involves only your intellect.

Each "Honeymooners" sketch was constructed according to an unvarying pattern. Ralph Kramden concocts a scheme or becomes the victim of a delusion. He is aided by his weak-witted friend, Ed Norton. Ralph's wife, Alice, sees through to the accurate heart of the difficulty and attempts to deflate Ralph's daydream bubble. Ralph bridles and blusters. He persists in his scheme, only to find that Alice was right all the time. Ralph is finally revealed for what he is—a blundering braggart whose bull-voiced confidence scarcely obscures his inner feelings of inferiority. At the denouement, with the help of muted violins playing George Gershwin's "Our Love Is Here To Stay," the Kramdens are reconciled and Ralph is the object of the viewers' sympathy. It is all wonderfully familiar and predictable, like a well-loved comic strip. On radio its life expectancy might have been fifteen years. I guessed at the time, that "the TV mortality rate to date leads me to believe audiences will continue to be fascinated by 'The Honeymooners' for about three more years, or till about 1958." I was wrong. The show didn't last that long. But the one season of fine programs is still being enjoyed in syndication.

"You know," Leonard Stern said when I discussed the Gleason series with him, "almost all the first few years of the show are gone now. The old films have fallen apart, been lost, or purposely destroyed. All that's left are those thirty-nine "Honeymooners" shows, which are now recognized as classics. And those shows were the season in which we were cancelled."

Like Carroll O'Connor's Archie Bunker, Gleason appealed to the good-natured lower class slob in all of us. Though he was never a professional Irishman of the Pat O'Brien or Dennis Day type, he was very New York-New Jersey Irish nevertheless.

Most conceited people pay at least lip-service to humility. Indeed sometimes they are honestly big-headed at one moment and appropriately modest at another. Again, Gleason played the instrument of himself at full throttle. His enormous, and deserved, success was simply not enough for him. He wished to be taken seriously not only as a successful and popular comedian, but as "the greatest" among comedians, taken seriously as a musician, even as a thinker.

He was not, needless to say, in his private life the same loud-mouthed life-of-the-party he played on the air, although it would not be correct to say that this aspect was totally absent from his off-camera guise. Gleason's "hiya, folks" attitude actually served to keep the rubes at a distance. If everybody was addressed as "pal" the word was robbed of its meaning so that there were, in reality, surprisingly few pals. For the most part, his friends were those he worked with.

Although young people today consider Gleason an "old-fashioned type," the odd thing is that he was an old-fashioned type even at the height of his success in the 1950s. His public image was somehow that of a vaudeville or speak-easy hot-shot from the '20s or '30s. Even the earlier comedian he admired so much, Jack Oakie, whose influence he acknowledges, had been a typical 1920s-'30s type—a fedora-brim-turned-up, hail-fellow-well-met sort of guy, the likable con-merchant charming his way through various scams and scrapes. This, as I say, was already the case at the moment of Jackie's greatest popularity.

Writing about Jackie in 1956 I said, "Is Gleason's hold on the top rung of the TV ladder secure? I think so. His popularity is a little like Godfrey's, not at all like Fred Allen's. Fred was always the critics' darling and the favorite of the intellectuals. All a rival network had to do to knock him off was put on the air a substandard give-away show that drove intelligent listeners to distraction but openly pandered to the tastes of the mob. Gleason is secure, I believe, because his appeal is to the mob."

Well, it turns out that none of us could remain forever in the Top Ten, but Gleason's reputation, at least, is still secure.

We'll always laugh at Jackie, thanks to those old films. He and Art Carney were the Laurel and Hardy of the 1950s and '60s generation. I can pay them no higher compliment.

Bob Hope

Bob Hope

*I*N EARLY 1976, JAYNE AND I FILLED our house with flowers, lit the candles, and threw one of the best parties of all time. The credit for its merits, however, goes to the list of guests; we had for some time talked about the fact that it might be fun to have an all-comedian's party.

Practically every funny man and woman in town on the date of the event accepted. Among those who joined us for a warm and hilarious evening were Groucho Marx, Bob Newhart, Jack Albertson, Bea Arthur, Sid Caesar, Harvey Korman, McLean Stevenson, Red Buttons, Jack Oakie, Carroll O'Connor, Jean Stapleton, Rob Reiner, Phil Silvers, George Gobel, Maury Amsterdam, Alan King, Bill Daily, Dick Martin, Jan Murray, Jack Carter, Tim Conway, Bill Dana, Louis Nye, Tom Poston, Foster Brooks, Joe Bologna, Renee Taylor, and—just for the hell of it—Alice Cooper.

I have a terrible suspicion I'm leaving out several other important names, but in any event the evening could hardly have failed to be great fun with such a cast of characters. One reason I recall the event is that the comedians present related to each other as what they were—peers, equals—but the one visitor by whom all the others were most impressed was Bob Hope.

The reason for this was not that such a knowledgeable assemblage of professionals were of the opinion that Bob was the funniest among them. Had a poll been taken they probably would have so honored Groucho or Sid Caesar. But Bob was, far and away, the most successful. Even among creative artists it is not talent alone but success that excites the greater interest.

Of all the comedians I have known personally, Bob is in some ways the most difficult to know man-to-man. But there is considerable mystery to this, because Bob is by no means cold or aloof, as was Bing Crosby. He is affable, cheerful. It is not that he is off alone working on his own planet, as is Woody Allen. Unlike some show-biz relative loners such as Joey

Bishop, Red Skelton, Jerry Lewis, or Johnny Carson, Bob does mingle with his peers. But it always seems to be in the context of work or when he is publicizing one of his projects. At such times, however, he is unfailingly cordial, sometimes witty, always good-natured. All of this makes it even more puzzling that one has the sense of conversing with a sort of affable charm-machine rather than just one of the guys. It's relevant that when, in the early '60s, Bob was asked to identify his close friends, the only show business name he could think of was Fred MacMurray. So I wonder: does anyone ever call Bob Hope up and say, "Hey, would you like to have dinner tomorrow night?" I doubt it. He obviously doesn't need such calls. Being successful to the point of becoming a social institution, as distinguished from merely a popular entertainer, presumably suffices.

An old-time comedy writer once said to me, "You forget that Bob originally was a small-time vaudevillian. Despite his later success—and he's certainly the most successful comedian since Chaplin—I think somewhere inside himself he may still feel like a small-time vaudeville hoofer and emcee who got lucky. So maybe he's afraid to hang around, like at Lindy's in the old days, or the Friar's Club, or the Comedy Store with the young guys, or just at somebody's house for dinner. Maybe he somehow needs just to play the role of the famous Bob Hope."

Perhaps. But it is hard to envision Bob as personally insecure. Not only has he been eminently successful for over half a century, but even back in the days when he was struggling, suffering through financial hard times, he always had the brash self-confidence that subsequently became part of his public image.

Perhaps—if there is any area of insecurity involved—it might grow out of the fact that, although he has for most of his career been a great favorite with the people, he has not always enjoyed the respect of critics, none of whom have considered him as on the same plane as a Chaplin, Buster Keaton, Stan Laurel or—in more recent times—Woody Allen, Sid Caesar, or Richard Pryor.

It is fascinating that things said about Bob in the 1980s have been said for over thirty years. In his New York *Herald-Tribune* column of March 5, 1958, the witty John Crosby observed:

> This has not been a good year for the stand-up comic. In fact, the man who stands just behind the footlights and tosses naked jokes at the audience has been quietly going into eclipse for the last couple of years—all

except Bob Hope, who is an exception to just about all the rules. *Hope's intermittent television shows have frequently taken an awful critical lambasting and consistently run up awe-inspiring ratings anyway* . . . (Italics supplied)

If there is one word of praise that Hope's work most readily calls forth, however, it is *class*. Class itself is not a particularly classy word, but does have its function. Although Bob is obviously funny—extremely so, in certain situations—there is a certain authority, a kind of professional polish, that is quite separate from his ability to amuse. Watching Hope function in front of a camera, one never feels the mixture of sympathy and concern that often wells up at the spectacle of other and newer TV comics plying their wares. Even when he has had a bad show, Bob personally is still in command. He's still moving at high speed, tossing off his lines with a remarkable facility and timing.

The ability to stand up close and face an audience is a speciality of Hope's, and few can touch him at it. This seemingly run-of-the-mill assignment, incidentally, is difficult for many comedians. Jackie Gleason was never truly at ease until he stepped back into the protective arms of some scenery and went into a sketch. Sid Caesar is simply unable to address an audience and amuse them as himself. Milton Berle is a close match for Hope when it comes to firing jokes at point-blank range, but Milton at such times will often battle with an audience for laughs. He gets them, but not with the ease that Hope does.

A related quality is that Bob seems very much a gentleman. There was an ideal of the "gentleman" in American and European culture at one time. In the United States at present, the ideal seems little honored. Hope is, of course, neither the first nor the last gentlemanly comedian, but this was always an element of his appeal.

Yet another reason for Hope's success is the length and variety of his experience.

Hope was born Leslie Towns Hope on May 30, 1903, in Eltham, England. His mother, Avis Towns, was by all accounts a sweet, sensitive woman, a center of stability and love to her large brood. Her husband, Harry, was a hard-drinking, good-looking, womanizing stonemason.

By the time he was four, little Leslie was beginning to give evidence of a gift for entertaining. This is a common pattern among those who eventually become successful professional comedians. They garner attention, usually in early childhood, by some special quality of cuteness, eccentricity, energy, or playfulness. Since adults usually reward such behavior with laughter, compliments, and other kind attentions, the natural comedian quickly learns to keep such behavior in the act, so to speak. It may be a simple matter of behavioral conditioning. The subject increases the frequency of those acts for which he is especially rewarded.

In 1906 times were difficult for Harry Hope. His brother Frank had already moved to Cleveland, Ohio. Harry decided his fate, too, lay in America. It was not until almost two years later that his wife and children followed him. Young Bob (still called Leslie) and his brothers settled into a more-or-less typical life for young mid-westerners early in the century—they sold newspapers, engaged in sports, attended school.

Leslie had an interesting encounter one evening while selling newspapers at the intersection of Euclid and 105th Street. To quote William Robert Faith's *Bob Hope, A Life in Comedy*:

> Sooner or later each boy had the experience of selling a paper to "that man" in the big black Peerless limousine. Les caught him in the evening when the hand reached out from the back seat window with his two cents for the *Press*. His face was wrinkled, Leslie thought, like an old leather coin purse, and he seldom said a word when he took his paper.
>
> One night he handed Les a dime. Les told him he didn't have any change, but the man stared until Les said he would go get some. The youngster disappeared into the grocery and waited his turn at the front counter for his ten pennies. When he ran back to the side of the big automobile, the man leaned out slightly and said, "Young man, I'm going to give you some advice. If you want to be a success in business, trust nobody—never give credit, and always keep change in hand. That way you won't miss any customers going for it." All Les could think of was the customers he had already lost because this man was so stingy. When the chauffeur drove the car away, the trolley starter said to Leslie, "Know who that man was?" Les shook his head. "John D. Rockefeller, that's who."

Young Leslie quickly had to learn another art common among the poor in America, that of fighting. The remnant of his English accent, the name Leslie—considered sissified by his classmates—his English-style clothes were more than enough to make him the butt of teasing.

Out of embarrassment at the name Leslie he took to calling himself Les. But since most children are familiar with the word in the form of the adjective "less," the change did nothing to ease the cruel jibes at the boy's expense.

As a teenager, Bob learned a few dance steps, danced with various neighborhood groups, won a neighborhood Charlie Chaplin contest. A naturally husky physical specimen, he quit college after one year of studying dentistry to enter the prize ring. Since a friend had taken the name Packy West, after a great boxer named Packy McFarland, Bob, for a lark, took the name Packy East. It did not take him long to discover that prize-fighting was not his game. One night in an Ohio ring he was quick-frozen by Johnny Risko; he took the hint and retired.

By 1920, Hope had put together a dance act with a neighborhood girl of whom he was fond. After three years Mildred bowed out of the yet-to-be-successful act. Hope replaced her with a friend named Lloyd Durbin, a polished dancer. Little by little, Hope and Durbin placed increasing emphasis on comedy elements. By 1925, Bob had another partner, a man named George Byrne. In 1926, something happened that was significant in terms of Hope's later development as a performer. He and his partner were booked at Detroit's State Theater.

According to Faith, "The M.C. at the State was Fred Stitt, and Hope watched him carefully, more because of his material than his style. Though Stitt sang a lot in his act, his comedy was patter based on 'the latest happenings in the *Daily News.*' That intrigued Hope."

Bob recalls the first time he thought of being a comedian. "I always wanted to be a dancer in those days, but as I knocked around theaters I saw a comic named Jim McWilliams. He got 1,500 dollars a week. He'd come in, didn't even put on make-up, deliver his gags, and then head for the saloon across the street. It looked like the perfect life for me. That's when I decided I wanted to be a comic."

In the summer of 1927, Hope and Byrne at last broke into the big time when they were hired as chorus dancers for a show called *Sidewalks of New York.* The success the boys had assumed would follow their first Broadway break was nowhere evident, however. Quite the reverse. After the musical show closed, they could not at first get work of any kind. An important agent named Johnny Hyde told Hope that he wasn't even interested in looking at his act because he had heard that it was not very good. He advised the boys to go back on the road, change their act, and make a whole new start.

Back to playing small-time theaters, Bob had another lucky break at a minor house in New Castle, Pennsylvania, when, on the spur of the moment, the manager asked him to walk out after the last act and simply make some announcements about the coming attractions. "The show is called the 'Whiz-Bang Revue,'" the manager said. "It features a Scotchman named Marshall Walker. That's all I know about it."

The meager bit of information was enough for Hope. He swaggered on stage and said, "Ladies and gentlemen, next week's show features a Scotchman named Marshall Walker. He must be a Scotchman; he got married in his own back yard 'cause he wanted his chickens to get the rice." Surprised by a big laugh, he added another joke the following show. By the end of the night he had built up a short routine. A musician pointed out to him that while comics might be a dime-a-dozen, good MC's were hard to find. "Your double act with that dancing and those corny jokes," the musician said, "that's nothing." But, he argued, as a master of ceremonies Hope had just the right quality and attitude.

Hope and Byrne split up shortly thereafter. Bob was on his way.

After a siege of tough luck, he finally landed a one-week engagement as master of ceremonies at a theater I used to visit as a child, the Stratford, on Sixty-third Street in the wilds of Chicago's South side. A vaudeville agent named Charlie Hogan met Bob one day in front of the Woods building, a downtown Chicago booking center. Hope looked glum.

"How are you doing?" Hogan said.

"Not too good," Bob answered. "As a matter of fact I haven't worked in a while, and I could really use a booking right now to help pay the room rent for Dolores and myself at the Croydon."

To help Bob out, Hogan booked him for a trial weekend at the Stratford. The booking proved a turning point for Hope. Because of this, for years after, whenever Bob played a concert engagement in the Chicago area, he saw to it that Hogan received a 5 percent commission. The arrangement persisted until Hogan died, in the early 1970s.

At the Stratford, the neighborhood crowd immediately went for Hope's breezy patter and his pre-Pepsodent smile. He was held over once, then again, for a total of six months.

When I appeared as guest on one of his comedy specials in March of 1976, Bob told me that he had originally been brought to Hollywood in 1930 to do a screen test for producer William Perlberg. "Things didn't work out too well," he said. "Nobody met me at the station. There was no welcome at all. I went out to the studio, did the test, and it was terrible. My nose came on the screen 20 minutes before I did. Nobody even seemed to know that I was around so I just got back on a train and went right back to Salt Lake City where I was working at the Orpheum."

Fortunately important bookers became aware of Bob's talent and he headed for New York, where work in musical comedies added to his polish. In *Smiles* (with Fred Astaire) *Sidewalks of New York, Ballyhoo of 1932,* and *Red, Hot and Blue* (with Jimmy Durante and Ethel Merman) he began to stand out. From the night he opened in *Roberta* he was a Broadway star.

Even today being a big man in New York can still leave you a complete unknown to the country at large. It was radio that exposed Bob's talent to the nation.

Hope's comedy style was basically what it is now, but then it had the impact of being fresh and different. Before long he was a sensation, signed for his own program. His rapid patter took the country by storm. Even as today, his jokes were full of fantastic comparisons, exaggerations, snappy, timely references. Instead of saying, "This girl was so fat that . . ." Hope switched it to, "I won't say this girl was fat, but . . ." and somehow the negative approach made the line funnier. His jokes were up-to-the-minute, brazen, and above all, good. From the first Bob has had the good sense to spend whatever was necessary to hire the top comedy writers. He is not a humorist, but his judgment is good, and he knows what he likes. A list of the graduates of Hope's writing stable reads like a *Who's Who* in the field of mass-produced humor. Like Jack Benny, he has a superb editorial sense. He will sometimes take a dozen or more pages of jokes contributed by several of the best gag-writers in the business, read quickly through them, and, in just a few minutes, select those that are best for him. He would not argue that they are necessarily the best per se, merely that they are lines that he feels comfortable with, that he believes will make his audience laugh. Writers practically never argue with a comedian about such choices, by the way; there is, after all, no way they can get into the performer's head and make such choices for him.

The jokesmith will often later grouse privately that, "He skipped over the best damn joke of the whole lot," or "How do you like that? What I thought was my weakest line, he liked more than the good stuff." An impartial jury would almost certainly agree with the writers, who are, after all, experts on the subject—if not always about the jokes that they personally create. But the important decision must be reserved for the comedian since he alone has that peculiar sense of what will work for *him.*

One secret of the success of Hope's comedy style lies, I think, in the fact that his personality is peculiarly American, uniquely representative of the culture in which he functions. He is the perennial wise guy whose braggadocio is made palatable by the fact that in the last analysis *he* gets it in the neck. He seems to know all the answers, yet he comes off no better in a given situation than the average man. He exhibits all the customary traits, all the faults common to the rest of us; cowardice, an exaggerated idea of his sexual prowess, a talent for getting into trouble without trying, and a penchant for trying to *talk* his way out of a tight spot. The average middle-class American would never envision himself as a Milquetoast Wally Cox, a New York-neurotic Woody Allen, a wild and crazy Steve Martin, or a leering Groucho Marx; he would probably picture himself as something like Bob Hope.

A joke that, in this connection, I think, reveals the true Hope image is a line from one of his "Road" pictures with Bing Crosby. The boys had gone into a saloon and had been warned to act tough, as the place was a den of thieves and murderers. But when the bartender said, "What'll you have?" Bob's absentminded answer was "Lemonade." "What!" Bing reacted, nudging him. "In a dirty glass," Bob added.

And yet—oddly—there is always an unreal, unlifelike quality to Bob's routines. Perhaps nothing dramatizes the essential unbelievability of Bob's radio and television sketches of the last 40 years as the combined facts that (a) he is widely publicized as a married man with children but (b) he does sketches in which, as *himself,* he plays the flirtatious, over-sexed roué.

There is no such thing as a comedian totally free from influence by his predecessors. At various times, in separate interviews, Bob has conceded learning a trick of the trade or two from Harry Fox and Richie Craig, two vaudeville old-timers whose names are now obscure, as well as from Frank Fay and Lynn Overman, Fred Allen, Jack Benny, and W. C. Fields. He does not work exactly like any of these older performers; influence rarely works in so direct a way. But young comedians are always influenced by at least a few of those who precede them. The lasting impressions are usually absorbed during the young performer's late teens or early 20s. It is at that age that one generally first sees the masters of one's profession. They have a certain polish that only experience can provide, and watching such practitioners of one's art is always an educational experience.

Hope himself has also been an instructive influence for many comedians. In 1940 when he was new at the comic trade, Danny Thomas was working as master of ceremonies at the Morocco Club in Detroit. Hope was in town one rainy evening and had agreed to make a brief appearance on "celebrity night."

"I was afraid that if any celebrities showed up at all," Thomas recalls, "they'd be playing to a very small audience. Anyway, I came on and began knocking myself out with gag after gag. I got the usual scattered applause. After all, I'd been working there for two years and the crowd knew me, and I guess they knew a lot of the jokes, too. I knew that I was only a stage-wait for the guest stars. The original Lone Ranger from radio was supposed to show up, and also Betty Hutton. Anyway, Bob came in and we got him on right away. He taught me a great lesson because he's always very well-dressed, you know, but mud and rain had gotten on his slacks from the storm outside. So the first thing he did, he looked down at his wet pants cuff and said, 'Those Detroit cabdrivers come mighty close.' The audience really broke up. The joke itself wasn't all that hilarious, but the point was, it was topical. It took advantage of that situation."

An even more important point: "I never realized until that night what *authority* meant, and how important it was to size up and understand your audience. Up 'til that time I had never really done that. I just rattled off my jokes and stories. But Bob Hope taught me that night that the most brilliantly written material in the world can fall flat unless the delivery is authoritative."

Danny has put his finger here on what has always been one of Hope's strong cards. He has always had a remarkable degree of self-confidence. Even before he was a star, he carried himself like a star. That quality isn't always endearing, but he "got away" with it for a number of reasons: he did good-natured comedy, he was good-looking, had a cute salesman's smile, and was willing—like Jack Benny—to submit to jokes at his own expense.

You might suppose that anyone who *is* a star acts like one. But this happens not to be the case. Many comedians, in fact, have an appealingly humble quality, which may or may not be a professional advantage. Will Rogers, George Gobel, Fred Allen, Herb Shriner, Sam Levenson, Bob Newhart, Woody Allen, W. C. Fields, Stan Laurel, Bill Cosby—these and other eminently successful performers have seemed not to take themselves too seriously. As against this there are the entertainers who work in a deliberately conceited manner: Bob, Danny Thomas, Don Rickles, Milton Berle, Jerry Lewis, Jackie Gleason, Phil Silvers.

Having set this brash, over-confident character firmly in the public mind, Hope always "plays himself," regardless of costume or locale. He does no dialects or regular characterizations, preferring to always play the breezy guy who somehow manages to get loused up for all his flip assurance. In a well-written sketch, he can deliver strongly without overplaying, which is another reason the public has never tired of him during five decades. The following scene with singer Rosemary Clooney from one of his TV shows is typical. It's from the 1950s, but the style has not changed to the present day:

HOPE: I'd like to tell you a little about my frandfather, Robert Casanova Hope.... He was a sort of a Casanova of the Gay Nineties—he had a notch in his cane for every woman whose heart he had broken. That's what killed him—one day he leaned on his cane.

He was a gay old dog, and the men of his day copied his style of dress. As a matter of fact, he invented spats. . . . Well, he didn't exactly invent them—he just used to let his long underwear hang out over his shoes. All the women chased him, but none of them ever caught him—he was known as Robert the Eel . . .

This is the home of one of the young ladies grandpa was courting back in the days of the mustache cup, the horseless carriage, celluloid collars, and the overstuffed bustle. Dig those crazy outfits.... No wonder they called it the *Gay* Nineties—people just looked at each other and got hysterical. All right, you folks—action!

MOTHER: Rosemary, I'm going to forbid you to see that young scoundrel Robert Casanova Hope unless he states his intentions. After all, he's been courting you for seven years now.

CLOONEY: But, Mother, I've tried everything to get him to propose. You have no idea how he wriggles out of it.

FATHER: I won't have my daughter resorting to trickery.

MOTHER: Oh, hush, Clarence. You're simply not trying hard enough, daughter.

CLOONEY: How can you say that, Mother? . . . Just yesterday I pretended to faint in front of the marriage-license bureau.

MOTHER: Good thinking, girl, good thinking!

CLOONEY: When he took me inside to revive me I said, "As long as we're here, Robert, isn't there something you'd like to get?"

MOTHER: Yes. . . . What did he say?

CLOONEY: He said, "I'm not ready for marriage yet. Why don't we take out a learner's permit?"

(Doorbell sounds)

CLOONEY: Oh, good heavens! That's Robert now.

MOTHER: Keep plugging, girl. *(Mother hikes daughter's dress)* There. If a man doesn't see what's in the back of the store, he won't ask for it!

FATHER: Here now, none of that. That's trickery.

MOTHER: Oh, quiet, Clarence. How do you think I hooked you? Just get him to propose, and your father and I will see to it that he doesn't get away today.

FATHER: Trickery, That's what it is—trickery! *(As they exit)*

(Doorbell rings again.)

CLOONEY: Come in.

(Hope enters)

HOPE: Sorry I'm late. I was busy pollinating my avocados—it's the mating season, you know. Flowers for my lady.

CLOONEY: How lovely!

HOPE: *(Handing her candy)* You didn't know they had a licorice counter, did you? I better sit over here. *(Hope sits. Reacts uncomfortably. His jacket is made of the same material as the couch.)*

CLOONEY: What's wrong? Don't you feel at home here?

HOPE: Oh, sure—and I go so well with the furniture! What's your upholsterer's name?

CLOONEY: Jim Clinton. *(Los Angeles low-price clothing chain.)*

HOPE: I thought so. He's my tailor! Must have a talk with that boy— This sofa has better shoulders than I do.

CLOONEY: *(Dropping hanky)* Oops, I dropped my hanky.

(Hope tries to scoop it. Stares at cane)

HOPE: I knew I'd never make it with a wood. It's a four-iron shot.

This is an example of a device Hope has always put to good use: the seeming ad-lib, the slightly out-of-character aside to the audience that seems to come from Hope himself rather than from the character he is playing. Both the reference to the wood shot and the "This sofa has better shoulders than I do" line above were received with the special reaction audiences reserve for an ad-lib.

> *(Hope gets to his knee)*
> CLOONEY: While you're down there, isn't there something you'd like to do?
> HOPE: Sure, but I didn't bring my dice with me.
> CLOONEY: I'm talking about something else. When Father proposed to Mother he was kneeling on that very spot!
> HOPE: Well, don't worry—a little Carbona will take that out!

This is another typical Hopeism, the timely, local reference. The word *Carbona* is such a down-to-earth household term that it greatly multiplies the laugh. The audience does not expect to hear a performer refer to the particular things and places that are associated with the "common people." The joke would be funny with the words "cleaning fluid," but it's funnier with Carbona.

> CLOONEY: Oh, Robert, don't you realize we're the only ones in our set that haven't been married?
> HOPE: Yeah, I was thinking about that.
> CLOONEY: What do you think we should do about it?
> HOPE: Join a new set?
> CLOONEY: Can't you see what I'm hinting at? We have so much in common, haven't we?
> HOPE: Well, it's true that we have one important thing in common—we both like me.
> CLOONEY: We could be so happy together. The two of us could be one.
> HOPE: Won't there be some parts left over?
> CLOONEY: Oh, Robert, what have you got against marriage?
> HOPE: Nothing! Nothing at all! I think marriage teaches a man patience, consideration, kindness, thrift, and a lot of other things he wouldn't need if he stayed single!
> CLOONEY: Oh, Robert!
> HOPE: Besides, I'm not your type. You're a sweet girl, a charming girl, a lovely girl, and I'm none of those things—I'm a boy!
> CLOONEY: I don't care, I like you as you are! You're the only man in the world for me. Say you'll marry me.

HOPE: But think of your parents. Your father would never consent to our marriage.

(Father pops out from behind the sofa.)

FATHER: Congratulations, my boy. You have my blessing!

HOPE: Where'd he come from?

FATHER: Now, then let's get on with the wedding. *(He hands Clooney bridal veil and bouquet.)*

HOPE: Well, I'll see you later! *(Starts for the door.)*

CLOONEY: Robert, where are you going?

HOPE: You can't rush into weddings. It takes weeks of preparation. You've gotta hire a parson and . . . *(He opens door. Parson enters.)*

PARSON: Dearly beloved, we are gathered here . . .

HOPE: *(Walking to the other door.)* Wait a minute—let's talk it over first. I want a wedding with a best man and bridesmaids . . . *(Bridesmaids enter, one sings)*

HOPE: This is ridiculous. When I go I'm goin' first-class. I want a big wedding with organ music and everything. *(He has reached opposite door. Mother pushes organ on. Organist plays. Best man and Father carry Hope. Place him next to Clooney.)*

PARSON: Do you Rosemary, take this man to be your lawful wedded husband?

CLOONEY: I do.

PARSON: Do you, Robert, take this woman to be your lawful wedded wife?

FATHER: Remember, son, I laid out the money for this wedding. You owe me five hundred dollars.

HOPE: I do?

PARSON: I now pronounce you man and wife!

HOPE: Trickery. That's what it is—trickery!

I quote this old sketch because, while it is far from the quality of the better sketches seen on the more creative comedy programs, it is nevertheless a typical Hope sketch. The structure is basic, primitive, essentially unchanged from Bob's radio style of the 1930s. A high percentage of these sketches, over the years, have had Hope playing opposite an attractive woman. The flirtatious banter is almost invariably part of the act. Bob's characters sometimes are simply on the make and at other times—as in this instance—trying to escape responsibility. He is always the likeable con-man, the big city sharpster trying to put one over on somebody, and usually suffering some indignity himself as a result.

Hope did not invent the idea of topical humor, but he has carried it to great lengths. In his autobiography, *Have Tux, Will Travel* (Simon and Schuster), he says, "For my money, the No. 1 joke of them all is the topical joke, a quip based on today's newspaper headlines. When you use one everybody is with you as soon as you tee off." Hope's insistence on topicality, of course, gives his humor a transient appeal. You can read a 20-year-old Jack Benny or Fred Allen script and still find it amusing, but a Hope monologue does not age well since so many of his jokes refer to popular interests of the moment.

Bob originally instructed his writers to devote their greatest creative energies to his opening monologues, for he likes these to tap the popular mind-set. The formula has now been established for years. With five minutes of good topical jokes to depend on, Bob is off to the races and feels more confident about the rest of the show. His dependence on the humor of the moment is greater than that of any other funnyman since Will Rogers. Will, of course, was the humorist-philosopher, always able to put his finger on just what the public wanted to hear about, and able to say something original, pithy, and discerning about the issue. Hope's approach is only on-the-surface. The jokes do not have to have any philosophical or satirical content; they just have to be snappy. If there is anything peculiar on the front pages tonight, you may be certain that the next Bob Hope special will include references to it. Johnny Carson has followed Bob's lead in this regard.

Pick up a Hope script from the war years and you'll find jokes about blackouts, foxholes, the sugar shortage, draft boards, the Germans, Japanese, Chinese, Vietnamese, gas ration coupons, and jeeps. One reason the men in the armed forces like Bob (besides the obvious fact that he spent time doing shows for them overseas and in hospitals) is that his jokes concerned the men themselves:

"You know what an officers' candidate school is. That's a concentration camp on our side."

"I stopped off in Paris on my way here. They had quite a few artists there, sketching the girls in a show I saw. I thought I'd try it but they threw me out—they said no fair tracing."

"Last night I slept in the barracks. You know what the barracks are—a crap game with a roof. What a place to meet professional gamblers. I won't say they were loaded, but it's the first time I ever saw dice leave skid marks."

Incidentally, the common Hope formula of stating a straight line in the negative sense—"I wouldn't say this girl was fat, but . . ."—was apparently borrowed from a comedy writer of the early 1920s named Tommy Gray, who created material for a good many vaudevillians.

Bob has always had a clear understanding of the dimensions of his ability. "In all honesty," he says, "I think I have pretty good timing. . . . At times I have good material; at other times I have great material. But I know how to cover up the merely good and make it sound better by timing. In fact, timing is my greatest asset, especially on radio or television."

Audiences are so conditioned to Hope's timing that he can get away with jokes no other comedian could get a titter with. Milton Berle once argued with a friend about the value of timing. "It's almost more important than material," he said, and proceeded to prove his point by telling an audience a joke and then substituting for the punch line the meaningless words "last Thursday." The audience roared, sucked in by Milton's adept handling of the words. He had given them the phrase "last Thursday" in such a way, with such confidence and finesse, that they laughed before they realized they had laughed at nothing.

"I know how to snap a line," says Hope, "then cover it, then speed on to the next." This is the most typical mechanical trick to Bob's mono-logue style. He doesn't stop and wait when he gets to the last word in a punch line. He races ahead and pretends not to be aware that he has said anything worth waiting for. At an Academy Awards show he said, "We have a special prize for the losers—a do-it-yourself suicide kit. And I want to tell you . . ." And that's where the laugh comes in. "You have to get over to the audience that there's a game of wits going on and that if they don't stay awake they'll miss something—like missing a baseball someone has lobbed them. What I'm really doing is asking, 'Let's see if you can hit this one.' That's my whole comedy technique. I know how to telegraph to the audience the fact that this *is* a joke and that if they don't laugh right now they're not playing the game and nobody has any fun. At least that's my comedy technique for personal appearances. I have other comedy styles. In pictures I work with broader material and use my face a lot. . . . I also have a sneak attack, where I make a line seem nothing.

This is called throwing-it-away technique, which is the opposite of hitting a joke too hard. Anybody can learn a lot about this technique by studying the work of such artists as Helen Broderick . . . and Bea Lillie, who tries to hide funny lines from you instead of ramming them down your throat."

Hope is funny by nature, but he also understands his nature. He is without question the champ as an all-around comedian. Others are big in one field or two. Only Hope has been equally at home in vaudeville, on Broadway, in motion pictures, radio, television, and the drawing room. He is not confined, as are most buffoons, to playing the comedy second-lead in a picture. He is that rarity among comedians, the clown who can also be the leading man. Indeed, he first won the hearts of the American public when he sang, with considerable tenderness, "Thanks for the Memory" to Shirley Ross in *The Big Broadcast of 1938*. Since then he's given us all a lot of happy memories to be thankful for.

But despite this, no one has ever fully understood the reasons why Bob Hope is the most successful, most famous of American comedians. It is simple enough to point to the various steps, the highlights of his career, the time in vaudeville and Broadway shows, the radio success, the films with Bing Crosby, etc. But these components are in no sense explanations. They are simply what he did. But a fascinating result of the mystery of his success is that it has led to some forty years of public speculation characterized chiefly by its inanity and irrelevance. In reference to Bob's doing occasional jokes at his own expense, a prominent satirist has said, "This, I think, is the basis of true American humor."

It is nothing of the kind.

A critic, addressing the mystery of Bob's phenomenal success, has said, "Hugh Downs expressed it best. Bob Hope cuts across every strata of America and reaches everyone with a TV set or a GI dog tag . . ."

Both the critic and Hugh are speaking largely unintelligibly. The adjective "best" certainly cannot be applied to Downs's observation, nor does the fact that Bob reaches a large audience explain why he does.

Bob, himself—so far as one can judge by his public comments—has very little idea as to why he has been successful for so many years. Asked about the reasons for his longevity, he digressed. "Our concept of what's comic and what's fair has changed. You can get away with a lot more now." This first part of his statement is true, but has no relevance to the question of his long popularity. "But you still have to edit, to ride the fine line. If you go overboard they reach for that knob and turn you off."

Again, a fuzzy statement, and one with no relevance to the question. "But it's always been fun. You've got to walk a line. You're playing to everybody. You can't be silly." The last part of the statement, too, has no possible connection with Bob's success.

If Hope is regarded only in the context of television, it would be an exaggeration to say that the reasons for his continuing eminence are mysterious or hard to identify. The reality is that they do not exist. Such evidence as is available all points in one direction: that Hope would *not* succeed in this particular medium. He does, after all, do old-fashioned, 1930s verbal comedy. He is not a particularly gifted acting-comedian like Jack Benny, Jackie Gleason, or Art Carney. He is not a creative genius of sketch comedy such as Sid Caesar. He is not able to strike spontaneous comic sparks as can Jonathan Winters, Robin Williams, or Richard Pryor. He is not able to address audiences in a relaxed, lifelike manner as do Johnny Carson and Bob Newhart. He does not have the rough-and-tumble burlesque vitality of Phil Silvers. Even more strangely, he has no specific appeal whatever to that segment of the American population that the entertainment industry insists dictates ratings—the under-35 group—as do Lily Tomlin, Chevy Chase, or Steve Martin. Bob Hope does not, in sum, do anything at all that is supposed to assure success in television comedy: anything, that is, except the one thing network executives care about to the literal exclusion of everything else. He almost invariably gets enormous ratings.

One part of the explanation of such a paradox—at least in the last twenty-five years—is quite simple. Bob is less an entertainer, less a comedian at this stage of his career, than he is a social institution. He does not have to be good now; he has only to show up. Indeed if he—or his programs—were somehow suddenly to become creative, original, fresh, truly funny—in the sense that a Chevy Chase or Lily Tomlin special is freshly funny—not only would network officials become uneasy, it is quite possible that Hope would pay for his courage in tackling new directions by suffering a rating loss. It would be rather as if the Lawrence Welk orchestra suddenly began to play new, authentic jazz or Bob Dylan suddenly developed a fine singing voice. The improvement might work to their disadvantage.

Another part of the explanation, as I suggested earlier, lies in the human tendency—nowhere else on our planet so pronounced as in the United States—to be infatuated not with talent but with success. For some thirty years interviewers have professed to be amazed at my ability to predict which young entertainers would ultimately achieve one degree or another of stardom. Perhaps because of my early conditioning—growing up around vaudeville theaters—I am as puzzled at being singled out for praise for this ability as I would be if complimented on being able to perceive the color green.

I have, of course, in time become aware that there *is* something unusual about this ability, for most people have a remarkably tin ear for talent. They will repeatedly contrive to suppose that a freakishly interesting personality such as Elvis Presley is talented, while being relatively insensitive to a true artist, a near-genius such as Anthony Newley. But if they often can't distinguish art from schlock they do, on the other hand, have sensitive antennae for picking up the slightest signs of success and it is to this they flock. Hence the explanation for Bob's continuing success adds up to a circular statement: he is successful because he is successful. Or, more precisely, he is successful today because he was successful yesterday. The public responds both subliminally and consciously to all the playing golf with presidents, hobnobbing with admirals and generals, booking—like Ed Sullivan—whatever astronaut, movie star, or sports hero is newsworthy at the moment.

Dominant, needless to say, among the reasons for Hope's continuing importance has been his overseas entertainment of troops during the wars in Europe, Korea, and Vietnam. And much has been written, both serious and humorous, about Bob's choosing in so many instances to be away from his family at Christmas and throughout the year, particularly when his children were younger. Bob has told of one instance with his son Tony as his father prepared to leave home once again. "Tony was about eight at the time. I hugged him and said, 'Good-bye, Tony.' And he said, 'Good-bye, Bob Hope.'"

One hears two points of view about Bob's junkets to entertain the troops: (a) He's done a fine, heroic thing over the years at considerable inconvenience and cost to himself and (b) it's been a well-planned if by no means necessarily cynical campaign to keep Bob's name in the news, to ingratiate himself with the American people and to address a generation of youngsters who otherwise would have sought out comedy favorites of their own age while ignoring Hope, Benny, Cantor, Jessel, et al. Evidence has been assembled to support both points of view. The argument, typically, goes as follows:

BELIEVER: Bob Hope is a fine, patriotic American who would much rather be home with his family on holidays than overseas entertaining troops.

SKEPTIC: Bob's patriotism has never been questioned but it's irrelevant. He would, in fact, *not* prefer to be home with his family. He gets itchy and restless sitting around the house and even in the absence of war is constantly off performing in one corner of the world or another.

BELIEVER: Are you saying that there's something questionable about all these wonderful people like Jerry Lewis—who puts on the annual Muscular Dystrophy Telethon—Danny Thomas—who works so hard for St. Jude's Hospital—Eddie Cantor—who helped start the March of Dimes?

SKEPTIC: Yes, Virginia, there is sometimes more than meets the eye to such labors. Nobody denies that good comes from such campaigns. I'm just telling you that the performers involved are perfectly aware that they're reaping enormous publicity benefits for themselves, creating vast reservoirs of good will and—in some cases—making substantial amounts of money while they're at it.

The debate, in any event, has never been settled, even among knowledgeable show-business veterans. The two points of view, oddly enough, are not really mutually exclusive. Each embodies facets of a larger truth.

Parenthetically, Bob's rubbing shoulders with political figures—who may be prominent for only a few years—is counterbalanced by the impression in the minds of presidents, governors, and secretaries of state that their own status is reinforced by playing golf with Bob. Perhaps they sense that long after they have left office his name will still have its peculiar power.

Most Americans would probably consider Hope the unchallenged master of the monologue. The popular judgment on this point is in some ways mistaken. First of all, he does a monologue *to* an audience, not *with* it. He lets people watch him perform, rather than making personal contact with them or addressing specific individuals at ringside tables, ad-libbing with them, sliding in and out of prepared material as the occasion seems to demand or permit. Hope never does this.

He was actually better at monologues when he was younger. A quarter-century of television specials, and the momentum of his reputation as superstar, has perhaps weakened his natural abilities. Since he generally works with *timely* material he does not have the benefit of that long-running, trial-and-error system by means of which most comedians hone their routines. With Bob almost every show takes place on an opening night basis. Since even the best comedians and writers can never totally predict audience response, perhaps one of every five or six of Bob's jokes will not get much of a laugh. He wastes no time with Johnny Carson-type savers—cracks about the writers, the audience, or himself that other comics might do—but simply plows ahead, pausing slightly to accommodate the tape-edit that his experience tells him will subsequently take place.

Or, if for some reason of timely interest the joke *has* to stay in—bomb though it did—that is no problem either. At a later recording session an audio engineer simply tapes in a resounding laugh and the at-home viewers, who may see the program hours or days later, are none the wiser.

Over the years Bob has become not an expert, polished monologist, but something of a parrot, a joke-machine, who simply throws lines out in a mechanical fashion as if to say, "These are the jokes, folks. Laugh or not, I don't care."

It seems to me that only a comedian who has achieved—if he did not always have—a certain degree of isolation from meaningful social contact could work as Bob does. I personally am so sensitive to audience reaction that even my standard routines are never the same twice; they are always modified in terms of what the audience is giving back. But Bob, as I suggest, may work in his straight-ahead, come-what-may style because even on the street or in other social contexts he has the same sort of not-quite-with-you quality for which the late Bing Crosby was noted.

Most comedians, of course, have a sort of front, a special face, a mask from behind which they work. It may be an attitude, a manner of speech, a certain style of comedy—something that distinguishes the public clown from the actual person. Most comedians set the front aside, however, in a private setting—backstage, on the street, in the home, sometimes even on a talk show. In the case of Bob Hope, however, the world is rarely permitted to see the self of the man. All one gets is that good-looking, glib, likable front.

There was a fascinating contrast between Bob's absolute triumph at the Universal Theater in 1980 and his NBC television special, aired a few nights later. Although it had its clever moments, the style was pure 1952 TV Bob Hope. Eye contact between performers was rare, cue-card reading was undisguised, rehearsal time for the guest-actors had obviously been inadequate for some of the sketches, and the use of recorded laughter, added to the legitimate audience response, was intrusive.

Bob's Christmas special during the December 1980 season was interesting in that his three chief guests—Loni Anderson, Loretta Swit and country-and-western singer Larry Gatlin—all spoke in a remarkably natural manner. In comparison, the talking-machine quality stood out in even sharper contrast.

The most remarkable thing about Bob's few weaknesses as a comedian is that none of it matters. Such details matter so little, in fact, that the angle-of-vision established by the cue-card holders on Hope's specials is the widest in television comedy history. On the conventional comedy series or special, the cue-card people stand almost directly behind the opposite players so that if two people are in a scene they seem—to the viewer at home—to be actually speaking to each other, particularly as long as they are sensible enough not to keep looking first at the cue-cards and then at each other, which gives the situation away.

But Hope and his guests literally seem to look in two separate directions. It is almost as if Hope is standing at home plate, the person he's speaking to is on the pitcher's mound, and the man with Bob's cue-cards is standing on first base.

To return to the explanation of Bob's long success, I'm reminded of an insight that occurred to me in the summer of 1976 when Jayne and I were performing for one week at Chesaning, Michigan. One afternoon in our motel, near the town of Flint, I happened to be watching television and was fortunate enough to see a motion picture that, while it could not be described as being of top quality, was nevertheless important: "The Big Broadcast of 1938." It starred W. C. Fields, Martha Raye, Shirley Knight, Bob Hope and Ben Blue. The story is a flimsy structure about a race between two giant ocean liners. Bob played the part of what he was, in fact, at the time—a popular radio comedian. Somehow, although I have been enjoying Bob's work for forty years, and have earlier analyzed his comedy for publication, it never occurred to me until watching this ancient film that Bob Hope is today, as he was then, and will be until he enters the grave, essentially a *radio comedian*. It is irrelevant that he has not done comedy on radio for a great many years. His successful motion pictures came about because he had already established himself as a radio favorite, but more importantly he continues to work in the radio *style* of the 1930's, even though his primary medium is now television. His monologue technique, even his sketch technique, are on the radio wavelength.

On an "NBC Magazine" show in early 1981, David Brinkley said to Bob, "You're known all over this country, all over the world. You have done very well financially; you're much admired and respected. Why do you still push yourself as hard as you do?"

"I just do what I want to do," Hope said, explaining nothing. "I don't consider it pushing myself. I get my schedule kind of wrapped around because, unfortunately, I enjoy it. I enjoy entertaining. I enjoy the challenge of getting up new routines. I enjoy hearing laughs, and so I get myself all loused up schedule-wise once in a while."

"Haven't you had to give up a lot to do that? In terms of family life?"

"Yes. I think so. You sound like my wife."

"She told me to ask that question."

"Yeah. No, but truly, she harps on me about that."

Bob Wynn, a TV producer who has worked with Bob, says "He *has* to go out on stage. He *has* to hear the applause. He has to hear the laughter. He thoroughly enjoys it. It's a very healthy addiction, but it is indeed an addiction. If there's no laughter, there's no life for Bob. I think the most important thing in Bob's life is laughter. Did the joke work, did the sketch work?"

The program also featured a television first, a look inside Bob Hope's joke vault, literally a vault, with a heavy steel door and combination lock. File after file of jokes labeled by date and subject, the accumulation of more than forty years.

Said Brinkley, "When he entertained troops in popular wars, he was popular. A patriotic hero. Then the sour notes. After an unpopular war—Vietnam—he got the first bitter attacks in his life, some quite vicious. He was called a right wing warmonger, and worse. It infuriated him.

"It became *necessary* to go at that time," said Bob. "Especially the last year, because the kids were waiting for peace, and they wanted us over there, the kids *wanted* us over there. You can't worry about whether it's a controversial conflict, you know? We're still doing the same thing we did in 1942, and '44. You can't worry about if somebody didn't like it. The ones we were entertaining loved it."

Hope's formula, as I've indicated, hasn't really changed since the late 1930s. Many of the jokes are strong. Some only pass because it is good old Bob delivering them. His 1980 show at Los Angeles's Universal Amphitheater is an example of this.

As part of his opening Bob explains that he was born in England.

I left there when I was four because I knew there was very little chance of me becoming king. . . . This is a beautiful setting. . . . I've played most of these places. They've asked me to play Vegas for years but . . . I'm a lousy gambler. When I'm $4 out I look like I'm in the middle of open-heart surgery.

They wanted me to open Resorts International in Atlantic City but I couldn't get together with them. They don't care about shows down there. They just want to gamble. They're flakey. I saw one guy playing the stamp machine.

Won enough to ship himself to Hawaii.

I saw another guy put a quarter in a parking meter. I said, "Are you crazy?" He said, "Look at the odds—8 to 5."

So I get around to places like this. I enjoy it. And this is nice outside like this—if we live, huh?

I'm used to playing different kinds of spots. I usually have to play those big auditoriums following those rock groups and it's really something. I use the same dressing rooms that they've used for ash trays, you know. There are foot prints on the ceiling.

It's a funny thing when you walk into one of those dressing rooms after the rock groups. You take one deep breath and immediately you can play the drums. . . .

I'm playing all over the world. Peking, Shanghai, Moscow.

I had a wonderful trip to China last year. Met nine hundred million people that never heard of me.

And didn't give a damn.

But I got great service over there. They do wonderful laundry over there—while it's still on your back.

They gave me a nice suite at the Peking Hotel. And I walked in and I said, "That's a beautiful statue of Buddha." And the captain said, "No, that's a mirror."

I live right down the hill on the Lakeside Golf Course. This is where I play every day. I had a wonderful day today. I only fell off the cart twice.

And that's when I was putting.

I had a frustrated kind of caddy. He kept looking at his watch so I said to him, "Are you in a hurry? What are you looking at your watch for?"

He said, "This isn't a watch, it's a compass."

I said, "You must be the worst caddy in the world." He said, "Naw, that would be too much of a coincidence."

I try to go down to Palm Springs every year. I tell you these celebrities are marvelous. Sammy Davis, Jr., plays every year and hits a nice ball, about 90 yards.

And his jewelry goes 110.

He's very small. We lost him in the ball washer last year.

And Lawrence Welk plays every year, but I don't play with him. He can only count up to two.

And Jimmy Stewart plays every year. But he's so damn slow, he starts in my tournament and finishes in the Andy Williams.

He talks so damn slow, by the time he yells "fore" the guy's in an ambulance on the way to the hospital.

And Liberace plays every year. He's colorful. He's got pink clubs. And pink balls. I've never seen them.

As David Brinkley and others have observed, Bob has taken a certain amount of criticism in recent years for his strongly conservative views on some social issues, although this has obviously done him more good than harm, particularly during the conservative counterrevolution of the late 1970s and early 1980s—a force so strong it was able to put an out-of-work actor into the White House. But again, the strange thing is that all of Hope's flag-waving cliches, his John Wayne sort of political philosophy, his lack of understanding of American youth, of the peace movement, of honest, law-abiding American concern about the pollution of our air and water, about nuclear radiation, nuclear war, the general American loathing of the crimes of Watergate—all of his well-intentioned wrongheadedness, like his occasional old-fashioned or weak sketches, doesn't hurt him. No matter how poorly informed he has sometimes seemed politically, Bob is still good old Bob Hope.

Long may he wave.

Laurel and Hardy

OR WHATEVER THE POINT IS WORTH—and I say this as a Chaplin fan—from early childhood I have considered Laurel and Hardy *funnier* than Chaplin. I certainly would not go so far as to demean his talents, as did W. C. Fields, who dismissed him by saying, "The bastard is a ballet dancer." Perhaps the point will be clarified if I refer to the modern comedy of Lily Tomlin. Lily is unquestionably one of our *greatest* comediennes. She is, however, by no means always the *funniest.* In some of her shows, in fact, she seems to deliberately eschew laughter.

Part of the explanation for the great superiority of Laurel and Hardy over other comedy teams—the Marx Brothers, for example—is that you cared about them as human beings. There was no reason—nor even any way—to care what happened to the Marx Brothers. Their antics were merely wonderfully silly nonsense and, since their films were written by talented people, there were often good jokes in them. Jokes, as such, were of little importance to Stan and Oliver. Stan and Oliver simply *were* funny, just by showing up.

Stan Laurel grew up in England, where his father was an actor, writer, and producer named Jefferson. Young Laurel made his debut in English music-hall comedies. In 1913, the year Hardy started in films, Stanley came to the United States with a touring show called *A Night in an English Music Hall.* His job was to serve as understudy for a better-known English comedian, Charlie Chaplin. The show broke up during the tour, when Chaplin was lured to Hollywood by Mack Sennett. Laurel remained in America to try his hand at vaudeville. Four years later, he, too, began to appear in short films.

We often assume that after a perhaps brief fledgling period successful entertainers emerged full-blown as stars of major magnitude. This is not usually the case. It certainly was not as regards Stanley and Oliver. Stanley's first ten years as a film comedian were by no means what one would expect from a performer who eventually emerged as one of the handful of true masters of the art of comedy. His first short film, *Nuts in May,* won him a contract with Universal, but not long thereafter his film career seemed at an end and he returned to vaudeville. Hal Roach, for whom he made many of his films, let him go twice. By 1926, Stanley himself had come to think that his true gift lay in writing and directing rather than in performing comedy.

At the Hal Roach Studios in Culver City, Stanley and Oliver were members of a silent-film group called the Roach Comedy All-Stars. In 1926, Roach decided to cast them as a starring team, which they remained for twenty-four years, surviving not only depression and war but the revolution of talking pictures. With the advent of sound, Stan and Oliver began talking their way into their predicaments. And, almost invariably, the story situations were those anyone could identify with.

One of their favorite subjects was the trouble you can get into when you lie to your wife. In a scene from one of their classics, the boys tell their wives they are going to Honolulu for a rest. Instead they sneak off to a convention of a fun-loving group called "Sons of the Desert." The wives hear a report that their boat sank on the return trip from Honolulu, but learn the truth when they attend a newsreel theater and see Stan and Ollie having fun at the convention. When the boys return from their escapade, they think they'll be able to fool their mates. As usual, they're wrong.

Someone once asked Ollie to explain why he and his partner were so popular. He guessed it was because the moviegoer had fun feeling superior to them. Hardy said he played the role of "the dumbest kind of guy there is: the guy who thinks he's smart." Laurel and Hardy believed that they got most of their laughs by combining dumbness with dignity. "There's nothing funnier than a guy being dignified and dumb at the same time."

One indicator of Laurel's uniqueness is that he was among the first to develop a form that would years later become a staple of radio and television humor—the broad satire or parody of serious works. All of us in TV who have done take-offs of soap operas, Japanese samurai films, Westerns, World War I pictures, and gangster movies, are in Laurel's debt. Even the kind of titles we have given our take-offs were originated by Stan. He called his comedy version of the serious film *The Spoilers,* for example, *The Soilers.*

In defense of those who seemed insensitive to Laurel's greatness, it did take him several years to find his proper film role. In his first picture he is—like most other comedians of his time—the aggressor, the one who drives the action, who attacks others. This phase persisted even during his first work with Hardy. Then gradually something unplanned and consequently eminently natural occurred. The peculiar, unique relationship between the two men—the relationship with which we are now so familiar we think it must always have existed—came to the fore. The larger, seemingly more threatening Hardy begins to browbeat his smaller companion. The change made all the difference.

Properly sensing that comedy is a manipulation of negatives rather than positives, they made themselves look less attractive on the screen, more bizarre and ridiculous. Stan did it in part by wearing a whiter than normal facial makeup, like a mime, and making his normal-sized eyes appear smaller through the use of makeup and squinting. His hair—which was in no way unusual—he deliberately scooped upwards in ragged handfuls, which made him look both somewhat silly and frightened.

The great French pantomimist Marcel Marceau has said that one of his pantomime idols was Stan Laurel. Marceau said Laurel worked in the tradition of the old comic troubador, performing silent comedy that looked utterly simple but was actually supremely graceful and therefore funny.

In an early Laurel and Hardy film, *Putting Pants On Phillip,* Ollie had taken Stan—a newly-arrived immigrant from Scotland, wearing kilts—to a tailor to be fitted for a conventional American suit of clothes. Starting from this real-life situation Stan built it to the kind of absurd lengths of exaggeration that would rarely be seen after Laurel and Hardy until, in the early 1950s, Sid Caesar did some of the same sort of things. Shying like a nervous horse at each attempt by the tailor to apply a tape measure to his ankles, legs, or thighs, Stanley twitches and jumps. Before long, the tailor and Hardy are actually grappling with Stanley, forcing him to the floor, to get the measurements made.

Exaggeration was as important to Stan and Ollie as it would be later to Sid Caesar. In the film *Blockheads* the boys are in the trenches during World War I. Hardy and the rest of their platoon are sent over the top; Laurel is left behind to guard the trenches. He dutifully guards them for over twenty years, not realizing that the war is over. Finally he's picked up and put in an old soldier's home. Now that's exaggeration.

Garson Kanin, in his *Together Again!,* a study of great Hollywood teams, makes the insightful observation that although on screen Oliver Hardy was dominant, the pattern was completely reversed in reality. Stanley was the writer, the creator, the director. Ollie, for the most part, did as he was instructed. To his credit, he repeatedly conceded that Laurel was the more creative member of the team and deferred to Stanley on practically every question where judgment was required.

At some undetermined point in the historical development of the art of comedy it was discovered that a relationship between a smart character and a dumb character provided a certain tension or structure out of which funny jokes or situations could be developed. Around the turn of the century some of these comic confrontations involved a city slicker and a rube. Part of the comedy was that the hick—a farmer, back-woodsman, mountaineer—would often outwit the supposedly wiser city man. There is an old joke which dramatizes the point perfectly.

A city fellow, driving through a back country section, was having difficulty relating what he read on a road map to the actual terrain through which he was passing. Finally, spotting a farmer sitting on a rail fence, he pulled up alongside him and said, "Say, I wonder if you know the way to Route 52."

"Nope," was the laconic response.

"Well," said the city man, "do you know how to get from here to Highway 7?"

"Nope," the hayseed said.

"You don't know a helluva lot, do you?" snapped the annoyed city man.

"I ain't lost," said the farmer.

The same sort of comic dynamics have frequently been employed in countless husband-and-wife argument sketches such as "The Bicker-sons," "The Honeymooners," or Archie and Edith Bunker's exchanges on "All in the Family."

In the case of Abbott and Costello, the smart guy-dumb guy relationship was quite clear. Oddly enough, although Stan Laurel's character was clearly played as a lower IQ-type than Oliver Hardy's specialist in exasperation, both were somewhat dim-witted characters.

The "plots" of most of Laurel and Hardy's short subjects could usually be expressed in just a sentence or two. In their classic "The Music Box" the boys—having gone into the furniture-moving business—are required to deliver, with their horse and wagon, an upright piano purchased by a wealthy woman. Pianos are, of course, very heavy and unwieldy, so already, in the absence of any other detail, there is humor looming as we envision these two men, naturally inexperienced at their trade, trying to maneuver so large and weighty an object. But that premise itself would not sustain fifteen or twenty minutes of comedy action. The real fun starts when they get to the specified address in the Hollywood Hills and learn that their destination is at the top of a tremendously long flight of stairs running up the side of a hill. In reality, getting a piano up such stairs would be impossible for two men. Reality is therefore stretched a bit. We simply adjust our expectations and know that Stan and Ollie are nevertheless going to make the attempt to wrestle the enormous wooden packing crate up the seemingly endless flight of stairs.

With this much set up, we now proceed into a digression typical of their films. Indeed, it seems to be one of Laurel and Hardy's main devices that everything, every move that either of them makes, leads to some sort of complication. In this case, it comes in the simple attempt to get the piano out of the wagon and onto the ground. Stanley, with typical stupidity, starts to pull the box toward him off the back of the wagon. Ollie wisely points out that that would be the worst possible way—and very dangerous. He kneels down and instructs Stan to gently lower the box onto his back, after which it can be lowered to the ground. But as Stanley follows this instruction it occurs to the horse, who has not been tethered, to move a few feet forward. This has the result of suddenly crashing the piano box down on Oliver's back, crushing him to the pavement.

The boys now enact something like the myth of Sisyphus, who attempted to roll an enormous stone to the top of a mountain but suffered the fate that every time the stone reached the top it rolled back down again. After they get the piano perhaps a third of the way up the hill, with great physical effort, they encounter a woman coming down the steps with a baby carriage. She politely asks if they can move aside to let her pass. Always gentlemanly fellows, they tip their hats to oblige. But when they take their hands off the piano box it starts to roll back down the hill. They watch in dismay as it bounces all the way down and back into the street.

At this point in the original story conference it probably occurred to some member of the production team to have the piano roll down the hilly street, too, but the idea, if it occurred, must have been discarded because of the time-limitations of the film itself; there would be more than enough comic business in getting the piano up the steps and into the house.

Having again moved the piano part way up the incline, Stan and Ollie now encounter a loud, officious fellow with a funny foreign accent. The role is played by comedian Billy Gilbert, who some years later became famous for doing his sneezing routine in a number of feature-length comedies. In "The Music Box" Gilbert is a crazy professor who is immediately infuriated by the two bumblers. Needless to say, in the resulting confusion the piano rolls back down again, this time with the helpless Oliver bouncing along behind it, attempting to delay its descent.

It is remarkable what a tremendous amount of violence there was in many of the Laurel and Hardy films and, for that matter, in hundreds of other early comedies. But no one then ever raised the question as to whether such mayhem—an endless parade of falls, crashes, bumps on the head from heavy objects, punches, slaps, kicks, pratfalls—was having a negative moral effect on impressionable young minds. The reason there was no such outcry is that there was no such danger. It is when violence is shown within a realistic context, and photographed in a realistic way, that harm may be done, if only on the basis of showing bad example. But the violence in the films of Laurel and Hardy, Charlie Chaplin, Buster Keaton, Harold Lloyd, et al, was rather like that of the later animated cartoons. It was all for fun. No one ever bled. No one ever died. No matter what battering or pummeling a character was subjected to—as in the case of Ollie being dragged down a long flight of concrete stairs by a runaway piano—the injuries sustained were always minor. The character would simply pick himself up, dust himself off, straighten his tie or derby, and get back into action.

When the boys finally get the piano to the front door of the house they meet a mailman who tells them that he doesn't understand why they've gone to all the trouble of approaching the house on foot from the front when the road actually curves around the hill; they could have driven right up to the back door. All the heart-and-back-ache caused by the stairs was completely unnecessary.

In one of their many wonderful and typical moments, the boys exchange a look that says, "How could we be so stupid?" and with new determination never to be that dumb again, they carry the piano all the way down the stairs in order to load it back on their wagon and drive it up the hill.

At this point additional problems present themselves. Thinking he is backing up the steps to the house Oliver tells Stan to push the piano forward "just a little more." The push has the effect of dumping Hardy backward into a raised garden pool. Of course Stanley and the piano shortly follow him.

When the boys ring the front doorbell nobody is home. With the aid of a block-and-tackle they decide to move the piano into the house through an upstairs balcony window. This phase of the action provides several minutes of laughs. The ladder on which Oliver is standing falls forward and bangs against the front door, which opens. Oliver walks into the house and heads upstairs to join Stan, who is on the balcony. We cut to a shot of Stan hearing the footsteps on the stairs, suddenly horrified to think that someone is in the house after all. He steps out onto the balcony to share this intelligence with Ollie. Not seeing him below, he calls and whistles to attract his attention. Hearing the summons, Ollie—who is almost all the way up the stairs—walks back down again, goes outside, looks up and asks Stanley what he wants. Stanley explains that there is somebody else in the house.

"How do you know?"

"I just heard them coming upstairs."

It takes some time before the boys get this simple problem worked out.

Inasmuch as almost all silent-screen comedy was devoid of the sort of sexual and scatological components presently so common, the occasional lapses from the norm acquire a special interest. One thinks, "How did they ever get away with it?" when seeing such moments in an old film. In *We Faw Down,* for example, the boys are being chased by their two angry wives, one of whom is carrying a rifle. As they are running behind two apartment buildings a shot is fired. Instantly men leap from windows on every floor of the buildings. But the astounding thing is that each man is carrying his trousers in his hands. One can say at least that children would simply have laughed at the sight of men running around in their undershorts, without realizing the sexual implications of the action. Today all entendres seem singularly single.

On our old Westinghouse show in the early 1960s, we once set some sort of record for the most pies thrown in a single comic situation. It was hysterically funny, yet could not hope to achieve anything near the philosophical greatness of Laurel and Hardy's famous pie-throwing sequence in their film *The Battle of the Century.* Our sequence was good silly fun, but had no true justification. Theirs, on the other hand, clearly showed a step-by-step logical process that justified the pie-throwing sequence. Stan is a prizefighter—a funny idea already—and gets knocked out in the very first round of a match. Stan himself described what follows, in talking to biographer John McCabe.

Fade out. Fade in. The arena again, only now it is completely empty. I am still out on the deck. Hardy is leaning on ringside, looking into the camera and showing plenty of weariness. Fade out. Next day we're sitting on a park bench, looking miserable. A guy passing us (played by Eugene Palette) is an insurance agent and he suggests to Hardy that he should take out an insurance policy on me as I am very likely to get hurt, and that means money in the bank. It's a cut-rate insurance company he owns. The company gives five hundred dollars at a two-buck fee for a single broken leg or arm. Hardy borrows the two dollars from me and pays up. (Hardy has taken the guy aside so I can't hear any of this.) Hardy then takes me for a walk around town, trying various methods to get me in an accident. He walks me under ladders where construction is going on and he gets conked instead. He passes a fruit stand and buys a banana. As we are walking along, he peels it and throws the skin in front of me so that I'll slip on it. I, unknowingly, step over it. He picks it up, drops it in back of him and leads me around to walk on it again, and of course, he slips on it and crashes to the ground.

Now Stanley explains the set-up for the pie-fight.

We come to a bakery shop with a pie wagon standing in front. Hardy drops the peel for me on the sidewalk there and the pie man comes along with a big tray of pies and slips on the peel. He's covered with pies.

As he clears his eyes, he happens to see Hardy pushing the banana into my hand and realizes that Hardy is trying to put the blame on me. An argument starts, ending up with the pie man pushing a pie in Hardy's face. I resent this and push a pie in the pie man's face. Hardy laughs at this, and the guy, instead of hitting me back, hits Hardy with another pie.

At this point, a stranger passing by tries to stop the argument and *he* gets a pie in the face too.

Gradually, one by one, other people get into the argument, until finally the entire street, the full block, is pie crazy. Everybody is pie-throwing happy. The camera goes up to take a panorama view of all these people throwing, throwing, throwing. There are pies thrown into a dentist's office, in windows, out of them, nothing but pies, thousands of them.

Then a cop, who of course is all covered with pie, arrests us and is taking us away when he slips on the banana peel and he falls down a manhole for the finish.

It is commonly assumed that because Stanley and Oliver were chiefly physical sight-comics that there were no other important components to their work. On the contrary, they were quite prepared to do plays-on-words and wonderfully silly banter.

> LAUREL: How long did you say it would take us to get up there?
> HARDY: Oh, just a jiffy.
> LAUREL: How far is a jiffy?
> HARDY: Three shakes of a dead lambs tail.
> LAUREL: Hmmmm. I didn't know it was so far. Surprising—the distance.

It is probable that Oliver Hardy invented the business of looking directly into the camera as a means of conveying utter exasperation, as if to say, "Look at what an idiot I'm involved with here." It is an open appeal to the jury. But because the act was so natural, so casual, its importance might easily be overlooked. First of all it was a daring, truly remarkable thing to do. The camera is, in a sense, the equivalent of the fourth wall in a theater. Even in the most meticulously realistic sets there has never been a downstage wall for the obvious reason that if there were the audience could not see what was taking place on stage. In the early theater—at the time of Shakespeare, for example—playwrights would include, as part of the script, "asides" to the audience. The convention persisted through the nineteenth century. But the advent of motion pictures and medium and close shots meant that the audience in a movie house was not at all the same as an audience in a traditional theater. Their point of view could be very close. Films make us not merely distant observers but in quite a different sense almost part of the action. We see fists apparently coming right into our own faces, lips parted as if to receive our own kiss, cliffs and window ledges from which we almost feel that we ourselves might fall. Because of this factor—the close positioning of the camera—the *aside* no longer had any rightful place.

But rightful or not, Oliver Hardy did it, and the effect was richly amusing. Stan did it, too, but the character he played was so dopey, so helpless and bumbling, that he rarely seemed to be communicating with the audience at such times. It was as if he simply happened to be facing front while making one of his marvelous faces expressing bewilderment. Ollie, on the other hand, communicated with us personally, purposefully. It never for a moment seemed to destroy the reality of the story-line or situation, as it would in a conventional film. A host of other comic entertainers subsequently used the device.

Another of the important components of Oliver Hardy's comic image was dignity. No matter how ill-fitting his clothes, no matter how impoverished he might be, no matter how many middle- or lower-class characters he came into contact with, he seemed eternally struggling to retain at least a shred of sedate composure. Not only was this funny in its own right but as contrasted with the naive, bewildered Stanley—who had no true dignity but instead a childlike willingness to please—the contrast made many a comic moment richer than it would have been if both characters had been either low-class or high-class. Laughter growing out of the pathetic attempt to preserve dignity is almost unknown in American comedy at present. There are, needless to say, other ways to get laughs, as the success of Richard Pryor, John Belushi, Steve Martin, Rodney Dangerfield, and others demonstrates. Perhaps the reason for the absence of Hardy's kind of character in American comedy at present is that there is precious little dignity of the traditional sort in our entire society.

Hardy's dignity was no mere comic pose. His father was a prosperous lawyer in Harlem, Georgia, where Oliver was born in January of 1892. Although the elder Hardy died when Oliver was still a child, the boy nevertheless acquired the manners of his social station. After a period of financial hardship following his father's death, the family fortunes took a turn for the better, and Hardy was sent first to military school, then to the Atlanta Conservatory of Music. He completed his education at the University of Georgia, planning to follow in his father's footsteps as a lawyer.

By 1910, when Hardy was eighteen, he became smitten with the newly developed motion pictures and opened a modest room in which he exhibited films. Not content merely to show pictures made by others, he sold his small theater and went to nearby Jacksonville, Florida, where films were being produced. Securing employment almost at once, he worked in Florida for over a year. On the basis of this experience he moved north to Fort Lee, New Jersey, another production center, and in time on to Hollywood. Several years were to elapse—during which Hardy attracted little public attention—before he was teamed up with Stan Laurel.

I have earlier noted that in the successful Laurel and Hardy formula Ollie was the aggressor. But the relationship is much different from that which prevailed between Abbott and Costello. Bud Abbott was always sharp, demanding, strongly manipulative. It was never thus with Oliver Hardy. He dominated in a gentle, if-you-will-permit-me way. From time to time Stanley's ineptitude would drive him to moments of fury, at which times he might slap, kick, or yank his luckless companion. But the dominant element in his character was his strange, silly courtliness, his niceness and decency. Oliver Hardy played straight to Stan Laurel but was brilliantly, richly funny in his own right. As my wife, Jayne, has pointed out, in many filmed sequences Hardy is actually doing funnier things than Laurel, but is more subtle. His tie-twiddling, drumming of his fingers on air, and his ways of conveying exasperation are among these.

There is nothing noteworthy about my one meeting with Oliver Hardy, which took place in 1956 while I was in Los Angeles doing a film. An agent had invited me to the Lakeside Country Club for lunch and, as we were walking through the sitting room, I noticed a grotesquely overweight man in a large chair. At first I did not recognize him. The agent introduced us. I told Hardy that I was honored to meet him. He smiled weakly but seemed more or less in a stupor. I did not learn until later that he was seriously ill. He died on August 7, 1957.

In 1959 some of my writers and I visited Stan. All of us reminisced about particular favorite films, scenes, and comedy routines we remembered having seen Laurel do, and were thunderstruck when it became apparent that he was more interested in talking to us about our shows and sketches than recalling his old films. He was a gentle, soft-spoken man and could not have been more charming. I later learned that it was typical of him to be generous and complimentary about other comedians. This may seem a simple matter of courtesy or decency, but I regret to report that one does not always find it among comedy performers. For example, Charlie Chaplin was notorious for his unkindness to other comedians.

When I spoke to writer Leonard Stern recently we reminisced about the visit with Laurel. "He was a lovely man," Stern recalled. "As a matter of fact, after our show went off I was doing the Dickens and Fenster series. Stan used to watch the show every week and every so often he'd write me a critique of it."

"I'm not surprised," I said. "He was such a fine comedy director that he probably couldn't just watch a show without analyzing it and thinking of ways to improve it."

"Exactly," Stern said. "Another interesting thing Stan said—I don't know if you remember—is that those "Honeymooners" shows I did for Gleason probably wouldn't be appreciated until years later. He said that's the way it was with Ollie and himself. 'You know,' he said, 'except for one picture—*Babes In Toyland*—we never got great notices.'"

Because Stan in person seemed like his screen image—though much more intelligent—I was surprised when a painter who did some work at my home early in 1982 told me that when he had worked as part of the crew on a Laurel and Hardy film many years earlier, he had liked Oliver but not Stan.

"What was wrong with Stan Laurel, in your opinion?" I asked.

"Oh," replied the painter," he just seemed stuck-up. He was too much of a perfectionist. He always wanted everything to be just right and if it wasn't, he could be kind of a son-of-a-bitch about it."

The same might be said, I suppose, of every talented perfectionist who ever lived. It was Laurel, after all, who was the inspired creative genius of the team, and it can be frustrating if an artistic person has a vision and those he assigns to flesh it out do not properly do so.

Stanley continues to be a major figure in American comedy, and above all among other professional comedians, those best able to appreciate his genius.

Jerry Lewis

O NE OF THE MOST ILL-ADVISED decisions ever made by a network's programming department was the one made by ABC in electing to hire Jerry Lewis—a truly funny comedian—as host of a late-night talk show. When the program went on the air in the fall of 1963 the first night struck me as a disaster of such hilarious proportions that on the spot I wrote a parody of it and performed it on my own show a few nights later.

Jerry did his program from the Hollywood Palace Theater, subsequently known as the Merv Griffin Theater, on Vine Street, near Hollywood Boulevard. Today a disco club, it had been a good comedy house for years, but for some reason the vibrations were not right during Jerry's tenure. His program opened with cameras deliberately picking up shots of other cameras. Most talk shows are photographed by three units that can move about but generally remain rather stationary. In this instance Jerry had several cameras, rolling in all directions; the director made fast cuts, showing seemingly dozens of Jerry Lewises in a long shot, medium distance, close-ups, from the left side, from the right, from the back, etc.

In my sketch, I reproduced this factor and had myself—playing Jerry—momentarily in danger of being crushed to death as four cameras converged swiftly on me from different directions.

Jerry also had his lovely wife and fine children in the studio seated in a specially protected box, at stage right. This element, too, we reproduced, having gun-toting guards surrounding the family.

But the real program itself was in immediate difficulty, even before other comedians began to make it the object of their humor. Like most comedians, Jerry is a poor interviewer. More importantly, he's too funny and too hyper to be on every night. When Jerry is funny, he is so exceptionally funny that you have to go on a sort of vacation to get over it. He's not subtle or warm or gentle or sophisticated or fey. He's down your throat, in your ears, buzzing in your brain. The jokes come so fast, the Seltzer bottle squirts so often, the pratfalls are so hilarious, that once every so often is enough.

Mel Brooks made the same essential point in speaking to the late Kenneth Tynan. Of Lewis, for whom he once wrote the first draft of a screenplay called *The Ladies Man,* Mel says, "He was an exciting, dynamic creature and I learned a lot from him. But high-key comics like that always burn themselves out. Lewis could do thirty-one different takes and when you'd seen them all, that was it. Low key, laid-back comics like Jack Benny are the ones that last."

Dick Cavett discerned the reasons for the failure of Jerry's late-night program:

> The show was an ill-conceived idea from start to finish. Because of Jerry's ability, as a guest on other shows, to break things up, somebody had thought it would be a great idea to give him his own show, and somebody else had thought it would be an even greater idea if his own show were two hours long and, on top of everything, literally live-as-it-happens, not taped or filmed.
>
> The point everyone overlooked was that Jerry had been hilarious partly because he was a guest. It may be funny to see a man tear up someone else's place, but it is embarrassing to see him tear up his own. It was bizarre and funny to see Jerry go on Ed Sullivan's show, push Ed into the wings, and pull the TelePrompTer apart and rip the paper out of it. But when he did that kind of thing on his own show it wasn't funny so much as it was puzzling. I went around pointing this out to people on the production staff, and was told to sharpen some pencils and stay out of the direct sun. But the fact was that Jerry's comic definition—God, how do you avoid such phrases—was taken away.

Jerry has a self-destructive side that is sometimes revealed in poor judgment. With some comedians their problem is not simply that they depend upon off-color material—there are places and times when vulgarity is appropriate—but rather that they lack an editorial wisdom or, to put the matter more plainly, seem not to have common sense enough to know when it is right to do dirty material and when it is not. This generally grows out of insecurity on the part of the performer involved. It is a fact, rightly or wrongly, that a dirty joke will get a hearty laugh from most audiences. Comedians of a certain type live from joke to joke anyway while performing and it is understandable that they can grow to depend on particular laughs at certain moments of their routines. I know from personal experience that when performing at a church benefit, or for an audience with children or senior citizens, one can miss those big laughs. But they must be sacrificed, nevertheless, when the occasion demands. Jerry happened to entertain at the Starlight Theater, a large outdoor auditorium in Kansas City, several years ago, two weeks before Jayne and I opened there. Even though he knew that a great many children were in his audience on opening night, he did blue material of the most vulgar sort. One of the jokes later quoted to me was the old one involving stepping on a rake and hitting a certain portion of one's anatomy with the handle, in the context of a golf game. There was a great deal of local shock and criticism as a result, understandably enough, all of which could have been avoided if Lewis had simply taken six or seven jokes out of what was quite an amusing and pleasurable production without them.

Jerry Lewis, nevertheless, is a wonderfully funny visual comedian. Like Chaplin, Lewis's appeal is largely physical. Although Charlie was physically funny by virtue of the necessity posed by working in silent pictures, Jerry's greatest appeal lies in his actions, even though he has appeared in radio, television, nightclubs, and motion pictures—media that also involve the spoken word.

When a comedian has attained a certain peak of popularity, it becomes difficult to dissect his talents and classify them separately. You are so used to laughing at the overall impression the man creates that at first it may be hard to believe that you laugh at what he says chiefly because of the face he makes when he says it. Lewis has the fortunate faculty of bringing to his verbal delivery such a powerful physical assist that only through the medium of radio can one notice how lopsided his comic talents are. Listening to a Martin and Lewis broadcast one immediately wonders at the riotous reaction of the studio audience. The answer is that those fortunate enough to be present in the studio were enjoying an in-person performance, and in person Dean and Jerry were unfailingly entertaining.

Gifted with the emotional ability to plunge into complete physical extroversion, Lewis can pull out all the stops in his attack on an audience. There are those who would not appreciate the subtlety of a literary allusion by Robert Benchley, the witty sarcasm of a thrust by Groucho Marx, or even the bizarre rendering of a character by Andy

Kaufman, but there is not a person alive who can suppress a guffaw at a perfectly timed pratfall.

Lewis is a master at gathering laughs at his own physical expense. He will pretend to allow a piano top to fall on his hand, will take a pie in the face, trip and fall on his face while dancing, he will get a coworker's little finger accidentally hooked into his ear, and in the performance of all these antics will prove that there is something to the theory that laughter has its basis in a feeling of superiority on the part of the observer. Slip on a banana peel and you are not amused. Watch someone else do it and it's funny.

Jerry's knack of *doing* funny things is to some extent shared by Red Skelton, Lou Costello, and other physical comedians. Lewis's advantage over most of his competitors lies in his comic appearance. In recent years he has seemed physically more attractive, but the young Jerry Lewis, with his close-cropped, monkeyish hairdo, his limber, impish face and thin, angular body, was equipped with a vital plus that made his success as a clown seem to have been predestined. It is difficult to imagine *not* laughing at Jerry Lewis. If he had not become an entertainer it is likely that he would still have been an awfully funny stock clerk or shoe salesman.

Another of Jerry's assets is his youthful, almost childish appearance, even now that he is in his 50s. It allows him to indulge in the physical lunacies that have become his stock in trade. Milton Berle or Red Skelton may also take a pie in the face or a fall over a chair, but somehow these older men have a certain stature and dignity under their clown's clothes. An Ed Wynn or a Groucho Marx might also slide down a banister or fall into a swimming pool, but they do so with the explicit if unspoken understanding that they had momentarily taken leave of their senses. When Jerry Lewis performs these same actions he does so with no dignity whatsoever. He is a *complete* buffoon, the hundred-percent fool, of whom insanity is expected and hoped for. Even now there is much of the child in Jerry; on stage he does not *revert* to idiocy; he sometimes seems to *be* an idiot, and the effect is wonderfully hilarious.

Writing about Jerry in *The Funny Men* in the 1950s, I devoted only a few lines to his then-partner, Dean Martin, though I emphasized the important debt Jerry owed to Dean. At the time, in fact, I doubted that Lewis could operate as successfully as a single as he had in partnership with Martin. His comedy was so completely, fiercely uninhibited that it required setting off. A straight man seemed then as much of a necessity to Jerry Lewis as it would have been a burden to Will Rogers. Jerry is not a true humorist, nor even a capable joke comic. He is not at his best alone on the stage. He is not unusually amusing in isolation; it is necessary that he be brought into contact with others. What they do to him and his reaction to what they do—therein lies the heart of Lewis's comic appeal.

Martin was, therefore, necessary to Jerry's early success, although if he were not predominately a singer his capabilities as a straight man would be somewhat more in question. Experience welded the two into so polished a team that I found it difficult to think of their separating. Not long thereafter, they did.

Except for his several brilliant performances in comedy films, Jerry rarely seemed quite as funny on a nightclub floor after leaving Dean as he was before, though being greatly talented he still does a strong comedy act.

Dean Martin is difficult to analyze. His image as an easygoing singer prevented a true appreciation of his own comic gifts so long as he worked with Jerry. Since their separation he has, of course, established himself as an immensely popular comic performer. But he has never been a true comedian in the sense in which most of his peers are. Nor—to my dismay—did he ever take himself seriously as a singer, despite the fact that as a young man he had a very pleasant, Crosbylike crooner's voice. As a singer he is a bit like Victor Borge at the piano. He sings, and Victor plays, but each seems reluctant to complete a number straightforwardly. Every few bars the performance is interrupted for a joke. But if Dean is not truly a singer, in the sense that Frank Sinatra is, and not truly a comedian, in the sense that Milton Berle is, what is he? He is perhaps something even rarer, a one-of-a-kind personality, one who projects a strange image that makes one smile even when one does not laugh. It is by no means just a matter of endless booze jokes. More importantly there is a wonderfully silly glint in Dean's eye. He never seems to take anything seriously. That is why his film performances in noncomic roles have always been essentially absurd. No matter what he was saying or doing on the screen, one could never take him entirely seriously. Dean is—to use the old high-school girl's word—cute. He is a good-time-Charlie, sort of an Italian early-Gleason, a party-boy, a the-drinks-are-on-me type.

Part of his image, too, is based on his long professional and personal relationship with Frank Sinatra. There is the association with the old rat-pack, the clan, the Mafia, Jack Daniels liquor, swinging with beautiful showgirls. That is why Dean has always been able to do an effective, enjoyable act in Las Vegas, whereas he would not make nearly so much sense as an attraction at the kind of state fair at which Bob Hope, Red Skelton, Steve Martin, or I sometimes perform. To be fully appreciated Dean should be seen by an audience numbering not more than a few hundred.

Despite the fact that Dean and Jerry's professional divorce was inevitable, Jerry was nevertheless truly shaken after their last performance together, an unforgettable night at New York's Copacabana in July of 1956. Jerry later recalled, in an article for *Look* magazine:

> When we finished the last show together, I went back to my dressing room. I was numb with fright and shaking all over, my clothes were drenched with perspiration. I sat in my dressing room, crying. I thought I'd never be able to get up before an audience again. I thought it would be impossible for me to work without Dean.
>
> After I finished crying in my dressing room, I phoned Patti in California. I said to her, "It's all over." She said, "Don't be afraid. I'm your friend"—and I cracked up completely. Then Dean came in and we both cried. We shook hands and wished each other luck.

A few days later Jerry had one of those breaks that seem to come in the lives of all performers. He and Patti happened to be vacationing in Las Vegas when Jerry suddenly got a call from Sid Luft, Judy Garland's husband and manager. Judy, Luft explained, was suffering from a bad case of strep throat, couldn't sing, and every other entertainer in town was working at other clubs. Could Jerry possibly fill in for Judy, just for one night?

The reader might think that Lewis's immediate answer would have been, "Certainly" and he would have run over to the New Frontier Hotel without a worry in his mind. He was, after all, a major star and a seasoned performer. There was, however, one problem. Jerry had no act. Everything he had done until now—since the days of his solo record pantomimes—involved working with Dean.

Jerry's fears about replacing Judy proved to be groundless. His performance—partly ad-lib and partly consisting of bits and pieces he had done before—was a triumph. Without this unexpected experiment he might for some time have continued to be victimized by fears that he could not successfully work alone.

This engagement was so successful, however, that Jerry was launched on his solo career as a comic performer and a singer. His recording of "Rock-a-bye Your Baby," made shortly after his appearance in Las Vegas, sold over a million copies. Soon after, Jerry accepted an engagement at the Palace in New York.

Anyone with a serious interest in the comedy of Jerry Lewis—or, for that matter, the art of comedy generally—should read Arthur Marx's biography of Dean and Jerry, *Everybody Loves Somebody Sometime —Especially Himself.* The book—although it is a comedy writer's view of comedians—reads, in parts, like a Greek tragedy. That the author is the son of a famous funnyman, Groucho, undoubtedly gave him special insight, although admirers of Martin and Lewis might have a difficult time adjusting their image of these two talented entertainers to conform to the sometimes shocking portraits drawn by Marx.

Jerry Lewis is the only leading comedian who regularly employs pantomimed effeminacy as a comedy device. Since the American attitude toward homosexuality is a confused one, there has been only confused and scattered resistance to this facet of Lewis's work. He is heterosexual. His effeminacy is tolerated because, I think, of his childishness. If a child is effeminate he is simply a "sissy," or a weakling. The condition is not perceived as an abnormality until the individual becomes an adult and it is observable that he has not become the sort of adult that one had expected.

Just as Jerry's childishness sugar-coats some comedy pills that would seem bitter if prescribed by Bob Hope, Milton Berle, or Red Skelton, it also, early in his career, made him attractive to the young. Teenagers who were unimpressed at the personal sight of Arthur Godfrey, Jackie Gleason, or Jack Benny reverted to near idiocy when Dean and Jerry appeared among them. In what is perhaps a reflection of Lewis's own lack of social inhibition, they descended upon him and Martin like locusts, ripping at the pair's ties, pleading to be allowed to cut fragments from their suits, stealing their handkerchiefs, and expressing their adoration in various other destructive ways.

One of the reasons they were attracted to Jerry is that they felt he was one of them. He didn't seem far above and out of reach like Fred Allen or

Sid Caesar. He seemed rather like an extroverted high-school boy who made good. Also it is probable that his disrespectful attitudes toward characters who represented authority enabled the young to rebel vicariously.

Lewis's humor is unique in that it has little relation to reality. His lunacy is often silliness for its own sake. As a child, Jerry showed signs of developing into a professional clown. He was the neighborhood "Crazy Kid," which did not surprise those who were aware that his father, Danny Lewis, was a burlesque singer and comic, and his mother, Rea, an accompanist for his father. Jerry broke into show business at the age of fourteen at Brown's Hotel in the Catskill mountains, training ground for so many comedians. While officially serving as waiter and busboy, he copied an old parlor entertainer's gimmick that involved pantomiming to phonograph recordings of operatic singing.

So enthusiastically were his efforts received that the following year Jerry made his theater debut at a burlesque emporium in Buffalo. A year or so later he met Dean Martin in New York and the two became friends. It was not till four years after that, however, in 1946, that they became partners while working on the same bill in the 500 Club in Atlantic City. Dean, working until that time as a singer, and Jerry, until that moment still doing his pantomime act, suddenly found themselves working on the same bill. With no real act, they began to improvise, telling old jokes, doing imitations, breaking dishes, insulting the customers, making things tough on each other. Dean would sing and Jerry would try to break him up. They were a first-night smash. In less than two years Martin and Lewis were in the $5,000-a-week class and were playing such important clubs as the Copacabana. Dean, with his romantic good looks and Crosbyish voice (Bing was his idol), proved the perfect basis on which to construct Jerry's insanities. He had a Mississippi river boat gambler's sort of charm (he actually had worked for some years in Steubenville, Ohio, as a roulette stickman and card dealer), which proved a fascinating contrast to Jerry's bad-boy brashness. Dean was not the same sort of polished, old-time straight man as George Burns or Bud Abbott, but what he lacked in technical know-how he made up for with a youthful charm and a fine sense of humor that made him better suited to working with Jerry than one of the old-timers would have been.

As creative as Jerry is, there is little of his humor worth quoting. He is a doer rather than a talker. His humor on stage is much like his humor off, which consists of practical jokes, cutting off his friends' neckties, kissing strange secretaries in offices, pouring water in people's pockets. I was sitting in Sherry's restaurant in Hollywood one evening in 1949 when Jerry came in. Seizing one of those canvas and alūminum frames on which waiters rest loaded trays, he began walking up and down the dining room shouting, "Deck chairs; get your deck chairs, right here! Fifty cents. Get 'em while they last!" The place was convulsed. Or he might call a friend long distance. "Hello, is that Sam?" he'll ask. When Sam says, "Yes, it is. Who's calling?" Jerry says, "I'll be seeing you," and hangs up.

It was in precisely one these telephone pranks that, in my opinion, Lewis reached one of his highest peaks of spontaneous comic achievement. Starting in 1952, when I was doing a daytime comedy-and-talk show for CBS, I had begun to make put-on phone calls on the air, calling actual people—while a good part of the nation listened in—and cooking up some sort of ad-lib nonsense.

The routine became a regular feature of my late-night show for Westinghouse in 1962, '63 and '64. In fact, two albums of recordings of these "Funny Fone Calls" were ultimately released on the Dot label. Some of the calls I made alone. Others were made with funny guests such as Mel Brooks, Peter Sellers, Carl Reiner, Shelly Berman, Louis Nye, Bill Dana. But the funniest call in the two albums was one made by Jerry. On the spur of the moment we placed a call to a food-caterer in Chicago. Note how fast, how wittily, Jerry's mind works.

> JERRY: Hello. Mr. Seigal?
>
> SEIGAL: Yeah.
>
> JERRY: This is Murray Resin.
>
> SEIGAL: Mullee?
>
> JERRY: No. MURRAY. Murray RESIN. R-e-e. Would you get that down right, Mr. Seigal? I was told to call you by Bartsy Overcall.
>
> SEIGAL: Are you from Columbia?
>
> JERRY: That's right.
>
> SEIGAL: Okay. What can I do for you?
>
> JERRY: If you recall we had the party two years ago for the entire affair.
>
> SEIGAL: Which affair?
>
> JERRY: :Your affair that you did for us two years ago. It was beautiful, Mr. Seigal. Just beautiful. You recall the Drake's cakes and all of that?
>
> SEIGAL: Yeah.

JERRY: Wonderful. Now, Mr. Seigal, we're going to have this affair next Saturday night.

SEIGAL: Yeah.

JERRY: Now can you handle it? It will be for 40 people.

SEIGAL: Right. This coming Saturday night.

JERRY: No. Any Saturday you *choose*.

SEIGAL: Uh-huh. Where would you like it?

JERRY: Well, we would prefer to have a stand-up rather than a sit-down.

SEIGAL: Uh-huh.

JERRY: Can we have it at the store?

SEIGAL: Which store?

JERRY: Your store.

SEIGAL: In my restaurant, you mean?

JERRY: No. I'd rather have it at the store, Mr. Seigal. We have a lot of money to spend.

SEIGAL: Yeah?

JERRY: And we'd like to throw it your way. You get the picture, sweety?

SEIGAL: Yeah.

JERRY: Right. Now, what do you say to Saturday? Is that all right?

SEIGAL: Which Saturday?

JERRY: You name it.

SEIGAL: In three weeks.

JERRY: Fine.

SEIGAL: When can you come and see me?

JERRY: We can be there Saturday.

SEIGAL: Saturday I'm closed.

JERRY: Then we won't have the party.

SEIGAL; Why not?

JERRY: How would we get in?

SEIGAL: Which Saturday?

JERRY: You name it.

SEIGAL: I mean you want a *Saturday* to make a party in my restaurant?

JERRY: It's no celebration. You know what I mean?

SEIGAL: What?

JERRY: I say whatever you want to do. Shouldn't you enjoy it, too?

SEIGAL: I see.

JERRY: What does it run?

SEIGAL: It's a question of what Saturday and when—

JERRY: Any one that follows Friday. I don't particularly care.

SEIGAL: You don't want it this Sunday or Monday?

JERRY: We'll have it Saturday, Sunday *and* Monday. It's a long celebration. You know, for the family.

SEIGAL: For the *family?*

JERRY: No. For the *famine* that we had. We're celebrating that it's over, and we'd like to go right through like the Romans and then just give it all up and start all over again.

SEIGAL: Yes.

JERRY: Now what would you say it would cost, Mr. Seigal.

SEIGAL: About around $5.50.

JERRY: For the 40 people?

SEIGAL: Yeah, a person.

JERRY: Now wait a minute. Now hold it a minute! Now I was told that you were *reputable* and that you knew your business.

SEIGAL; Yeah.

JERRY: Now don't pull any of that on me, baby.

SEIGAL: No, I'm not pulling—

JERRY: You said $5.50.

SEIGAL: $5.50 a *person.*

JERRY: *Now* it became a person. I *told* you it was 40 *people.*

SEIGAL: Forty people will be $200, and—

JERRY: Wait a minute. Hold it! Hold it!

SEIGAL: Yeah?

JERRY: I can add, Mr. Seigal.

SEIGAL: $5.50 a *person?*

JERRY: No. You first said $5.40 and I have already told them all we're going. But *not* for $5.40 a person!

SEIGAL: No? How much?

JERRY: $5.50 for the whole *party.*

SEIGAL: $5.50 for the *whole* party.

JERRY: Didn't you hear the president with inflation? What are you trying to do? Okay. Let's say $5.50 is fine.

SEIGAL: Yeah.

JERRY: Per *person.* Right. Now. When can you *be* there?

SEIGAL: Where can I be *where?*

JERRY: At the party.

SEIGAL: Anytime you want to.

JERRY: All right. Why don't you come over *now* and we can start?

SEIGAL: No. I can't come over there.

JERRY: Let me ask you this. Will you have all of the *stuff*?

SEIGAL: I *always* have all of the stuff.

JERRY: Fine. Now we'd like to start with as much goyish food as we can. You understand? None of that lox and pastrami jazz. We're having enough problems. You know the Arabian problem is still pretty hot. Is that clear?

SEIGAL: It's always clear.

JERRY: I tell you what. Why don't we meet in the morning?

SEIGAL: Which morning?

JERRY: At your place.

SEIGAL: Which morning would you like?

JERRY: You name it.

SEIGAL: Any morning you like.

JERRY: All right. What about tomorrow?

SEIGAL: Tomorrow morning? Impossible tomorrow morning.

JERRY: You're impossible tomorrow? I'm impossible tomorrow myself. But what about tomorrow?

SEIGAL: Tomorrow *night*?

JERRY: In the morning.

SEIGAL: In the morning?

JERRY: What time?

SEIGAL: Ahhhhhh. 10:30 in the morning.

JERRY: 10:30 I have an appointment with Sid and Buck. We're going to talk about the other affair. What about 11:30 tomorrow?

SEIGAL: 11:30 in the morning?

JERRY: Tomorrow night.

SEIGAL: Tomorrow night's impossible.

JERRY: Friday night. I can't make it Friday night. What about tomorrow morning?

SEIGAL: Tomorrow morning?

JERRY: What time?

SEIGAL: About 10:30 in the morning.

JERRY: I can't make it. What about *tomorrow* morning?

SEIGAL: Tomorrow? That's impossible.

JERRY: Impossible tomorrow *night*. I'm busy too. What about Friday?

SEIGAL: Which Friday would you like?

JERRY: Which Friday do you want?

SEIGAL: In three weeks.

JERRY: In three weeks we have to prepare for it.

SEIGAL: Yes, I know.

JERRY: I tell you what. Why don't I call you? Just hold it. Let me get a pencil.

SEIGAL: Okay, get a pencil.

JERRY: Okay, you start.

SEIGAL: D-E-2—

JERRY: Do you have a pencil? All right, take this down. Mr. Seigal? Why don't you take *my* number? Do you have a pencil?

SEIGAL: Yes.

JERRY: Does your pencil say Ticonderoga on it?

SEIGAL: Yes.

JERRY: All right then, fine. Then why don't we bring *that* to the party?

A certain part of Jerry's style is traceable to the influence of one of the great clowns of the present century, Harry Ritz. Jerry borrowed a few of his professional mannerisms from Ritz, including ways of walking, facial expressions, and gestures. There are dozens of comics, however, who have copied Ritz's mannerisms, but only a comedian of exceptional ability like Jerry could have risen above and beyond the scope to which purely imitative gestures would have limited him. There is some evidence that Jerry was also slightly influenced in his early period by the popular night-club comic Gene Baylos.

There's one complaint about Lewis that has been troublesome for him. Philip Minoff, writing in *Cue* magazine, once said, "There is nothing remotely comic in Jerry Lewis's repeated impersonations of imbecilic children. His portrayal of a teenaged baby-sitter who is himself petrified at being left without *his* mother would have been more suitable for 'Medic,' which doesn't even pretend to be a comedy show."

Complaints against this particular approach to humor on Jerry's part are based on a misconception. It is true that there would be nothing humorous about acting like an actual imbecile, but this would be the case only if a given audience clearly understood that such was the comedian's intention. I am sure that Jerry has been shocked to learn that his mugging and monkeylike speech have been interpreted as a thoughtless burlesque of handicapped children. (It is not entirely beside the point here that Jerry is among the most tireless workers in the country in the fight against cerebral palsy and muscular dystrophy.) But, one might also ask, what was funny about Chaplin's imitating a starving derelict? What was funny about Red Buttons's portrayal of a poor soul so mentally incompetent that he had practically lost the power of speech?

What was so funny about Peter Lind Hayes's impersonation of a prize-fighter who has been punched so often his brains are scrambled? Acting stupid, in any event, has been a part of clowning since the pre-Christian era. We are all born as imbeciles. We progress to being idiots, then morons, and at last, with luck, to relatively normal adults. It is late to notice that all the looking cross-eyed, blank-faced and idiotic, all the stuttering, howling and fumbling, all the mincing, staggering and skipping that comedians have been doing for a thousand years has a basis in tragic reality.

Red Skelton, parenthetically, has an interesting observation on the subject, having done considerable entertaining at children's hospitals. "I was leery about doing any funny walks," he says, "but they begged me to do Willie Lump-lump, the staggering drunk. Oddly enough, children crippled with polio laughed the most when I hobbled along. A couple of kids who hadn't walked in a long time decided to get out of bed and try it. They thought they could do as good a job as I did."

Jerry Lewis is, in my opinion, a great comedian. That more "authorities" do not recognize him as such may be due to his youthful image and his lack of adult dignity. Perhaps older critics are reluctant to admit to Olympian heights a comedian who seems to be only a "funny kid."

Oddly enough Lewis shares with most American jazz musicians the distinction of being more appreciated in Europe than in the United States, although his fame overseas is based entirely on his motion picture work. He still has a reputation, particularly in France, as an unusually creative director of comedy films. He is certainly able to direct his own pictures, but would probably not, like Carl Reiner, be well-adapted to the task of directing comedies for other entertainers.

One of Lewis's problems in recent years is that he has had a problem, in the public mind at least, with growing up. In his early work he acted like a teenage nut, and brilliantly. But now that he's in his mid-fifties that image doesn't quite come into focus. Lewis has, nevertheless, a vigorous and creative comic streak.

Film clips shown on "Sneak Previews" revealed this explicitly. He still does the funny things that in earlier years could be depended upon to amuse. The facial expressions, the bodily contortions, the wild clowning are performed as ably as ever. But the person doing these things is physically very different now. Twenty years ago Lewis still had the attitude of a manic teenager. He is now an attractive middle-aged man. The monkeylike, knobby-kneed kid is gone, replaced by someone who looks like a successful clothing industry executive or a Beverly Hills film producer. Jerry obviously cannot, by an act of will, simply turn into Cary Grant, or even Chevy Chase, but perhaps he could explore the possibilities for adult—as distinguished from teenaged—comedy. There are, after all, film scripts so funny that actors who are simply energetic and charming—without one-tenth of Jerry's natural funniness—get big laughs. Jerry has already demonstrated, certainly to the satisfaction of his European admirers, that he can direct the youthful Jerry Lewis to good effect. But it remains to be seen whether he can direct the middle-aged Jerry Lewis.

The problem is particularly apparent in one scene critiqued in "Sneak Previews" where Jerry, working as a bartender, finds himself in a low-class club where strippers strut their wares on the bar. The camera shows Lewis fixing a drink with a cocktail-shaker, while immediately in front of him two attractive legs move about in an erotic rhythm. Any man, new on such a job, would be distracted, and there are obvious comic possibilities in the situation. With the Jerry Lewis of twenty-five years ago, the naive, embarrassed, sexually frustrated teenager, the situation could have been hilarious. But when the Lewis staring up at the legs and, of course, the to-the-camera invisible nude body above them, is a good-looking middle-aged man, much of the humor is drained from the situation and it becomes somewhat vulgar.

I was doing a daily syndicated comedy-and-talk series when I got a message that Jerry Lewis wanted to discuss something important with me. When I got to Paramount he was somewhat behind schedule, working on a musical recording.

After some delay, he rushed up and greeted me warmly. I had no idea what the subject of our conversation would be. The only two possibilities that had occurred to me were either that Jerry wanted me to play a part in one of his films or perhaps to write a piece of special musical material for a picture or his act. I was wrong.

"Steve," he said, "you're a good writer and you understand comedy. I always liked what you wrote about me in *The Funny Men* and I think you're just the guy who should write my biography."

I explained that I was involved with a daily 90-minute television show that didn't permit a great deal of time for writing, but added that I was flattered by his invitation and would certainly give the possibility a good deal of thought. I suppose both of us forgot about the conversation not long thereafter.

Jerry's 1981 film, *Hardly Working,* was roundly assaulted by the critics but proved successful at the box office. Gene Siskel and Roger Ebert of the PBS Network's "Sneak Previews" program, like their colleagues, were harshly critical of the picture.

> ROGER: This was Jerry Lewis's comeback after almost a decade away from the big screen, and I was appalled by this entire film. It is so bad, so slow-paced, idiotically written. It's so badly-timed that even the usually reliable old slapstick routines don't work. . . .
>
> Later on in the film Jerry gets a job as a gas station attendant. I'd like you to look at this scene carefully. Jerry gets knocked over from the car-hood popping up. Notice in the very next shot the hood is back down again. Great editing. . . .
>
> This movie doesn't have fun *with* the character. It makes fun *of* the character. You'd have to be cruel to laugh at that guy. The movie advertises Jerry as the original jerk. Maybe they're cashing in on Steve Martin's big hit of a year ago. But the trouble is that this movie treats its audience as the original jerk. . . .
>
> *Hardly Working* is hardly bearable.
>
> GENE: I agree with you. He needs Dean Martin. He needs a partner who can play the romantic character. Those old films were quite entertaining. Lewis's comedy hasn't grown since the old days. I think it's an embarrassing kind of film.

Except for his solo set-pieces—in which he is usually very funny— Jerry does need someone to work with, to represent reality, to provide a contrast to his nuttiness. There is nothing of criticism in this comment; many of the greatest comedians of the century have required another person to play against.

The true humorist can easily perform alone. The joke-machine, too, does not require help. The clown may be effective alone in the spotlight. But comedians of Jerry's type depend largely on the humor of relationship, context, situation, predicament.

Martha Raye

Martha Raye

A GREAT MANY PERFORMERS OF THE present century have changed their names to conform to the Anglo-Saxon bias that has dominated American social consciousness for the last two centuries. Sometimes there is a certain sense to this, I suppose, in that if an actor looks like Cary Grant or Rudolph Valentino, it might seem funny if he had a name like Mortimer Katzenjammer. But why Martha Raye changed her name from Margie Reed is certainly not self-evident. Her parents were a vaudeville comedy team who specialized in physical comedy. Martha was born August 27, 1916, while her vaudeville parents were passing through Butte, Montana. While still a child she became a member of the act, working with her brother, Bud. Gradually the parents made their children more prominent, to the point where the billing was eventually changed to "Margie and Bud."

Vaudevillians suffered from the Great Depression, as did almost all other Americans. When Margie was 15, and bookings were slow, she took a job as orchestra singer with the then-popular Paul Ash. It was at this time that she changed her name.

I first saw Martha at the Southtown Theater on Chicago's south side in 1935. The Southtown was a glamorous new architectural wonder, a palatial film and vaudeville house with vaguely Moorish architecture. It was a block or two away from the Stratford, the theater where Bob Hope had started his rise to stardom.

Martha was about nineteen, and attractive, despite all the later jokes about her mouth and her willingness to mug outrageously for laughs. Her face was pretty enough and her body was certainly impressive. But more importantly she had a marvelous sense of comedy and a great singing voice. It is only the fact that Martha eventually became a world-famous comedienne that obscured the fact that in her prime she was one of the best vocalists in the business. From the first she had a jazz singer's sound, with a certain throaty breathiness to it. But unlike most jazz singers—even the best of whom are rarely able to convey emotion— Martha could very effectively perform an emotional ballad.

I am supported in this view, incidentally, by one of the important jazz singers of our time, Anita O'Day, who, in her autobiography *High Times And Hard Times,* says of Martha, "She danced and used her body as well as her voice to put across her songs. She was a presentation singer. She gave me the idea that I could sing jazz and still perform. To this day, when she sings, the back of my neck begins to creep. She's that *natural* who comes along every now and then. She doesn't pretend to know music, even though she was married to David Rose, a musician, and has associated with music people all her life. But she's rhythmical, a very good tap dancer, a show-business gal. She doesn't think of herself as a singer; she just sings."

Hollywood soon recognized Martha's talent and brought her into films. One of her first film performances was *The Big Broadcast of 1938.* Students of comedy should miss no opportunity to see this picture anyway, since so many important funny people appear in it. Martha does one of the most exciting song-and-dance specialties ever seen in films. The number takes place on the deck of a ship, with Martha wearing a sort of Eleanor Powellish sailor-girl costume; one, needless to say, which exhibited her attractive legs. She sings superbly, dances up a storm, is very funny, and—well, see the picture when the opportunity presents itself.

Unlike some film actors who work for years in relative obscurity, playing minor roles until they emerge into stardom, Martha was starred in her first film, playing opposite Bing Crosby in the 1936 Paramount hit, *Rhythm on the Range,* in which she was personally cast by director Norman Taurog. Not only was her performance engaging and funny but she had the good fortune to introduce the song "Mr. Paganini," which became a hit recording. To this day the number is one that audiences expect her to perform in personal appearances.

Among her other early films were *College Holiday* in 1936, *Artists and Models, Double or Nothing, Waikiki Wedding,* and *Hideaway Girls* the following year, *Give Me a Sailor, College Swing, The Big Broadcast of 1938, One Thousand Dollars a Touchdown* in 1938, *Never Say Die* in 1939, *The Farmer's Daughter* and *The Boys* in 1940, and *Keep 'Em Flying* and *Hellzapoppin'* in 1941.

In 1940 Martha had taken a break from film duty and costarred on Broadway with Al Jolson in the musical revue *Hold on to Your Hats.*

After a three-year absence from films, she was featured in 1944 in *Four Jills in a Jeep,* the story line of which was based on a USO tour of military bases in North Africa and England. The film itself was far from notable but, as usual, Martha was singled out for special praise.

The cultural highpoint in her career occurred in 1947 when Charles Chaplin selected her for an important role in *Monsieur Verdoux.* Archer Winsten of the *New York Post* was correct in observing at the time that "Only raucous Martha Raye holds her own with the . . . comedian. Her bull-in-a-china-shop personality is a perfect contrast for Chaplin's very precision."

After 1947 Martha did no motion picture work for a full 15 years. Then, in 1962, she returned to Hollywood in the MGM production of *Jumbo,* in which she costarred with Jimmy Durante.

The size of Martha's mouth has always been exaggerated, for purposes of easy laughs and publicity. In the 1970s and '80s, comedians as a class have done very little humor about their own actual or alleged faults and idiosyncracies, particularly the physical. Jokes about Eddie Cantor's "banjo eyes," Bob Hope's or Jimmy Durante's nose, Jack Benny's toupee, W. C. Fields' nose and drinking, and Joe E. Brown's mouth, are typical of the era from which they emerged. Such comic devices were like verbal caricatures, something that quickly identified the artist in the public consciousness, something that could be depended upon for an easy—and usually cheap—laugh. I don't suppose that it's possible for there ever to have been an actually brilliantly witty joke about Bob Hope's nose, but we were nevertheless subjected to thousands of them. In the modern day John Candy or John Belushi, so far as I'm aware, did not do jokes about being fat, Gary Coleman did no jokes about being short, Andy Kaufman did no jokes about his oddly vague quality. But because much of Martha's comedy was performed during the 1940's and '50s, writers and publicists who worked for her went for the easy jokes about her mouth. Martha, of course, cooperated by mugging and contorting her essentially quite normal face. Her eyes, by the way, were always remarkably pretty; one sensed vulnerability in them.

Martha, one of the minority of comedy performers who can be funny without a script, usually resorts to outrageous physical schtick rather than witty repartee to get laughs in such contexts. I was once the master of ceremonies at an industry luncheon given in her honor. Perhaps because she knew she was among friends and fans, she was particularly loose, creative, and wild. Since I was working without a script, at one point I reminisced that many years earlier, as a new comic, I had been awed at walking on the stage of the enormous, cavernous Hollywood Bowl, to entertain some 20,000 people. I recalled that I had been wearing a white suit and that the rest of the Bowl stage around me was in darkness. How I entertained for the next several minutes I could never later recall, but I did remember one line that had occurred to me as I stood alone on the giant stage. "I feel," I had said, "like the last tooth in Martha Raye's mouth."

At the luncheon, when Martha stood up to respond to my recollection, she actually took out her false teeth to get a laugh. A few minutes later, she tore apart a little piece of Kleenex and pasted scraps of it—quickly moistened in her mouth—over each eye. Then she put her left hand under her right arm and made the traditional double-pump gesture with which, for centuries, 14-year-old boys the world over have gotten laughs from easily-impressed friends.

When I went back to the microphone after she had finished, I said, "Ladies and gentlemen, I would like to announce that Martha Raye has just been presented a very special citation, the Dame Mae Whitty Award, for ladylike behavior under stress."

Martha's frequent lapses of taste are, at least in show business, notorious, but in no way detract from the lavishness of her comic gift. In some of her television appearances with Red Skelton—who is not only a great comedian but one of the Kings of Raunch—Martha's own similar tendencies came to full flower, at least during rehearsals. In his fascinating biography of Skelton, Groucho's son, Arthur Marx, describes a typical Raye-Skelton confrontation.

> But people still slipped away to see the likes of—for example—Martha Raye making a grand entrance that caught everyone's attention. She had a hand on each one of her breasts and was thrusting them upwards. The effect was that of a child playing with a big mound of Silly Putty. She next stepped over to the bar and ordered a beer, only to find that the bartender had slipped her the real thing. Hearing that it was real beer, Skelton rushed over as quickly as he could, guzzled down the entire mug, and let out a big burp, at which Miss Raye quipped, "Why don't you switch ends and save your teeth?" Red laughed about ten times as hard as when he has one of his usual laughing spells on the air.
>
> However, now he owed her one and he was quick to pay up. When Miss

Raye blew into her sweatshirt to indicate how hot the weather was, Red pointed into the air and exclaimed, "Look, a bat flew out!" The score was now even but by the time they had talked about closet queens and breast transplants, Miss Raye had a small lead. Red didn't let her keep it for long, however. Separating her breasts with his hands and peering into her ample cleavage, Red looked back at the audience and said, "My God, there are two of them."

Martha's war record, dating from 1942, endeared her to the countless men and women in uniform she entertained. Not long after the attack on Pearl Harbor, and before the formation of the U.S.O., Martha went to England with film actresses Kaye Francis, Carol Landis, and entertainer Mitzi Mayfair, to entertain the troops. The women then got permission to go to North Africa, and when the three others were taken ill, Martha stayed on for several months until she was stricken with yellow fever.

Later, when American troops were in Southeast Asia, she spent four months each year with them, for several years. When she returned from her last Asian tour she was cited by General Westmoreland for her work not only as an entertainer but as a nurse, the first citation of its kind. Martha had arrived in Soctrang, South Vietnam, on the morning of a major battle, just as the casualties were coming in. She donned fatigues, went to the field dispensary, put her training as a nurse into practice for thirteen hours, then resumed the duty the following morning.

Martha enjoyed great success in the mid-1950s as star of her own TV shows and specials. In time, however, she did not have the proper sort of writing support. This led to a period that was difficult for her both professionally and personally.

A large part of the explanation for Martha's personal difficulties as an adult is that, because she started entertaining so young, it was never possible for her to have a normal childhood. Those who know little of human psychology may assume that such deprivations are a matter of no great importance. They may think that much of our experience as children involves such trivial elements as carefree play, toys, going to school, forming innocent friendships, enjoying mostly mindless laughter, suffering a few soon-to-be-forgotten disappointments. Such experiences are part of childhood, but even they have far greater psychological and emotional importance than is commonly perceived. The reason is that childhood is the time during which we learn to be mature, responsible adults. That many of us never learn such lessons, that others learn them imperfectly, and that none of us learn them adequately, we see established daily by the countless physical cruelties, marital infidelities, broken marriages, abused children, psychologically induced illnesses, crimes, escapades, tragedies and stupidities that constitute the raw material with which the news media concern themselves.

If any common element of childhood is missing—one or both parents, the experience of forming peer-group friendships, education, contact with at least reasonably normal, mature adults, the traditional stages of relationships with members of the opposite sex—the deprived individual suffers as a result. The human predicament is notoriously difficult enough even for those who are not so deprived. It is far worse for those who are.

A number of such elements were missing from Martha Raye's early years. Fate further complicated her plight by providing her with a great deal of talent, a beautiful body, and an appealing face, which was actually far prettier than Martha sometimes permitted it to seem. These made her attractive to men, six of whom married her. But because she had no early training or preparation for the roles of wife or mother, it can hardly be surprising that she had difficulty performing them. What seemed most important to Martha was her profession, the expression of her gifts. She has always loved to make others laugh. Indeed, she is a classic case of the comedian who would "do anything for a laugh."

The ease with which she has amused us all her life at least facilitated her search for approval. All of us require the approval of others. Without it, in infancy, we literally wither and die. Comedians are perhaps distinguished from the rest of the human race by requiring the attention of others even more. Laughter is certainly an expression of approval, although this approval may be mixed with other emotions. But the funny man or woman, by the performance of his or her art, controls and manipulates us. This gives the funny person a certain important power. Not everyone literally requires the sound of a symphony, the sight of an inexpressibly beautiful poem, painting, or statue. But everyone naturally requires laughter. Those who are not able to laugh are in serious emotional trouble.

So Martha has had more than her share of the world's laughter and applause. But offstage, in intimate contexts, it has been difficult for her to achieve personal happiness.

Television in the 1950s was a natural theater for the accommodation of Martha's various talents. First of all, the period was indeed a golden age of sketch comedy, a form now notable chiefly by its absence from prime time television. But in the mid-1950s sketch comedy flourished in the hands of such important comedians as Ed Wynn, Milton Berle, Jimmy Durante, Jack Benny, Bob Hope, Red Skelton, George Gobel, Phil Silvers, Sid Caesar, and Red Buttons. Martha was one of the most talented of the group. Starting with a number of guest appearances on Milton Berle's program she moved on to the "All Star Revue" and later, on NBC, to her own "Martha Raye Show." By 1954 she was firmly established as what critic Marie Torre called her, "the country's number 1 comedienne."

During the mid-1950s, when personal and health problems began to interfere with her work, she acquired a reputation for undependability and as a result, despite her enormous talent, had trouble securing television employment. She continued, however, to perform in the nation's leading nightclubs, including her own Five O'Clock Club in Miami.

By 1958, I was doing a weekly comedy series for NBC—at 8 o'clock Sunday nights, opposite Ed Sullivan—and remember being startled to be told, when I first suggested booking Martha, "She's dead in the business. Forget her." I naturally refused to listen to such nonsense and instructed that she be booked immediately, and repeatedly. The result was something still recognized—at least among comedy writers in the over-55 age bracket—as something memorable in the 35-year context of television comedy. Martha appeared on the show twelve times. In each case the writers—all Martha Raye fans—wrote brilliant sketches tailored especially to exhibit her talents. But before her first appearance, Leonard Stern, our head writer and comedy director, producer Bill Harbach, and I had a meeting during which we agreed that one of us (it turned out to be Leonard) would have to have a little talk with Martha. The point of our message was that since we had already demonstrated our ability to stage top-quality comedy sketches and inasmuch, secondly, as we were determined to present her in the best possible light, she would therefore be wise to simply put herself in our hands and trust us to make all the right decisions. And that is precisely what she did with, as I have said, stimulating results. We had already done some sketches in what we called the "Right Way/Wrong Way" formula. This was a rather courageous form of sketch inasmuch as the "straight line," the set-up to the funny part, invariably took several minutes to perform, minutes during which there were purposely no laughs whatever. I naturally went to great pains, in introducing the sketches, to explain to our audience, in the studio and at home, that we were first going to show the right and traditional way of doing a certain dramatic scene and then were going to demonstrate that even such well-laid plans can often get loused up. Since this was the day of live television, when things frequently did fall into confusion before the eyes of millions of witnesses, the audience had some general familiarity of understanding of the premise of the sketches. The following is the first sketch of this sort that was prepared for Martha, written by Don Hinkley, Leonard Stern, and Bill Dana. In it she plays the melodramatic role of the wife of an escaped convict. As the escapee, I naturally show up at our home and confront her. I essentially played straight for Martha.

In the first scene she gets a phone call telling her that I have broken out of prison. The writers' original conception at that point involved first an extra ringing of the phone after the conversation had started and secondly, the audience's discovery that the phone was not plugged into the wall. Also crucial to the moment was a stagehand's attempting to place the phone into position after he has originally forgotten to put it on the proper table. But in rehearsal one of us got the idea of Martha being so anxious to grab the phone and start the conversation that she clutched it before the crew-member's own hand had been withdrawn from the instrument. The sight of Martha trying to hold a phone and trapping a man's hairy, bare arm was something that absolutely convulsed the audience. Here is the scene:

LOUIS NYE: It's time to return to Players' Playhouse and the fourth and final act of "Desperate Decision." Fay, played by the brilliant Broadway actress Martha Raye, has just told the police that Frank, played by the rising young star, Steven Allen, was responsible for the bank holdup, and they have arrested him.

As our scene opens, Fay returns to her apartment, a nervous and distraught woman, wondering whether she has done the right thing.

(Music: Eerie background.)

(Camera: Fade up on apartment. Martha enters, takes off her coat, hangs it on the coatrack in the corner near the door. She sighs, crosses tiredly to easy chair, and sits. She notices picture on wall behind couch is not straight. She gets up and straightens picture. She then walks to the

window, unlocks it, opens it, takes a deep breath, and closes the window.)

(Sound: Phone rings three times)

(Camera: Martha walks to the phone which is on small table next to easy chair. She picks up receiver.)

MARTHA: Hello. Yes, Captain. He what? Escaped! Does he know that I'm the one who turned him in? Then he'll come here. You've got to help me. Oh, you've sent an officer? Good! Thanks.

(Music: Dramatic phrase)

(Camera: Martha hangs up phone, quickly walks to door and locks it, then leans with back against door. She walks to table, lights cigarette.)

(Steve appears in window, lifts it, and enters room, unseen by Martha.)

STEVE: Hello, Fay.

MARTHA: Frank! Oh! You startled me. *(With a nervous laugh)* Since when have you started coming through windows?

STEVE: Since a cop started guarding your door. Why did you tell them, Fay? *Why?*

(Camera: Tight close-up of Martha as she emotes.)

MARTHA: I love you, Frank, and I did it for your own good. You'll get two, maybe three years, and then it's all over. No more hiding . . . no more being afraid. I did it because I love you, Frank. You've got to believe me. You've *got* to!

STEVE: Shut up! You taught me a lesson, sister. Next time I want loyalty, I'll buy it at a pet shop for five bucks.

MARTHA: Frank—I'm sorry.

STEVE: It's too late, Fay . . .

(Sound: Knocking on door)

STEVE: Who's that?

MARTHA: I don't know.

STEVE: Come on. *(He grabs Martha's coat.)*

MARTHA: I called the police.

STEVE: Swell! Okay, Fay . . . *(Starts backing toward closet door)* You said you were sorry. You said you loved me. Well, here's your chance to prove it. Get rid of him!

(Camera: Steve hides in closet. Another knock. Martha walks to door and opens it. Cop is standing at door.)

MARTHA: Hello, officer.

COP (Gabe Dell): Lady, I got a call to come over . . .

MARTHA: Everything is all right, officer. The captain just called and said Frank is on his way to Pittsburgh. He wants you back at headquarters right away.

COP: Oh, okay. Thanks, lady.

(Camera: Cop exits. Martha closes door and starts walking toward closet.)

MARTHA: All right, Frank. He's gone.

(Camera: Steve comes out of closet, embraces Martha.)

STEVE: Fay, I love you.

MARTHA: Frank, darling.

(They kiss and exit.)

(Music: Swells up as

(Fade)

(Camera: Nye in front of traveler.)

NYE: And thus concludes tonight's Players' Playhouse production of "Desperate Decision." And as is the custom of Players' Playhouse, let's bring out for a well-deserved bow, our director, Dwight Knotts.

(Camera: Don Knotts enters from the side, very smug and self-assured.)

KNOTTS: Thank you. It's all in a night's work.

NYE: And now our lovely star, Miss Martha Raye.

(Camera: Martha comes out through the curtain. Nye kisses her hand. They exit arm-in-arm.)

NYE: Thank you for a brilliant performance.

MARTHA: *(To Louis)* Thank you. *(To Don)* Thank you.

DON: Thank you.

NYE: Good night.

DON: Good night.

MARTHA: Good night. *(Takes Don)*

NYE: Good night to all of you—from all of us.

(Camera: Steve comes through the curtain.)

STEVE: Well, that was the way that scene was supposed to have been done when it went on the air.

But in television there are many people involved . . . actors . . . cameramen . . . stagehands . . . soundmen, and problems do come up, as those of us in television know, and as those of you who watch television know.

Let's do that same dramatic scene again and see what might happen when it goes on the air.

Once again here is Mr. Joe Pasternak to introduce the stars and set the scene.

(Camera: Cut to Nye in front of limbo traveler-curtain. The curtain is quite noisy. It moves jerkily, not smoothly.)

NYE: *(The noise bothers him, but he tries not to show it.)* Now once again it's time to return to Players' Playhouse and the fourth and final act of "Desperate Decision."

(Sound: Backstage noises—hammering; three seconds)

NYE: Fay, played by the brilliant Broadway actress, Martha Raye, has just told the police that Frank, played by the rising young star Steven Allen, was responsible for the bank holdup and they have arrested him.

(Sound: Glass crash, unexplained)

NYE: *(He winces)* As our scene opens, Fay returns to her . . .

(Sound: A heavy metal object falls. Sound of metal scraping)

NYE: . . . her apartment, wondering whether she has done the right thing.

(The scene is played legit, as dramatic actors would play it if encountering the ensuing difficulties.)

(Camera: Fade up on apartment: An overalled stagehand is caught on camera placing prop upstage. He has telephone in hand. Another stagehand enters, carrying cushion for easy chair. Offstage, Steve whispers "Psst, psst!" The stagehands realize they're on camera. Panicked, the man with the phone dives behind couch.

(Man with cushion runs offstage.)

(Martha enters, closes door, takes off coat, hangs it on coatrack. The coatrack falls down.

(She picks up coatrack and leans it against the corner of the room.

(She sighs and crosses tiredly to chairs, sits, and sinks terribly deep because there is no cushion.

(She now notices that picture on wall back of couch is not straight. She gets up, walks behind couch and obviously is stepping on stagehand. He yelps in pain. She manages to get the picture nearly level. She now crosses to the window, unlocks it, tries to open it. It is stuck tight. She gives up and takes a deep breath in front of the closed window.)

(Sound: Phone rings several times)

(She walks to the end table near easy chair where phone should be. There is no phone. She looks around for it, and sees the stage hand sneakily putting the phone on the end table near the sofa. Martha rushes over and in her haste grabs the phone, but grabs the stagehand's hand with the receiver and lifts them.)

MARTHA: Hello. Yes, Captain. He what? Escaped! Does he know that I'm the one who turned him in?

(Sound: Phone ring)

MARTHA: *(She looks at camera)* He does? Then he'll come here. You've got to help me! Oh, you've sent an officer? Thanks.

(Camera: Martha hangs up hand, arm and receiver. She quickly walks to the door and locks it. Then leans back against the door. Nervous, she goes to table, picks up cigarette and lighter. The lighter will not work.)

(She doesn't see Steve come to the window and try to open it. She finally realizes he can't get in and retreats upstage and unlocks stage door for him behind her back. She signals to him, also behind her back, for him to use the front door.)

(Steve then enters behind her.)

STEVE: Hello, Fay.

MARTHA: Frank! You startled me! *(With a nervous laugh)* Since when have you started coming through—er—*doors*?

STEVE: Since a cop started guarding your—window.

But why did you tell them, Fay? *Why?*

(Camera: Tight close-up as Martha emotes.)

MARTHA: Because I love you, Frank, and I did it for your own good. You'll get two, maybe three years and then it's all over. No more hiding... no more being afraid. I did it because I love you, Frank. You've got to believe me. You've got to!

(Camera: The close-up holds too long. Martha has to hold expression. Finally her eyes dart nervously to Steve and then to camera. Camera finally cuts to Steve.)

STEVE: Shut up! You taught me a lesson, sister! Next time I want loyalty, I'll buy it at a pet shop for five bucks.

(Camera: Steve advances on Martha threateningly.)

MARTHA: Frank ... I'm sorry.

STEVE: It's too late, Fay ... You don't realize how late it is ... *(Obviously somebody has missed a cue. Steve ad-libs.)* Fay—Fay, do you have any idea *how* late it is?

(Steve stops and looks at the door. Waits a few seconds.)

STEVE: Who's that knocking so silently at the door?

MARTHA: I don't know.

STEVE: Come on. *(He grabs her coat.)*

MARTHA: I called the police.

STEVE: Swell! Okay, Fay ...

(He starts backing toward the closet door.)

STEVE: You said you were sorry. You said you loved me. Okay, here's your chance to prove it. Get rid of him!

(Camera: Steve moves toward closet. He trips over the stagehand who is still behind the couch.)

(Martha walks to door and opens it. A cop is hastily putting on his coat. A hand from the side reaches out and slaps his cap on him. But it's the wrong hat: a Spanish dancer's hat.)

MARTHA: Oh, hello, officer.

GABE: *(Hurriedly getting coat on, he nods with billy club and hits himself on forehead.)* Lady, we had a call to come over.

MARTHA: Oh. Everything is all right, Captain. Er—officer. The captain just called and said Frank is on his way to Pittsburgh. He wants you back at headquarters right away.

GABE: Okay. Thanks, lady.

(Camera: Cop exits. Martha closes door and starts walking toward closet.)

MARTHA: All right, Frank. He's gone.

(Steve rattles door. Doorknob comes off.

(Steve can't get out of the locked closet. Martha walks over to closet door to help. At the window we see Steve running into the cop, as he tries to get around to the front door. He finally gets past the cop and tries to get in through the front door, but it is now stuck.—

(The knob comes off.)

(Steve goes back to window, taps window, and with his face against the glass, mouths the words, "Fay, I love you." Martha dashes to the window.)

MARTHA: Frank, darling.

(Music: Swells, as:

(Camera: Traveler curtain comes together from opposite sides but the two halves keep right on going so that we see the set again. Several angry people are on stage arguing, with gestures. Steve is furious.)

NYE: *(Wiping his brow.)* And thus concludes tonight's Players' Playhouse production of "Desperate Decision."

(Actors stop talking: realize they're on stage. Now traveller closes.)

NYE: And as is the custom on Players' Playhouse, let's bring out for a well-deserved bow, our director, Dwight Knotts.

(Camera: Knotts enters from the side. His clothing is disheveled, he is sweating and shaking badly.)

KNOTTS: *(Grimly)* Thank you. It's all in a day's work.

NYE: And our lovely star, Miss Martha Raye.

(Camera: Martha can't get through the flap in the traveler. After an unsuccessful struggle, Nye kisses her hand through the cloth; then she comes through.)

NYE: Thank you for a brilliant performance.

MARTHA: *(To Nye, venomously)* Thank you. *(To Knotts)* Thank *you*!

KNOTTS: Thank you.

NYE: Good night.

KNOTTS: Good night.

MARTHA: Good night. *(Takes Knotts.)*

(Martha and Don exit together arguing.)

(Prop flat comes in and covers Louis Nye.)

NYE: And now—from all of us—from all of you—good night.

(Music: Playoff.)

In another instance the sketch was based on the premise that when a major film star appeared on Broadway, producers would surround her with the best available talent—gifted supporting actors, the finest singers and dancers, directors, lighting men, costumers, scenic designers, etc. But—we explained—often the success of such productions led to the booking of a cross-country tour, which sometimes included appearances in summer stock houses. In such instances, I noted, it was unlikely that the all-star team assembled for the original Broadway production would still be available. The following sketch—in which Martha was brilliantly supported by members of our regular comedy team—Louis Nye, Don Knotts, Tom Poston, and Gabe Dell—was one of the funniest in television comedy history.

(Camera: Steve at home base)

STEVE: A couple of summers ago, my wife, Jayne, traveled the summer stock circuit starring in *Tea and Sympathy*. The children and I made part of the trip with her and I was amused by the fact that there's a great difference between the production of a play in a Broadway theater and the production of it in a small town where the play may be located in a converted barn.

You see, the producer usually sends out a star with perhaps one or two supporting players in principal roles, and then the company uses local talent for the lesser roles . . . with sometimes disastrous results.

Most of the people who did the bits in Jayne's production did a good job, but unfortunately all companies don't have this luck.

Tonight Martha Raye is going to show us the trials and tribulations of a less fortunate summer stock company. First, however, let's take a look at a portion of the *original* production on Broadway. We had our candid camera go into the theater and film this scene. Then we'll see what happened when the star took off on her summer stock tour.

(MUSIC)

(Camera: Open on set. Martha enters, followed immediately by bellhop carrying several pieces of luggage. Her clothes indicate she is a wealthy woman. She surveys the room with obvious delight.)

MARTHA: You can put the bags right here. *(Indicates to bellhop to put luggage down.)* Oh, this is lovely. *(Bellhop opens closet door stage left.)* Lovely.

WILLIAM: *Oui.* Monsieur Francois, the hotel manager, thought you would like it. It's one of our nicest rooms.

(Martha walks stage right, reaches in her purse for money.)

MARTHA: By the way, can you tell me why all the policemen were in the lobby?

(Puts her purse on small table.)

WILLIAM: *Oui,* Madame. There was a rumor that the notorious jewel thief, Reynard, the Fox, was seen in the hotel.

MARTHA: Reynard? Here?

WILLIAM: Only a rumor, Madame.

MARTHA: I see. Oh, here's a little something for you.

(She hands bellhop what is obviously a generous tip. Bellhop backs obsequiously toward door.)

WILLIAM: *Merci. Merci beaucoup.*

(Exits)

(Sound: phone ringing)

(Martha turns and moves to stage right. She picks up phone, which is on same end table as her purse.)

MARTHA: Yes? Oh yes, Mr. Francois, I love the room. It's beautiful. Yes, thank you. Goodbye.

(She hangs up phone, crosses to center of room. Takes off mink coat, brushes it, puts it on couch.)

(At the large bay window we see the silhouette of a man appear. The window flies open and the man poses on the sill a la Douglas Fairbanks, hands on hips. Martha doesn't see him.)

GENE: Is this where the woman I love lives?

MARTHA: *(Turns, is shocked)* Reynard!

(He leaps into room. Martha rushes to him)

Oh, Reynard, darling.

(They embrace upstage right)

You shouldn't have taken the chance of coming here. The police . . .

GENE: My darling, you didn't think a few gendarmes would stop the

Fox, did you? Let me take you in my arms.

(He picks up Martha in his arms.)

MARTHA: Oh, Reynard, this is madness.

GENE: Perhaps.

MARTHA: Put me down.

(He puts her down. Martha starts to walk back and forth on speech.)
What am I doing here? I never should have consented to this. You'll
never change.

GENE: But I gave you my word.

MARTHA: What has your word meant before?

(Martha goes downstage right.)

GENE: I tell you the Fox has made his last strike. *(He starts upstage
center.)*

MARTHA: *(Goes to Gene.)* Do you really mean that?

GENE: Yes, I have just won the biggest prize of all—the Reinhardt Stone.
(Pulls out jewelry box from inside pocket.)

MARTHA: The Reinhardt Stone!

GENE: *(Closes jewelry box.)* Yes, I just paid a little visit upstairs to
Madame Rheinhardt. Now I'll be able to fulfill all my promises to you: that
trip to the Riviera, the nights at Nice, the cabarets at Cannes. What do you
say to that?

MARTHA: *C'est magnifique!*

(Sound: Knock on door)

(They both react.)

GENE: Who's that?

MARTHA: I don't know.

GENE: *(He rushes to closet door)* I'd better hide in here.

(Opens closet door.) Whoever it is, get rid of them. *(Steps in closet,
closes door.)*

*(Martha opens door leading to outside. An inspector from the police
and a uniformed gendarme are there.)*

MICHAEL: Pardon, Madame, are you alone? *(Looks around.)*

MARTHA: Yes.

MICHAEL: I am inspector Ravel, the prefect of the Paris Police. This is
Sergeant Emile DuBois. May we come in?

(They come in and cross in front of Martha.)

MARTHA: Well, I really don't have time to . . .

MICHAEL: It will only take a moment, Madame. It is just a routine check.
Have you noticed anything missing? Any valuable, diamantes, etc.?

MARTHA: No. Why?

MICHAEL: Well, it concerns the thief, Reynard, the Fox.

MARTHA: Oh, yes. I've heard he's a very clever man.

MICHAEL: Oh no, Madame, he is not clever. Reynard is just a common sneak thief who has had uncommon luck. Right, Sergeant?

CHARLES: *Oui,* monsieur.

MARTHA: *(She starts to move.)* Perhaps he has uncommon intelligence. *(She sits.)*

MICHAEL: Perhaps. If you call it intelligent for a man to prey on unsuspecting women, and—poof—disappear with all their possessions. If you call it intelligent for a man to be a bigamist and a deserter of children. If you call it intelligent for a man to be a murderer.

MARTHA: *(Stands up.)* Murderer?

MICHAEL: Yes, he just killed Madame Rheinhardt—in the room directly above you.

(Martha is completely distraught. She walks slowly toward closet door. Her next speech builds with dramatic intensity to a climax.)

MARTHA: So, the Fox is a philanderer. So—The Fox is a bigamist and a deserter of children—(Now pounding her fists on closet door) . . . so the Fox is a murderer! Well—(She flings open closet door.) Here is your Fox!

(Camera: Push in to tight two-shot of the betrayed Fox and Martha.)

Music: Playoff)

(Camera: Steve at home base)

STEVE: That was the scene as it appeared on Broadway. Now, let's see the same scene—but this time, when our star Martha Raye goes to Vermont to appear with the Middlebridge Vermont Barnstormers Summer Stock Company.

(Music:)

(Camera: Fade up on summer stock set. This time the Parisian hotel suite is a bucolic fright. Since the stage has been built in a barn, it has a roof which slants steeply, making stage right almost impassable. Anyone moving in that direction must stoop.)

(All furnishings reflect the stereotype hick feeling.)

(Hold on set for a beat or two before Martha enters, followed by Tom Poston as the bellboy.)

MARTHA: You can put the bags right here. *(Indicates to bellhop to put luggage down. Tom puts luggage down in front of Martha. She doesn't see it and trips over it.)*

Oh, this is lovely. *(Martha goes over to closet door and can't open it.)*

(Sound: Door shaking.)

MARTHA: It's lovely . . . lovely.

TOM: *Oui,* monsieur Francois. The hotel manager thought you would like it. It's one of our nicest rooms.

(Martha crosses into slanted area. She stops as she realizes she can't walk naturally under the slanted roof.)

MARTHA: By the way, can you tell me why all the policemen were in the lobby?

TOM: *Oui,* Madame. There was a rumor that the notorious jewel thief, Reynard, the Fox was seen in the hotel.

MARTHA: Reynard? Here?

TOM: Only a rumor, Madame.

MARTHA: I see. Here's a little something for you.

(Looks in her handbag for tip but can't find any. She puts empty hand on Tom's hand.)

TOM: *(Looks at hand.)* Wow!

(Backing out) Mercy. Mercy.

(He backs into set, missing the door. The set wiggles noticeably. He exits.)

(Martha takes one step.)

(Sound: Phone rings.)

(Martha turns and her head bangs into low ceiling as she heads downstage.)

(Sound: Head hitting ceiling)

(Martha goes left to avoid wooden beam. Then she turns toward phone and hits top of head again.)

(Sound: Head hitting ceiling)

(She makes her way to phone, which is on table at stage right. She picks up phone which has only a short, dangling cord. She attempts to stick it back into wall.)

MARTHA: Yes? Oh, yes, Mr. Francois, I love the room. It's beautiful. Yes. Thank you. Goodbye.

(She hangs up phone, crosses to middle of room. Takes off cheap racoon coat, brushes it. Dust flies all over. She puts coat on couch.)

(We see a silhouette of Don Knotts trying frantically to get up on the window sill. Finally another silhouette helps him up.)

(He opens the window and stands there like Mighty Mouse. However, he is not too secure in his footing.)

DON: Is this where the woman I live, loves? Loves live?

MARTHA: Reynard?

(Martha rushes to him. Her velocity puts Don off balance. He falls off, seemingly into space, but of course lands on stage a few feet down, with a crash.)

Reynard, darling.

(Don tries to get back up on sill. Martha finally jerks him into room, angrily.)

Reynard, you shouldn't have taken the chance of coming here. The police . . .

DON: My darling, you didn't think a few jendarmees would stop the Fox, did you? Let me take you in my arms.

(Don tries futilely to lift her in his arms.)

MARTHA: *(As he is still trying.)* Oh, Reynard, this is madness.

DON: Perhaps.

(He struggles all around the stage with her and finally they fall on the couch.)

MARTHA: Put me down?

(She gets up.)

(To Audience)

What am I doing here?

(To Don)

What am I doing here? I never should have consented to this. You'll never change.

DON: But I gave you my word.

MARTHA: What has your word meant before?

(Martha goes downstage right but ducks, to avoid hitting her head. Don crosses to her.)

DON: I tell you, the Fox has made his last strike.

(He hits his head on ceiling, painfully.)

(Sound: Head hitting ceiling)

MARTHA: *(Still squatting, she doesn't realize she's free of ceiling.)*

Do you really *mean* that?

DON: Yes, I have just won the biggest prize of all. The Rheinstone Hart. The Hart Rheinstone. The Stonehart . . .

(Pulls out jewelry box from inside pocket.)

MARTHA: The Rheinhardt *Stone!*

(Don slams the box closed on Martha's finger.)

(Sound: Box closing on finger)

DON: Yes, yes, yes. Yes, I just paid a little visit upstairs to Miss Rheingold . . . Rheinhardt.

Now I'll be able to fulfill all my promises to you: that trip to the Riveera.

The nights at nice.
The cabarettes in cans.
What do you say to that?

MARTHA: *(Disgusted)* Sest mag*nif*-icue.

(Sound: Knock on door)

(They both react.)

DON: What's that?

MARTHA: I don't know.

DON: *(He moves to outside door.)*
I better hide in here.

(He opens wrong door. We see Louis Nye as Prefect of Police and Tom Poston as uniformed gendarme. Don does embarrassed take. Closes door.)

Whoever it is, get rid of them. I'd better hide in here. *(He moves to closet door.)*

MARTHA: Good luck.

(He steps inside. Martha crosses to outside door, opens it. Tom and Louis are there.)

LOUIS: *(A la Henry Armetta, Italian accent.)*
Pardon, Madame, uh . . .

(Knows he's caught.)

Are you alone?

MARTHA: Yes.

LOUIS: I'm Louie Ravelli, the perfect Paris policeman.

(Louis and Tom come in.)

This is Sargeant Emily DuBoys. May we come in?

MARTHA: Well, I really don't have time to . . .

LOUIS: Itsa only taka moment. Itsa just a routina check.
You got somethina missing? Any valuables? . . . Nice dress? Fur piece? Earrings?

MARTHA: No. Why?

LOUIS: You heard about Renaldo, da Fox?

MARTHA: Oh, yes. I've heard he's a very clever man.

LOUIS: Now justa minoots. He'sa notta clever. He'sa joos'a common sneaky thief, that getsa uncommon luck. Right, Sergeant?

(Louis and Martha wait for Tom's reply, which does not come.)

MARTHA: Right!

(She starts to move.)

Perhaps he has uncommon intelligence.

(She sits.)

LOUIS: Right!
(Tom nudges him.)
Oh, yeah . . . No, that'sa *wrong!*
(Walks to Martha.)
You tink it'sa smart go foolin' around with women and marry them? And then piff poof . . . Is it nice to be a bigamist?
Steal all their possessions? Hanky panky monkey business? You tink it'sa smart to be a murderer?
MARTHA: Murderer?
(She stands upright. Her head smashes totally through the ceiling.)
(Sound: Head smashing through wallboard)
LOUIS: Datsa right. He killed the lady *upstairs.*
You *see* the lady up there?
(Martha retrieves head. Straw falls down from hayloft above. She has some in her mouth.)
(Martha staggers to closet door, valiantly tries to get through speech.)
MARTHA: So the Fox is a philanthropist.
So the Fox is a deserter and a bigamist of children.
So the Fox is a murderess.
(Martha pounds with her fists on closet door, which finally breaks away.)
Here's your Fox.
(Martha opens door. A cow enters.)
(Sound: Cow Moo)
(Music: Playoff)
(Blackout)

Perhaps the reason Martha felt more comfortable on our show than on some others on which she appeared during the 1950s was that she knew of my family's vaudeville background. She was also aware that I had always considered her one of the funniest women on earth. We always do our best work—whatever our professional fields—if we know we are appreciated.

Serious or casual students of sketch comedy should study films or video-tapes of Martha's twelve appearances on our show, although not to the exclusion of her usually brilliant work in films. What they will see is a truly original, funny, likeable, vulnerable, imaginative artist at work. Martha was ready-for-prime-time when she was a teenager.

She still is.

Allan Sherman

Allan Sherman

*W*HEN, IN 1962, I WAS HIRED BY THE Westinghouse Broadcasting people to return to the television formula I had originally created for NBC as "The Tonight Show," I decided to hire Allan Sherman as producer of the new program. I was aware that there were others better qualified in a technical sense, more experienced at the nuts-and-bolts of production, but assumed that minor officers of our command, so to speak, could attend to most such details, leaving Allan largely free to function creatively. This he did, to a considerable extent. Unfortunately the minor officers he hired either were not properly instructed or were taking too long to perceive what Allan needed from them. The result, almost from the first, was something of a backstage shambles.

The initial preproduction phase of almost any television production is somewhat rocky. But what was involved in this instance was more than opening week jitters and a normal degree of wheel-spinning. There was out-and-out confusion in the production offices. I was able to disguise a good part of this while on camera so that the first few shows were at least acceptable and—at certain moments—entertaining and exciting. I was willing to go through at least a few weeks of this, but our employers, the Westinghouse executives, had no such patience. They came to me almost at once and said, "I'm afraid we'll have to let Allan Sherman go."

The first two times this was proposed, I said, in effect, "I grant that there's a good deal of confusion right now, but I honestly think that before long things will smooth out. Everybody on the staff is new to the job and the first few weeks, especially on a show of this sort, are always something of a shakedown cruise." The Westinghouse people agreed to watch and to wait. But what they saw when they watched was not less confusion as the days passed but more. Allan's fate, therefore, became inevitable. Jayne was in New York the day he was fired. Unfortunately, he had scheduled a party at his house on the very date. It was a sad, uncomfortable experience for all concerned. A Westinghouse official told Allan the bad news that "they" had decided he was not right for the job.

The scales of justice were balanced, at least to an extent, when Allan later made a series of successful appearances on the show. After his first performance, the executive who had fired him said, "They thought you were great."

"Thank you," Sherman replied, "and please tell 'they' that I am in excellent health and hoping they are the same."

Oddly enough it was the shock of being fired, and the necessity to continue to support his family, that drove Allan back to his true, basic gift—the writing of parodies. Success did not come immediately. There was the temporary delay of the insensitivity of a recording executive at Capitol who—believe it or not—said "We don't think there's a market for this type of thing" when Allan submitted a number of his best comedy lyrics. Fortunately, Warner Brothers recording executives had better judgment. One of the lyrics Allan wrote in preparation for his first album was the now-famous switch on "Frere Jacques," which came to him in less than two minutes. To perceive the humor of the number it is, of course, necessary to have some degree of familiarity with American-Jewish culture.

> Sarah Jackman, Sarah Jackman,
> How's by you? How's by you?
> How's by you the family?
> How's your sister Em'ly?
> She's nice, too—
> She's nice, too.
>
> How's your brother Bernie?
> He's a big attorney.
> How's your sister Doris?
> Still with William Morris.
>
> How's your Uncle Nathan?
> Him I got no faith in.
> How's your Cousin Ida?
> She's a Freedom Rider.

How's your brother Bentley?
Feeling better ment'lly.
How's your cousin Seymour?
Seymour joined the Peace Corps.

Allan sent me a tape of the album and asked me to write its liner-notes, which I was happy to do.

Stendahl observed that *gaiety* is the sign of the intelligent man. Lest there be any who disagree, let them listen to the lyrics created by Allan Sherman in this irrepressibly gay album and forever hold their peace. So much for the myth that only sober men are intelligent.

While I'm in a myth-disposing mood, I'd also like to say a few words about the absurd belief that the pun is the lowest form of wit. In the hands of a square, a pun may merit a groan. In the hands of a Thurber, a Perelman, or Allan Sherman, a pun may be funny as all hell. Consider, for example, lines like "the drapes of Roth" in "The Ballad of Harry Lewis," which opens this hilarious program of folk songs.

Sherman, indeed, is a master of the pun. "Gimme Jack Cohen and I Don't Care," "Sarah Jackman (Frere Jacques)," and "My Zelda (Matilda)" are humor of a high order, as is the line in "Sir Greenbaum's" Madrigal in which the medieval balladeer tells us that he hopes to "give up *smoting* for good." To deal with the album in its entirety, "My Son, the Folk Singer" is, in a certain obvious sense, Jewish. But unlike those forms of Jewish humor which, because they involve such a high percentage of Yiddish words and private allusions, are difficult for gentiles to appreciate, this package, oddly enough, has an almost universal appeal.

Allan Sherman, unlike some prominent and extroverted entertainers, is like a certain comic strip hero in that he is, by day, a mild-mannered scrivener and TV producer, whereas by night he becomes Supercomic, able to convulse tall audiences with a single joke. At present, of course, Allan is very much a specialist. He is not a monologist, nor a sketch-comedian. His chosen field is that of the comedy song, and in it he has precious little competition. Like Abe Burrows, to whom he bears some physical resemblance, Allan creates his own material and sings it in a loud, clear, and funny voice which somehow perfectly complements the amusing ideas involved.

A point worth mentioning is that these performances are top-notch *musically*. This is no voice-and-solo-piano entertainment recorded in a tiny nightclub. The arrangements, rather, are full, rich, and authentic (note the spirited chorale throughout), which of course makes the fey lyrics all the funnier.

The audience one hears is obviously comprised of people having a perfectly marvelous time.

You will too.

Although Allan stated for the official record, in his autobiography, "I am indeed the worst singer in the world," he was simply mistaken about this. For the type of material he did—parody—he was quite possibly the best singer in the world. Had he had a glorious voice like Enrico Caruso, or a pleasant voice like Perry Como, the result would have been deadly in terms of his intentions to amuse. Even if someone so handsome as, say, Tyrone Power had had a sense of humor, and if a film director had instructed him to do what Charlie Chaplin, Peter Sellers, or Stan Laurel might do in a comedy scene, the simple factor of Power's physical beauty would have made everything he was doing seem markedly less funny. Allan's voice had something inherently amusing about it. He sounded like what he was, a short, overweight Jewish fellow with a sense of humor. Not only was Allan naturally funny but he had a good understanding of his funniness. "There seems to be some quality, or lack of quality, in my voice," he said, "with which the average person can identify. I sing like anyone singing in the bathtub, not good, but with genuine enthusiasm, and that's why it's so important that the musical background and the chorus behind me should sound beautiful and legitimate, and lush. The music is never funny. So the effect is something like this; you're looking into Tiffany's most elegant show window, and in the window is a black velvet pillow, and right in the middle of the pillow is an onion. That's me."

People who understood less about the importance of contrast and incongruity in comedy would probably make the mistake of trying to cram extraneous funniness into the arrangements of Allan's songs. That sort of thing works perfectly well if you are taking the Spike Jones approach to funniness in music, but even Jones understood the value of contrast because many of his recordings were of beautiful songs, such as "Cocktails for Two," and it was the clash between the original beauty of the numbers and Spike's crazy, anything-goes arrangements that made everything seem so hysterical.

As for Allan's parodies he always wrote them to fit long-familiar and therefore well-known songs. His job was to sing the new comic words with perfect clarity so that the listener was, every few seconds, pleasantly shocked by the difference by the original lyric and Allan's version. Again, if he had sung like Frank Sinatra or Andy Williams, you would have been distracted by the sound and therefore attended a bit less to the contrast of lyrics.

In 1962, his head reeling from his first taste of top-level success, Allan was booked to play Carnegie Hall on December 28 and 31. A number of people advised him that it wasn't quite enough to simply stand at a microphone and sing his marvelous parodies. As he recalls in his autobiography:

> I had to do *something*. I couldn't just stand there in front of an audience like a big fat *shloomp*, and read lyrics from a piece of paper.
>
> So I went to Steve Allen and Jayne Meadows and I said, "Help me with an act. I can't just stand there. I've got to move around and do something."
>
> Steve suggested that I do an impersonation of Judy Garland singing "Over the Rainbow," sitting on the edge of the stage, with my feet dangling over. He even suggested calling the parody "Overweight."

Actually, I gave Allan the first two lines of the parody, "Somewhere—overweight people, just like me," knowing he would take it from there. His development of the idea is sheer brilliance, with a big laugh every few seconds.

> Somewhere, overweight people,
> Just like me,
> Must have someplace where folks don't count
> every calorie.
>
> Somewhere, over the rainbow,
> Way up tall,
> There's a land where they've never heard of
> cholesterol.
>
> Where folks can eat just what they want
> And still be trim and slim and gaunt,
> You'll find me—
> Where every little thing I taste
> Won't wind up showing on my waist,
> Or worse—behind me.

Somewhere, overindulging is divine.
If their waistlines aren't bulging,
Why then, oh why does mine?

If bluebirds weighed as much as I
You'd see some big fat bluebirds in the sky.

What had turned Allan's life topsy-turvey—for better and worse—was his recording, on August 6, 1962, twelve songs that he had already been doing for years at show business parties. The songs included "Jump Down, Spin Around, Pick a Dress o'Cotton," "Glory, Glory, Harry Lewis," and "Sarah Jackman." Several years later, looking back at that experience, which occurred at a time when he was out of work, Allan said, "In my wildest imagining I had no way of knowing or dreaming or predicting that that Monday night was going to turn my life upside down and hurl me into a whole new career and convert me into a Great American Success Story, and make me a real-life Walter Mitty."

The album, titled *My Son the Folk Singer,* was not only an immediate hit but one of the biggest of all time. Naturally there was an immediate demand—in television and the concert fields—for Allan's services as a performer. Far from pleasing him, the flurry of invitations scared him to death. Ed Sullivan called him at home and invited him to sing "Sarah Jackman" on his popular Sunday night CBS variety show. Allan told Sullivan that he was not a performer and was frightened out of his wits by the idea of going on television and making an ass of himself in front of thirty million people. But despite Sherman's initial unavailability, sales of the album continued to mushroom. President John F. Kennedy was overheard singing "Sarah Jackman, how's by you?" as he hurried through the lobby of the Carlisle Hotel in New York.

Allan's first important Los Angeles area booking was at the Pasadena Civic Auditorium. He was to share the bill with Harpo Marx. The morning of the concert Allan called our house, in a somewhat perturbed state. "Jayne," he said, "you've got to help me out."

"How, Allan?"

"Eydie Adams was supposed to do the 'Sarah Jackman' number with me tonight and she's just been taken ill and can't make it." Although Jayne has a delightful voice, and has made a number of recordings over the years, a last-minute call of this sort is frightening. "But Allan, I hardly know the song."

"You do, too," Allan said. "The melody is nothing but 'Frere Jacques.' And all you do is keep singing the name Sarah Jackman."

"Yes," Jayne said, "but I have to sing it in just the right places, don't I?"

In any event, because Allan was a dear friend Jayne was unable to let him down. So she and I reported to the auditorium. We had already planned to be in attendance anyway, since Allan was the hottest comedy attraction in the country at the time and, although we had seen him entertain at parties, we had never actually watched him work in a concert setting.

It was a truly memorable evening not only because Allan was richly funny, as always, but because his co-star on the bill was Harpo Marx. After Harpo did his always-delightful act, consisting solely of silent sight-gags and beautiful harp playing, Allan announced—to an instantly shocked audience—that we had just seen Harpo's last public appearance. We reacted as if we had been told that a popular president had just decided not to complete his term, no reasons being given.

Harpo had seemed as energetic and funny as ever. Allan himself was choked with emotion as he shared the shocking news with us. But at that point the most marvelous and unforgettable thing happened. Entirely unexpectedly, Harpo walked back on stage. He at once received a tremendous ovation. Since no one present had ever heard him speak— except, naturally, for friends and relations—we were startled when he went to the microphone, opened his mouth and began to address us. It was almost as if an individual long known as a deaf mute were to suddenly come up to you on the street and say, "Hi, Bob. How's it goin'?"

At the first sound of his voice, a wave of laughter rolled over the audience since we assumed he was speaking purely for comic effect. This turned out not to be the case. He simply began to express his gratitude for our kind reaction to his performance and to refer to the reasons for his decision to retire. There were cries of, "No, no!" as he got into this subject. But he persisted, speaking extemporaneously and charmingly about his feelings of the moment, reminiscing about his past experiences. Somehow we had all assumed, after he began to talk, that he would just make some brief explanatory statement and exit. When—about four minutes later—it became apparent that he was just going to ramble on at considerable length, that, too, struck us all funny, and he was greeted by another roar of laughter. Allan stood by, apparently also under the assumption that Harpo's remarks would be brief. After all, what would you expect from someone you had never heard speak before?

All in all, it was one of those magical moments in show business experience.

There was in Allan Sherman—as there is in the lives of many gifted comedians—a personal self-destructiveness that caused him considerable suffering, not to mention the cost to his wife and two children. For one thing, he was dangerously overweight. He could will, intellectually, to control his diet, to cut down his weight, but seemed unable actually to do so. In the last years of his life he suffered from emphysema, high blood pressure, and other complications. He was also—and this part was understandable—depressed when his career took a turn for the worse. Since there had never been any such thing as "The Allan Sherman Show," he was not able to enjoy the two, three, or four-year run that many television comedians have experienced. And even when he appeared as a guest on other programs, during the time of his greatest popularity, he could do only the one thing that he did so brilliantly; sing one of his witty parodies. That is to say, he could not perform in a sketch, do stand-up jokes, physical comedy, or any of the other things that are part of the comedian's stock-in-trade, although the sales of his albums had been phenomenal. At one point it seemed as if every twelve-year-old child in the country was singing, "Hello Muddah, Hello Faddah."

The idea for Sherman's classic "Hello Muddah, Hello Fadduh" occurred to him when his accompanist-conductor Lou Bush happened to be playing the melody of "Dance of the Hours" by Ponchielli and Sherman's wife, Dee, mentioned that their daughter Nancy was planning to go to camp. "Good God," he thought. "My little Nancy, my baby, going alone to some strange wilderness for the whole summer? I won't have it." The lines of the lyric occurred to him immediately.

> Hello Muddah; hello, Fadduh,
> Here I am at Camp Granada.
> Camp is very entertaining,
> And they say we'll have some fun if it stops raining.
>
> I went hiking with Joe Spivey.
> He developed poison ivy.
> You remember Leonard Skinner?
> He got ptomaine poisoning last night after dinner.

All the couns'lors hate the waiters,
And the lake has alligators,
And the head coach wants no sissies,
So he reads to us from something called Ulysses.

Now I don't want this should scare ya
But my bunk mate has malaria.
You remember Jeffrey Hardy?
They're about to organize a searching party.

Take me home,
O Muddah, Fadduh,
Take me home,
I hate Granada.
Don't leave me out in the forest where
I might get eaten by a bear.

Take me home.
I promise I will not make noise
Or mess the house with other boys.
O, please don't make me stay;
I've been here one whole day.

Dearest Fadduh, darling Muddah,
How's my precious little bruddah?
Let me come home if you miss me,
I would even let Aunt Bertha hug and kiss me.
Wait a minute! It's stopped hailing!
Guys are swimming! Guys are sailing!
Playing baseball! Gee, that's better!
Muddah, Faddah, kindly disregard this letter!

By August of 1963 Sherman was so successful that he was asked to replace Johnny Carson on "The Tonight Show" for a full week. At the beginning of Monday night's program he challenged Cary Grant to appear on the program and once and for all let the television viewers of America decide which of the two men was the more adorable.

Cary responded with a comedy telegram and a personal phone call.

On Friday night's program Allan made the following speech:

I want to thank NBC and Johnny Carson and everybody on "The Tonight Show" and everybody in the audience for letting me be Cary Grant for a week.

I know I'm not really Cary Grant.

But neither is Cary Grant. Mr. Grant and I and everybody else who presumes to step in front of the public—all of us—we are what you made us.

All of us are human beings, and the only thing we have that is really special is your trust and your warmth and your precious time. And the best of us are the ones who live up to that responsibility.

I want to thank the New York Post Office for delivering to me hundreds of letters that were addressed: "Cary Grant, New York City." I want to thank the beautiful girl with the hatbox—she must have been a model— who stopped me on Fifth Avenue this morning and said, "You look much younger in person, Mr. Grant."

I want to thank the hundreds of people who this week have asked me for Cary Grant's autograph. I proudly signed his name for every single one of them.

The thing is, I believe that we all have a right to be Cary Grant once in a while. Not all the time. But once in a while it feels good to be able to melt someone of the opposite sex with that look.

And so I've done more kissing in these last five days than I usually do in six months. For me, that's a big deal. But for Cary Grant it's nothing.

This whole week has been wonderful and crazy and much better than the usual type of thing that has been happening to me all my life. Thank you.

I'd better stop talking now, because if I talk any more I'll start crying, and if I start crying I'll be Jack Paar, and I'd rather be Cary Grant.

Allan was more than a comedian; he was also a humorist, which meant that he was able to perceive the humor in everyday life and make professional use of it. While he was performing at The Sands hotel in Las Vegas in January of 1963, he got a call from the National Press Club of Washington, D.C., inviting him to do a show celebrating the installation of the club's new president. Allan accepted the invitation. Two days later the press club executive called and said, "Mr. Sherman, I don't know quite how to say this but, uh, well you see, we were a bit concerned because your material is rather—er—ah—."

"Ethnic?" Sherman said.

"Yes, that's it. I just wanted to prepare you, Mr. Sherman, for the fact that the audience will be only about 10 percent Jewish."

When Allan performed in Washington, D.C., he noted that Chief Justice Earl Warren was in the front row. He opened the show as follows:

> Thank you very much. I am very proud and grateful to be in your elegant city, and among such distinguished Americans.
>
> I was warned before coming here that the audience tonight would only be ten percent Jewish. Perhaps they thought I would be disappointed. On the contrary, I am delighted.
>
> Mr. Chief Justice, I am delighted to hear that you are even ten percent Jewish. I didn't know you were Jewish at all.

It might be assumed—since the greater part of Allan's comic references involved Jewish terms—that he would be at his best in front of all-Jewish audiences. Such audiences certainly took him to their hearts. He broke attendance records at Freedom Land in the Bronx, played the famous resort hotels, Grossingers and the Concord in the Catskill Mountains, and was given tremendous ovations. "But," he later observed, "they were laughing at the wrong places all the way through and I realized I am at my worst in front of all-Jewish audiences because they seem to want something from me that I can't give them. They want me to fit into a mold that I never made but they did. They want me to be a professional Jew, an inside Jew, and they want to sit there and laugh their version of the hipster's laugh—'I dig you, but the goys don't' and I can't give them that—that's too much Jewish."

It is not surprising that Allan was ill-prepared for success. His childhood had been incredibly traumatic. Perhaps the only thing that saved him from even more serious psychological problems in later life was that his family was blessed with a sense of humor. "Everybody in my family was crazy," he recalled in his autobiography, *A Gift of Laughter*. "Not crazy-crazy. Nice-crazy. Sweet-crazy. All they ever had was trouble, trouble. When the great history of trouble is written, my family will stand extremely high in the Table of Contents."

Sherman's father, Percy Copelon, sounds more like a character drawn from fiction than reality. Although Allan describes him, facetiously, as "a typical Jew," he was a stock-car racer and automobile mechanic from

Birmingham, Alabama. Later he sold automobiles in Chicago. "He was a reckless, free-spending, high-living, dangerous-living man. He flew airplanes at a time when only lion-hearted lunatics flew planes. He flew a pursuit plane in World War I."

Allan's mother—maiden name Rose Sherman—was no better casting for the role of mother than Copelon had been as father. "She was called a 'flapper' in her day," Allan recalled, "what you would now call a swinger." She was married at fifteen, divorced a year later, then married Allan's father, "and later she had two more husbands and I don't know how many boyfriends."

I thought I had an unusually chaotic childhood in that I attended eighteen different schools. Allan topped me; he attended twenty-one. "Sometimes I was living with my mother and whatever husbands. When she was between husbands, she would park me with a relative or with her parents until she made a connection. She was frequently between husbands."

Allan derived his interest in matters theatrical from his grandfather, who used to sing comedy songs at Jewish weddings. In time he became an alcoholic. Among Allan's chief early home towns were Chicago and Los Angeles. When he was six years old, a horrible thing happened.

> We were about to sit down to dinner one evening—I remember it clearly. There was the smell of lamb chops broiling in the oven. The table was set in the kitchen. I was playing outside in the courtyard. Mother called me to come in. I was very hungry. I always had this big appetite. But instead of serving dinner, she asked me to come into the living room. My father was sitting in the kitchen, at the table, with a bottle of whiskey and a shot-glass. He didn't say anything. My mother closed the door so we were alone. She was crying. I can't stand it when women cry. To this day, I fall apart when a woman cries.
>
> She put her arm around my shoulder. She said, "Your father and I are going to separate."
>
> My eyes filled up with tears. I didn't know what to say. I could smell the lamb chops burning. I could see she didn't care if the whole house burned down.
>
> "Allan," she said, "you have to choose. Which one of us do you want to live with?"

Allan later realized that the indecision and disorganization of his adult life came from having been forced to make such a painful decision at so early an age. "It's absurd, it's damaging to a child's soul to be asked to choose between his mother and his father at the age of six. Well, I chose my mother, because she was in the room with me and I didn't dare reject her to her face. If my father had asked me the same question, I would probably have chosen him. Since that day, I can't say no to anyone; I can't reject another human being.

"When I had made my choice, my father moved out of the house. I did not see him again until I was eighteen years old."

In junior high school in Los Angeles, a pretty girl who Sherman asked to go to a school dance with him laughed in his face and said he didn't appeal to her because he had a hooked nose.

"From that day until June 6, 1944—for ten years—I felt such a shame about my ugly nose that I would not sit in profile to anybody. If I was with a person, I always sat directly in front of that person. If I was traveling in a bus or streetcar full of strangers, I would sit with my hand over my nose, pretending to be rubbing it thoughtfully. I had the sense of shame that I had something awful on me—something that I couldn't cover up, and people could see it wherever I went."

In 1941 Sherman was a student at the University of Illinois, where he had the good fortune to meet Sheldon Keller, who years later would be an important television comedy writer. The two shared a sense of humor and began to write sketches for themselves. At the same time he began reading Robert Benchley, Mark Twain, Dorothy Parker, James Thurber, M. S. Perelman, and Stephen Leacock—suitable study indeed for a future humorist.

Sherman and Keller began a bit of amateur work as a comedy team. The father of a fraternity brother arranged an introduction to comedian Danny Thomas who, at the time, was popular in a southside Chicago room called the "1500 Club." Thomas offered to let them exhibit their wares, and they decided the following evening would be as good a time as any. Danny gave them a complimentary introduction after which Sherman went into immediate shock and forgot the entire act. As if the humiliating experience was not bad enough on its own terms, Allan discovered—when he walked off the stage in a daze and through the hooting, jeering audience—that his own mother, who was drunk, had witnessed the disaster from start to finish. He gave up all hope of ever becoming a performer on the spot.

Sherman had done a short tour of Army duty but had been mustered out because of a serious asthmatic condition. In 1945 he went to New York to look for work, wearing his Army uniform as a deliberate appeal for sympathy. A brief attempt at songwriting was so unsuccessful that he gave up the art for a full eighteen years.

Through a chance meeting he landed a job as comedy writer, although his employer was unaware that he had never written a joke in his life. He solved the problem, as many a fledgeling jokester has, by going to a book store and buying every joke-collection in stock.

By now he had married his University of Illinois girlfriend, a sweet woman named Dee. But his move to New York began "seven years of poverty, squalor, starvation and economic insecurity." Sherman was at least fortunate in that by the late 1940's a whole new world called television was starting. Since comedy was, from the first, one of its staples there was suddenly a good deal of work for joke writers, even if they had had very little experience. Allan was hired by comedian Jerry Lester, the star of a program called "Cavalcade of Stars." That job lasted thirteen weeks. His next assignment, to write jokes for NBC's "Broadway Open House," lasted only three.

Sherman's first approach to actual economic security came in 1951 when he and a friend, Howard Merrill, decided to create a television program. Since game shows were beginning to become popular, they thought they might do something like "What's My Line?" Their solution was "I've Got a Secret," a program in which my wife, Jayne, was later to be featured for seven years as a panelist, working with host Gary Moore, comedian Henry Morgan, Bill Cullen, and Faye Emerson, who was later replaced by Betsy Palmer. The program's producers actually submitted to Sherman and Merrill—on the spot—a contract that specified that all rights to the series were being turned over for the sum of *one dollar*. They were given jobs as associate producers on the program at 125 dollars a week each, plus a 125 dollar-per-week royalty. Since a salary of $250 for an associate producer would have been modest enough, this meant that the production company had actually acquired the idea for what would turn out to be one of television's most popular programs at no cost whatever. "Seven years later," Sherman recalls, the production company "sold 'I've Got a Secret' to CBS for something like 3 million dollars. I sent them a wire: NICE PROFIT, FELLAS."

By 1958 Sherman was also working as producer of an occasional comedy special. One starred Victor Borge, another Phil Silvers.

A year or so later CBS sent Allan to Los Angeles to work on a new game show, "Your Surprise Package." The move made it possible for him to meet pianist Lou Bush, who would later serve as his accompanist and conductor. After the game show was cancelled, Allan went into a period of depression. "I go in for enormous orgies of self-pity during which I am very nice to myself because the world has treated me so badly. I doubled and tripled my consumption of calories; I found escape in coconut-cream pies, chocolate malted milks, corn-beef sandwiches and spare ribs. I found absolution in mashed potatoes."

Theatrical success, though it is statistically rare in the context of the general population, is nevertheless repeated hundreds of times each year for individual entertainers and other creative artists. It always brings problems, as well as rewards, but for most who enjoy its blessings the problems are not overwhelming and the benefits far outweigh them. The reason is that most of us who experience success with a capital "S" do so by a series of stages. There is usually a long period, sometimes lasting many years, during which one learns one's craft, enjoys a number of small successes, even an occasional triumph. Thus one becomes gradually accustomed to any dramatic shift of role—whether it is becoming rich, becoming poor, getting married, becoming a parent, suffering or recovering from a serious disease, moving to a foreign country, etc. But when success comes almost overnight, that is truly a shock. On Monday you were just yourself, either completely or relatively unknown to the world at large. You almost certainly had financial problems of one degree of severity or another; you were an anonymous figure in crowds or public places. You knew that there were beings on your planet such as Marilyn Monroe, Elvis Presley, Marlon Brando, Barbra Streisand, The Beatles, presidents, Popes, kings, great artists, authors, scholars, or athletes, but they seemed a breed apart from humanity in general. And then, before the week is over, you wake up one morning to learn that you are now, quite officially, one of that rare breed. The suddenness, the sharpness of change in your life—of many changes, in fact—is breathtaking. Your former financial problems have vanished in the instant, although you will at first have no way of knowing that money problems of another sort loom in the distance. Thousands of people who formerly would not, as we say, have given you the time of day, now want to give you all sorts of things, including a great many that you do not want to be given. People wish you to have dinner in their homes. They wish to introduce you to their daughters or sons. You are suddenly sexually attractive to women, or men, who before your celebrity would have considered your own advances impertinent if not revolting. People keep running up to you with pieces of paper, asking you to sign your name on them. You can no longer enter a restaurant or other public building in the normal way but are now expected to stand for a few moments—even in rain, snow or sleet—while bystanders photograph you. As they often put it, "My wife wouldn't let me in the house tonight," or "My mother would never forgive me if some physical evidence of having made contact with you was not brought home." You are suddenly considered a subject for interviews. A week earlier, had you tried to tell any of the disc jockeys, radio announcers, journalists, or TV newspeople what you customarily ate for breakfast, how you and your wife settle arguments, how—physically—you went about writing your songs, or jokes, you would have been either insulted or reported to security personnel. Now the very same answers you would have given earlier are considered utterly fascinating. As you and I know, you are exactly the same person. You are not a whit more handsome or beautiful, wiser, more virtuous, talented, or superior in any way. Except, that is, the one way that in the modern mind counts for more than anything else. You are now successful. You ought not to be deluded, incidently, that it is your talent that is suddenly of such interest, although it will be to a few sensitive individuals, mostly those in the theatrical profession. But what is profoundly fascinating is your success. It is a truly magical factor, which makes everything else about you glow with a new light. You appear more physically attractive, wittier, smarter. People will, incredibly enough, solicit your advice about matters concerning which the degree of your knowledge may be abysmal. Your political views, if any, your smattering of theories about economics, religion, health, diet, or medicine, your interests in sports—all such factors will be bathed in the new glow.

If all of this happens gradually, as I say, you have ample time to make at least most of the necessary adjustments. Indeed, the degree of public hysteria about you will itself be considerably modified. But if it happens in an instant, as it did to Allan Sherman, your life can never be the same again, for even if you later sink back into obscurity you are by no means restored to your original lowly state. It is true that you may be back living in a modest apartment, trying to survive on less than adequate money, having the old difficulty getting reservations at restaurants, etc. But to these traditional inconveniences there is now added the element of disgrace. You are now something of a pariah. There may still be a few personal friends who will not let your failure affect the essential warmth of your relationship, but you will be astounded at the smallness of their number. Indeed, you will be fortunate if your own wife, husband, mother, father, or children are not among those whose respect for you is greatly diminished. Dramatic overnight success, therefore, is, in part, a no-win situation. Your lack of emotional preparation for your sudden good fortune creates one kind of problem and, if the Fairy Godmother suddenly takes it all away at the stroke of midnight, your original supply of problems is fully restored, but now added to a third category of difficulties, the particulars of which you could not have imagined.

There are very few performers, even among the most famous, who at the moment of their death are enjoying the peak of their popularity. If they are, they have almost certainly died very young.

Well, the point is that this strange drama happened to poor Allan Sherman. His marriage was destroyed, his health suffered, his new-found money was lost. Nor did he even have the benefit of long years of success and that sort of gradual sliding into obscurity that happens to some entertainers without their ever fully becoming aware of it. Allan's performing career was tremendously compressed. Everything—the good and the bad—happened quickly.

After Allan's marriage to Dee fell apart, in 1966, he wrote a musical based on the theme of divorce, titled "The Fig Leaves Are Falling." It closed the night after it opened. Undaunted, he began work on a book, *The Rape of the A.P.E.* (an abbreviation for American Puritan Ethic).

One of the odd aspects of Sherman's story is the Mystery of the Missing Manuscript. One evening in the mid-1960s Allan called me to say that he was so excited about a manuscript he was just completing that he wondered if he could run over to the house and read some of it to me. I told him I would be delighted to hear it and invited him to dinner. After the dishes had been cleared away, Allan placed his manuscript on the table and began to read from it. The title, as I recall, was *It's About Time* or *About Time*. It was an utterly fascinating and witty account of the subject of time itself. There were references to Genesis, Plato, Aristotle, Einstein, the phrase "time immemorial," sun dials, water clocks—a thousand-and-one factors related to man's methods of measuring his progress through space. The book's observations were wise, scholarly, thoroughly impressive. There was some discussion about my writing a foreword for the book, which I was certainly willing to do. A few years later, after Allan's death, it occurred to me that I had never heard more about the matter. Eventually I got in touch with Allan's son, Robbie, who seemed to know nothing about the book; nor did Allan's agent or any of his friends. Somewhere then, I assume, is a brilliant manuscript which ought to be printed and distributed. Perhaps some enterprising publisher will have better luck than I did in tracking it down and sharing it with the world.

Incidentally, I recommend to you—purely as literature—Allan's autobiography, *A Gift of Laughter*. It is unusual, first of all, in that Allan actually wrote it, and very well, too. I doubt if the news can come as a surprise to anyone past the teenage years, but very few celebrities actually write their own autobiographies. They obviously contribute, usually by spending several weeks being interviewed or tape-recorded by the professional writers who put the words on paper. But everyone on earth is capable of being interviewed. Less than one percent of the population of planet earth is able to write well. Allan was a member of that small group.

I talked to Sheldon Keller recently about Allan, whom Keller described as "the most self-destructive person I've ever known." Since Shelly liked Allan, his description cannot be taken as a thoughtless criticism by an enemy. "You know," he said, "some people aren't very nice, and their attitude toward the world is 'f— you.' Well, it always seemed to me that Allan's motto was 'f— me.'"

Near the end of his life Allan was living at the Motion Picture Country Home. I suppose this means he had run out of money, since the home is a haven where performers may at least enjoy peace and comfort in their last years or periods of illness when they cannot afford to support themselves. I went out there to visit him one day and we spent several laugh-filled hours together. Although his emphysema seemed to be troubling him, he appeared to be in good spirits.

Allan's last project was a parody on golf titled "Hallowed Be Thy Game," which he recorded at the Comedians Golf Classic at La Costa and which he was preparing in both a recording and a printed version.

When Allan died in November of 1973, his family asked if I would deliver the eulogy at the nonsectarian memorial service in his honor. On November 23 I addressed a group of perhaps two hundred of his friends, relatives, and admirers, as follows:

It will be difficult to add anything especially significant to the eloquent and very moving tributes the other speakers have delivered.

There is no good time for death. But certain times—such as the Thanksgiving season—surround the sadness of a friend's departure with a background that makes the loss even more painfully felt than would otherwise be the case.

There is something like an arithmetic of grief at times such as this. Saddest of all is the death of a young child. Least sad is the death of someone who is very old and for whose story death seems, therefore, a suitable last chapter.

In mourning Allan Sherman we refer to his age. "Too young," we say. There should have been much more time for him. Much more of his company for us. But the situation cannot be changed, despite our wishes. And so we gather together.

What we undertake at this moment is a ritual. For whose sake? Primarily our own. It is a formula, a means, a drama that man has developed over the long centuries to assist in dealing with the mystery and tragedy of death. But in whose honor? Allan's, and his alone.

And perhaps, mingled with the sadness and sense of loss at such moments, there is always a certain amount of guilt, too, that this ritual helps us to dissipate. Did we see him enough? Did we spend enough time with him? Were we supportive enough? And what does the word "enough" mean, in regard to such questions? Can there ever be enough love, enough respect, enough affectionate contact? Perhaps not, for as we ourselves are less than perfect so will all our relationships be less than perfect.

But the other side of this coin is gratitude, for the good moments there were, for the times of warm companionship, for the hours of sharing and understanding and affection.

Allan was not the kind of man who would expect monuments to be erected to his memory. Nor is there any need for physical monuments. For we will remember him without them. Because he was—is—a memorable man.

Allan—I think—was a genius. A humorist. A wit. He was gifted and was, in turn, generous with his gifts.

I never shared his company without being made to laugh. Just recently we spent a wonderful afternoon together. There was much laughter. And there were ideas.

For Allan was the kind of man who had so many interesting ideas of his own that he stimulated you to be creative, too.

In a field where that allegedly sincerest form of flattery—imitation—is far more common than originality, Allan was a fresh, inventive, and truly original artist.

At the art of parody he was—quite simply—the supreme master. And his recent writings—serious and comic—revealed his emergence as a perceptive philosopher.

It is a tragic loss, therefore, that he is taken from us just at the time in his life when he was developing as a Socratic gadfly, able not only to amuse but to stimulate, to instruct, to inform.

But the loss of creative people—whether in the arts, the sciences, or the humanities—is at least softened by the anodyne of the preservation of their work.

So we still have that part of Allan. His songs. His recordings. His books. Indeed they will outlast us. He will have admirers at this moment not yet born. And that is fitting because he was a particular favorite with children.

He appealed to the child in all of us. For children sensed in him that warm nature, that willingness to help, to participate, that those of us who knew him especially appreciated.

Because—like all the young-in-heart—he hated sham and pretense, he would not want to be eulogized today in phrases interchangeable with those of a tribute to Abraham Lincoln, Ghandi, or Schweitzer.

No, the simple truth about Allan is quite enough.

Such mistakes as he made in life he paid for in the coin of personal suffering.

There is something about man—specifically a faculty of his brain—that leads him to try to perceive purpose and significance in the frequently chaotic flow of events in which he finds himself immersed and borne along.

So, when a friend is taken from us before what we consider his rightful time, we look for meaning in the loss.

To be able to find it may be comforting. Not everyone is able to find it.

There is the obvious-enough sense in which death is as natural as life, part of the great pattern of physical movement through time. But that pattern itself is essentially mysterious. So the search for meaning is in a sense circular.

We locate ourselves in this universe according to two measurements—space and time. But the irony is that each of these is fundamentally mysterious.

Either time began one day—which is preposterous—or it never began, which is equally absurd.

As for space, either it ends somewhere—which is impossible. Or it never ends, which seems equally impossible.

All we can be certain of, therefore, is our existence. Of the necessity for that existence no man has ever been told. Of the purpose of that existence there is—among the best of men—a great variety of opinion.

It is death, that terminates that physical existence, which seems invariably to give rise to such speculation, and particularly the loss of a loved one or a dear friend.

If our existence continues on another plane after our physical death, then perhaps at this moment Allan knows secrets 'til now withheld from the rest of us.

If he does, I'm sure that among his reactions to his new discoveries a smile is included. For humor—like all forms of beauty—is partly in the eye of the beholder. And the sensitive eye is able to perceive the amusing element in everything.

Yes, even in serious and tragic matters, which should not surprise us inasmuch as the raw material of almost all comedy is tragedy.

So—if there is an otherwhere—we may believe that Allan will be one of its most perceptive and appreciative observers.

And, no doubt, if there are such things as heavenly music, as choirs of angels, the possibilities of parody are already occurring to him.

There is much more one might say of so warm and interesting a man, but it would not be correct to say that we gather here today to say that we loved him. Rather that we love him.

Red Skelton

Red Skelton

ONE DAY SEVERAL YEARS AGO, MOTION picture producer Irwin Allen and Groucho Marx stopped at a grocery store in the Palm Springs area to buy some supplies. They found the store's shelves almost empty.

The proprietor said, "I'm sorry, but Mr. Skelton was in here a little while ago with three men and practically cleaned us out. He thought perhaps the war was going to affect this area, and he wanted to stockpile all the food he possibly could."

Steve Martin plays the role of "a wild and crazy guy," but in reality is nothing of the sort. Martin is well-educated and has a clear grasp of the personal and professional reality through which he moves. Red Skelton—through no fault of his own, needless to say—was scarcely educated at all, had a painful childhood, has a distorted vision of reality, and *is,* in a sense, a wild and crazy guy.

I hasten to add that this is by no means merely my own assessment; it is also Skelton's. "I'm nuts and I know it," he once told journalist Dwight Whitney, "but as long as I make 'em laugh, they ain't going to lock me up." Columnist James Bacon, a long-time Skelton friend and devoted admirer, has described him as "downright nutty." "If I weren't making 2 million a year, I'd be in Camarillo [a mental institution]," Skelton once said to Bacon. But if he is at times wildly eccentric, Red is nevertheless one of the century's great comedians.

Of all the stand-up night club or concert comedy acts Skelton's is quite possibly the best. At no point during his approximately one hour and twenty minute presentation does he coast along with passages of relatively lightweight material or chit-chat, as do most of the rest of us. His act consists of one powerhouse routine after another. He does individual word-jokes, physical comedy, funny-hat schtick, makes remarkable comic faces, and—in some of his pantomimes—truly touches your emotions. His rightly famous mime of an astronaut leaving his command module on an "umbilical cord" of the sort that became famous when the United States first sent men into space, is a classic. And when, at the end of it, Red tries to pull himself back to the space ship but suddenly realizes that the cord has become detached, the audience falls totally silent, completely absorbed in the almost-believable drama of the moment. Red does a remarkable, almost invisible step, sliding his feet, flat-footed, backwards slowly, so that the audience has only the impression that he is getting smaller as he drifts off into space. It is a truly chilling theatrical moment. Only a gifted artist could pull it off. It is no surprise that Marcel Marceau is among Skelton's greatest admirers.

His impression of an old man watching a parade passing by also combines humor and pathos, and his imitations of drunks or babies trying to walk are masterpieces.

Another gem comes when, after a vigorous routine, he removes his hat and slowly combs his long red hair neatly back into place. Then, with a suddenly violent sneeze, the hair goes all wild again.

Groucho Marx thought that Red was the logical successor to Charles Chaplin. "I've seen most of the great, legendary clowns of the circus," he once wrote, "but I confess I've rarely seen one who could amuse me for more than a minute. True, they all wear funny clothes and funny hats and paint their faces, but it takes much more than that to be a great comic.

"The last time I watched Skelton perform . . . with one prop, a soft battered hat, he successfully converted himself into an idiot boy, a peevish old lady, a teetering-tottering drunk, an overstuffed clubwoman, a tramp and any other character that seemed to suit his fancy. No grotesque make-up, no funny clothes, just Red."

I agree with Groucho; Skelton is a giant of comedy. He is, however, a rather odd fellow.

The fact that Skelton is a great natural clown is perhaps not surprising in light of the fact that his father, Joseph Skelton, was a professional clown early in the century with the Hagenbeck and Wallace Circus. The senior Skelton married Red's mother, Ida Mae, in 1905. Three sons were born to her before Red was conceived. Two months before his birth Red's father died of the ravages of alcoholism. Since Ida Mae and the children were literally penniless she had to accept work as a charwoman in a small vaudeville theater in the family's home-town of Vincennes, Indiana. While her meager earnings were enough to prevent starvation, they could do nothing to lift the family out of the most degrading poverty. Red has early memories of sleeping in an attic infested with rats. Hunger was a constant companion.

There was another frightful childhood recollection when Red's mother arranged for him to spend the night with an uncle who ran a small grocery store. While Red was sleeping in a crib in a room behind the store, an arsonist lit a drum of gasoline. The child was rescued while the building burned down around him. From that day Skelton has been nervous near fire, even to the point of backing away when a match is suddenly lighted near him. His own cigars are never lighted.

His difficult early upbringing was in some respects like that of his idol, W. C. Fields. The two men greatly respected each other's talent. Fields once said, in fact, that if ever his life story was done in films he wanted Skelton to play the role.

Skelton has been making people laugh since he was a child. "When I was ten years old," he recalls, "I went to a medicine show in my home town of Vincennes, Indiana. I told the head man I wanted to work for him, singing or something, but the Doc had no ear for music, and he sent me out into the crowd to hustle his bottles of elixir. Running back to the platform for a new supply, I tripped on the steps and took a nose dive. It got a big laugh and I was hired. As a diver!"

Like many poor children in the early years of the century, Red survived by odd jobs—selling newspapers, racking up balls at a pool hall. Because of his mother's work he had occasional access to local theaters and had seen entertainers in action. He would sometimes perform on street corners, singing and dancing in the hope of attracting a few coins from passersby. A high point of his early years came from a chance meeting with the then-important comedy star Ed Wynn while Red was selling papers across the street from a theater where Wynn was headlining.

Some forty years later, when Wynn's days of great popularity were long past, he was given a serious acting role in the Playhouse 90 drama, "Requiem for a Heavyweight," written by Rod Serling. Red agreed to play a bit part on the show, without being paid for his services, as a way of thanking Wynn for his long-ago generosity in giving an unknown child a ticket to his vaudeville show.

Oddly enough it was his lack of formal school training that facilitated the development of what were probably natural gifts at pantomime. Because he read so poorly, Red had trouble learning, memorizing, and delivering jokes. Consequently he developed the ability to get laughs doing falls, making faces, almost any kind of spontaneous and/or rehearsed schtick.

While still in his teens, Red began to work with small-time stock companies. He put in a tour of duty on a Mississippi riverboat, the *Cotton Blossom,* on which he joined the troupe of a certain Captain Hittner.

Skelton worked next for a time as a circus clown, in the very profession that had been his father's. By the time he was 17 he had had to do so many things to keep body and soul together that he had learned how to sing, dance, tell jokes, do pantomime routines and pratfalls—all invaluable training for a young comic. In 1930 he was hired to work at the Gaiety Burlesque Theater in Kansas City for $75 a week.

The next phase of his career also provided invaluable training for the years of stardom ahead. Red was hired to work in the dance marathons or walkathons of the early 1930s. The duty was murderously hard; few comedians could have done it at all, much less carried it off as well as Red did. From 5 P.M. until 3 in the morning he was on, competing with half-passed-out dancers, bored bystanders, jaded or rude audiences. He did every old joke he had ever heard and used routines he recalled having seen others perform. He sang, danced, did imitations of other performers, fell down—as would Chevy Chase forty years later—comedy-flirted with lady visitors, climbed up the walls, purposely spilled soft drinks on himself, imitated assorted hicks, drunks, children, topped hecklers, did a bit of card magic. I can not think of even one other comedian who could have handled an assignment of this sort so ably.

Besides the training, perhaps the only other good feature of Red's walkathon days was that he married a bright, resourceful woman he had for some time been in love with, Edna Marie Stillwell.

"We were so hungry in those days," Skelton has recalled, "that sometimes I'd just lie in bed and cry. Edna would reach over and put the blanket around my shoulder and pat my cheek and keep saying, 'Go to sleep, honey. You have to get your rest. Go to sleep.'"

The recollection is interesting because it reveals the little-boy side of Red, a part of even his public stage personality that he has never fully abandoned.

The characters that some comedians do are purely whimsical creatures of their, or their writer's, imaginations, but they are sometimes drawn from aspects of the entertainer's own personality. Red Skelton's Mean Widdle Kid, I suspect, was part of the real Skelton buried somewhere inside the now-elderly man. While comedians as a class are not generally models of strength and sobriety as husbands, fathers, employers, some are, as human beings, less mature than others. They do not make a conscious decision to be so. The roots of their instability may easily enough be traced to chaotic childhood experiences. Red Skelton, whatever the Freudian realities, has been more influenced by his childish streak than have most of us. Even to those who know nothing of his personal life the little-boy element is evident. Skelton, although nearing seventy, still speaks in something almost like baby-talk when he does his sincere good-night, thank-you, and God-bless speech. I have heard other show-business figures criticize Red for playing the innocent little boy at the close of his act when—according to their argument—the real Skelton, a foul-talking, cigar-chewing wild man, is anything but. The conclusion such critics draw is that the cliche if-I've-done-anything-to-offend-anybody speech is a model of phoniness.

I disagree. I think that at such times Red actually believes every word he says. The emotional waves of repentance, innocence, and sugary sweetness are, I suspect, totally honest. Red Skelton is a comedian who entertains chiefly by submerging himself in imaginary characters. The combination Professional Nice Guy-Little Boy that he becomes at the close of the act is, then, one more of his characters, but one that is honest and consistent within the context of its own assumptions.

The combination of the poverty and generally chaotic nature of Red's early life—his three older brothers frequently bullied and tormented him out of jealousy—plus his interest in entertaining, meant that—as mentioned—he acquired little or no education. At the age of fourteen, when most students are preparing for high school, Red was still in the fifth grade, embarrassed at being surrounded by younger children.

An actress who performed on his television program once told me a sad story, the explanation for which is clear from Red's early lack of interest in learning to read and write:

> When I was doing his show once, in my dressing room I had the book of *Mad-Libs*. Red came into the room and asked me what I was doing. I told him it was the game called Mad-Libs, and he said, "What's that?" I said, "Oh, it's a game." And he said, "How does it go?" I said, "Well, you see this sentence where a noun and a verb are left out? Here, I'll show you. Give me a noun." And he said, "Blue." And I said, "No, a *noun*." And he said, "A

noun—um, *singing*?" I said, "No." And he said, "What's a noun?" And I said, "It's like a person or place or a thing." And he said, "Oh, you mean like *me*?"

Finally he told me he had hardly ever gone to school. He said he had worked from the time he was very young.

The director of Red's show was Seymour Berns. I happened to say to Seymour, "Gosh, I just had this interesting experience with Red." He said, "Oh, it's absolutely true. Why do you suppose I sit next to him in rehearsal the first day? He can't read very well." And I said, "What do you mean? He reads the script." He said, "Not really. Watch the next time."

I watched in rehearsal. They used to sit Red at one end of the table with Seymour on one side and the producer on the other side. Red would have the script read to him, and rehearsed, before he went into the meeting with the cast, and then they would sit there and when he would come to a word he didn't know how to say, he would say, "I want the—" and then they would say *ottoman*—or whatever—very softly, and you wouldn't even notice it.

It was not until the mid-1930s that Red was able to get into vaudeville. He enjoyed his first success as a vaudevillian in Montreal, where he became a particular favorite and introduced his eventually famous doughnut-dunking routine.

RKO producer Pandro Berman caught Red's vaudeville act at New York City's Loew's State and cast him in his first film *Having Wonderful Time*. The picture worked well for Red, partly because he was able to incorporate the doughnut routine.

An interesting—and not untypical—show business story concerns what happened to Red after *Having Wonderful Time,* in which his own work was deservedly quite well received. Because the picture itself was faulty, part of the blame somehow rubbed off on Skelton and he could, for the time being, get no further work in films. He was back in vaudeville, many months later, playing a Baltimore theater when he received a call from an advertising executive named Freeman Keyes. Keyes had seen Red at a Chicago theater sometime earlier, liked what he saw, and had been trying to track the comedian down ever since. Since he was aware that Skelton was handled by the William Morris Agency, he called that organization and asked to be put in touch with Skelton. While there would be no point in introducing the information by saying believe-it-or-not, the fact is that no one at the Morris office was aware that Skelton was a client. They agreed to track him down nevertheless only because Keyes was insistent. Eventually an office boy in the agency's New York quarters had the faint recollection that the office did represent Skelton. And this, mind you, was after he had distinguished himself in *Having Wonderful Time.*

Keyes asked Skelton if he would be interested in radio work and arranged to have him do an audition show for NBC. Thanks to Keyes, Red finally made his radio debut in January of 1938, on a program hosted by country-and-western singer Red Foley. Because Foley's fans liked simple, country humor, of the sort popularized a generation later on "Hee-Haw," Red began to develop some of his country-bumpkin characterizations.

The first time I saw Red I was about fifteen years old. The year must have been 1937. He was playing the Chicago theater, headlining, doing the doughnut bit. This involved sitting at a table, showing the various methods people employ to dunk doughnuts. (There was the sneaky dunker, who looked around to make sure nobody was watching and then slid the cruller furtively into the cup. There was the "Oh, look what I did" type who pretended "accidentally" to drop the whole doughnut into the cup.) During the bit Red used to eat eight or ten doughnuts. Doing five shows a day—well, you can see why his doctor finally had to order him to cut the routine. Fortunately he had plenty of others. One of them, the Guzzler's Gin monologue, is a true comedy classic. Red gives an impression of an announcer doing a commercial for a brand of gin. After each paean to the gin, the announcer takes a little sip. Naturally he soon is too drunk to speak clearly. The result is hilarious, whether you're seeing the bit for the first or the fiftieth time.

Interestingly enough, it later came to light that the Guzzler's routine was not entirely of Skelton's creation. When Metro studios decided to put the monologue on film in 1944, screenwriter Harry Tugend happened to see the routine and thought it looked familiar. Indeed it was. Tugend had written a very similar routine while working on Fred Allen's radio show. The biggest difference between the version done on Allen's program and the one done by Red was that Skelton worked alone, while Fred Allen had done Guzzler's supported by other cast members.

Tugend, although understandably upset, settled quietly out of court, in part due to his respect for Red's talent. In Red's defense, it is possible that he never knew the routine's lineage. Although no one has ever managed to confirm or deny the story, it might have happened like this, according to his biographer Arthur Marx: At a time before Red could afford many writers—and when he needed them most—Skelton was very dependent on his wife of the time, Edna, who knew what was best for Red's style. At this time—in the glory days of radio—it was common for actors reading a script on the air simply to drop each page to the floor as they finished it. After a broadcast the studio floors were littered with such pages. Edna, the theory goes, found the pages containing Guzzler's on one of her trips to NBC and, recognizing that the bit would be a good one for Red, simply kept the pages.

As Marx may be unaware, there were always people in the 1930s and 1940s who discovered that by looking through the trash bins behind the NBC or CBS studios, among others, they could find either partial or entire scripts of various popular programs. Some of those who scavenged through the wastepaper were just fans looking for souvenirs. But the resource was a rich strike for those who dealt in a sort of black market for jokes. I discovered this by accident when from time to time fans would come up and ask me to autograph old scripts from my various shows. When I began to ask them where they got the scripts they would say, "Oh, we just found it in a waste-paper basket," "It was just being thrown away out behind the building," etc.

Although Skelton would later become temperamental and to a degree personally irresponsible, he was usually on good behavior during his early days at MGM. My wife, Jayne, who was under contract at the studio at the same time, recalls that often, when she was shooting a particularly emotional scene, Red used to stand quietly behind the camera, watching her work, even though he had nothing to do with the film she was in. "I asked who the fellow was who kept staring at me," Jayne recalls. "They told me it was somebody named Red Skelton. He seemed very nice, but was too shy to introduce himself."

Red was not then in the habit of standing about the sets of films in which he was not working. The reason he watched Jayne was that she was his type, as his long-time producer, the late Seymour Berns, once told her. Jayne did bear a slight resemblance to Red's second wife, Georgia, in that both women were tall, red-headed, glamorous-looking. A few years later, when Red was doing his weekly comedy show for CBS-TV, he booked Jayne as his guest star on several occasions.

"I remember once," she recalls, "Red had a kissing scene written into the script. But we went all the way through the rehearsal and the show and the kiss never took place. After the show, I said to Seymour, 'The kissing scene was cut, right?' 'Oh, no,' he said, 'Red doesn't like to do that sort of thing in front of an audience. So as soon as the studio's empty, we'll start up again, do the kiss, and edit it in later.' Well, it was sort of creepy. The studio was empty except for the cameramen and the technicians. There were no jokes; just a line or two of dialogue and then Red was supposed to kiss me. But right in the middle of my cue line—before I even finished my line—he reached over and gave me a big, sexy kiss. It was sort of embarrassing. I always liked Red, but not that way."

Another odd thing about Red's career—considering the degree of his talent—is that although he has always been a highly visual, physical comedian, he was never really at his best in films.

Like Abbott and Costello he was generally well-received when doing the sort of routines with which he was familiar—such as the doughnut-dunking bit—but otherwise suffered from film's lack of audience contact. Perhaps it is Red's very insecurity that has made him so effective in front of audiences. He is so sensitive to audiences, even to individual laughers, or starers, perhaps from the early days of vaudeville and dance marathons when he had to play to small groups of sometimes inattentive people. In any event it is fair to say that one could not possibly judge the real Skelton by seeing him only in motion pictures. To be fully appreciated he must be seen in concert, in front of a live audience. After Jackie Gleason's television career concluded, Gleason could not, like Skelton, go on a life-long concert tour since Jackie's basic act was not the sort that would work in Las Vegas, Carnegie Hall, state fairs, college campuses or the other situations in which Skelton is so wonderfully effective.

Continuing the litany of personal idiosyncracies, Skelton's discomfort with his comedy writers is notorious. If he can avoid it, he simply will not talk to them at all.

Writer-comedian-humorist Jack Douglas—who first attracted popular attention on Jack Paar's version of "The Tonight Show"—worked for Skelton for several years early in his radio career. Even at that point, apparently, Red's difficulties with writers were serious.

Although Red's wife, Edna, could not herself write a joke, she was mistress of the enormous gag-file she and Red had compiled. It was her custom to keep the individual writers isolated from each other—God knows why. Because of this peculiar system each writer had to contribute an entire script. The combined scripts would be turned over to Edna who, in cooperation with Red, would select what she thought to be the best of the jokes. With scissors and paste they thus made up an acceptable script.

"The scripts would be in terrible shape by the time they went to mimeo," Jack Douglas later reported to biographer Arthur Marx. "And no wonder. Christ, I'd go over there to deliver a routine and I'd see Skelton on the floor, cutting and pasting things. And he cut so quickly with the scissors you knew damn well he was probably cutting off the most important lines in the whole routine. As you've probably heard, he wasn't much of a reader anyway. When I'd go over to the house, he and I and Edna would be sitting around his great big dining room table, he'd want me to read stuff aloud because he couldn't read it. Well, not couldn't—but it would take him a lifetime to read four pages."

Another of Skelton's early writers, Ben Freedman, said to Marx, "Red was suspicious of anything new, didn't always understand the humor of it right away. He might have to mull it over for a couple of weeks or perhaps months. Later he'd pull it out of the joke file and offer it as something he'd just originated and put in the script, and then say, 'Now why can't you guys come up with something like that?' If any of us dared say we already had, he'd blow his stack."

Despite his brilliance, Skelton had certain problems adjusting to television. He did not slip into the medium, like many of us, from below. He entered it from the top down. That made it tougher for him to be accepted, as it did for Bob Hope, Bing Crosby, Frank Sinatra, Fibber McGee and Molly, among others.

Red was so good on the radio, so funny in films (when they were good pictures), that most of us could hardly wait to see him on TV. When we finally did we had oversold ourselves. "The Berles and the Gleasons and all the rest who were not successful on radio and in pictures," people said, "are doing okay in television. But just wait until the real giants step into the medium. Wait 'til Hope and Benny and Skelton and Fred Allen go to work. Then you'll see something." Nobody can follow a build-up like that. Too much was expected.

At the time it seemed that some of the giants had stayed out too long. Some major performers stayed out of radio so long that when they were finally willing to visit the medium nobody cared. New stars had been created and there just wasn't any demand for all the old-timers from the theater, vaudeville, and night clubs. There wasn't room for everybody.

The same situation had existed when motion pictures were new. Some stars of the theater chose to bide their time, to make pictures only after it became important to make them. But when the stars finally informed Hollywood that the time was ripe, Hollywood wasn't interested. It had made its own stars. So did radio. So did television.

Now as to Skelton: what had he to offer to television?

A great deal. Physically he is one of the funniest men in the world. With the possible exception of Leon Errol, nobody else has even been able to give such a wonderful impression of a drunk trying to walk across a room. Red's struggle with gravity, his breath-taking battle with equilibrium, always amuses. His face, too, is his fortune. An attractive face in repose, it becomes a mask of comedy with very little distortion. Combined with Red's knack of twisting a hat into the right sort of shape to match a particular facial expression, it is a tremendously valuable asset.

Skelton, by the way, is one of the few remaining comics who does hat schtick, which was important in vaudeville. Ted Healy used to get a lot of mileage out of a hat. Joe Penner couldn't work without one. Joe Frisco, Jack Oakie, Ed Wynn, and Jimmy Durante were hat men. Skelton does a lot with his. When he's not turning it upside down to give a sort of college graduation mortarboard effect, he's rounding out the crown and pulling it down over his ears to establish that he's intoxicated. Or else he's just fondling it, using it the way some comedians use a cigar, musical instrument, or microphone, as something to play with while moving from one idea or routine to another.

Another standby is Skelton's ability to take a fall. His falls into orchestra pits are famous, and TV audiences took a long time to tire of the routine in which, while trying to say goodnight in front of a curtain, Red was suddenly yanked from sight by two men who reached under the velvet, grabbed his ankles, and pulled back hard. His drunk's falls, too, are classic.

A friend once asked me what was so funny about a man falling down. Well, it's all in the way you look at it. It's not funny if a baby falls down. It's cute, or sad, or normal, but not funny. What distinguishes a man from a baby? What quality does he have that makes his falling funny?

Dignity. A baby has a number of qualities, but no dignity. Only a mature adult can have dignity, and every adult has some shred of it. When he falls down he momentarily loses it. Skelton's comedy makes much of defects and ugliness and falling down and stumbling and getting sea-sick and looking cross-eyed. These things all represent a loss of man's normal stature; the loss, if it's sudden enough, shocks us in a pleasant way. When you are shocked in a pleasant way, you laugh.

Another factor in Skelton's favor is that he is not weak "as himself." Many comics are strong only when in a sketch or playing a part. Sid Caesar and Jackie Gleason, to name only two, are both happier when in character. Skelton is a fine stand-up comedian, a good story-teller, and handles one-liners better than most.

Red is also a better actor than the average comedian. He also brought to television an established line of comic characters. Clem Cadiddle-hopper, Freddie the Freeloader, Cauliflower McPugg, and the others were already established favorites. A TV producer, discussing Red's characters in the early 1950s, said, "They were all surefire on radio, but only time will tell whether they'll hold up for television audiences." For quite a few years they did.

But that the question should even be raised points up an interesting difference between television and radio. TV calls for more realism. On radio Jerry Colonna could say to Bob Hope, "Well, here we are on the moon," and the imaginations of listeners would construct a complete landscape. But on television the imagination is not a help. It may even be a hindrance.

So, too, with a character like the Mean Widdle Kid, audiences could visualize a three-foot brat of any particular form that appealed to them. On TV the eye is merciless. The imagination is weakened. The character of the Kid goes down the drain. If the brilliant Fanny Brice were still with us she would have the same problem with her Baby Snooks character. There was a different Baby Snooks in the mind of each of the millions of radio listeners whom Fanny entertained so wonderfully, but there was never any actual physical Snooks that would have had a long career in television. For the young reader, perhaps I should explain that Baby Snooks was like Lily Tomlin's Edith Ann.

On this negative note we now arrive at an examination of the reasons that, by 1955, seemed to be militating against Red Skelton's full success on TV. His characters, as I was saying, lack realism. There are successful comedy characters that lack the quality, but those that score most strongly are the ones that have the closest semblance to reality.

Jackie Gleason, for example, was most successful as Ralph Kramden, the bus driver, and less so as Reginald van Gleason, the baggy-pants playboy. TV audiences will laugh at exaggeration and fantasy, but when it comes to an enlistment of their emotions they find it impossible to become seriously involved with an entirely make-believe character. Gleason never destroyed the realism of a sketch by an aside to the audience, whereas a great part of Skelton's comedic approach in a sketch was the "ad-libbing" he directed toward his studio audience.

It is an axiom of the TV-comedy business that the less realistic you are the bigger your jokes have to be. If you're not being at least a little true to life, your script has to blast a laugh out of the audience every few seconds because their emotions are not much involved. But if the audience is intensely interested in what happens to your characters, they will laugh at almost any little joke. Consider Wally Cox's Mr. Peepers. His adventures resolved into a dramatic presentation. A Peepers script rarely contained a single rich belly-laugh, but it was delightful nonetheless. Once you became interested in what was going to happen to Robinson Peepers and his friend Wes (Tony Randall), and their addle-pated colleague Mrs. Gurney—the wonderfully funny Marian Lorne—you were a pushover for any little quip. But when you watched Skelton it had to be one big joke after another or your interest lagged. Red was being funnier but you didn't always laugh as much.

Another low card that Red holds is his habit of laughing at himself. I learned this by accident one night while watching one of his shows. The living room was full of people. About every fifth joke Red would join the audience in a brief appreciation of it. He would pretend to try to go on with his lines, but would apparently be overcome by his risibilities and succumb to a brief fit of the giggles.

"I wish he wouldn't do that," said one of the women in the room.

"Do what?" I asked.

"Laugh like that," the woman said. "He was there for rehearsal. He's heard the jokes all week. What's he laughing now for? A comedian is only entitled to laugh at an ad-lib or a mistake."

There followed a very unofficial survey, which revealed that about fifty percent of Red's audience wished he would just tell the jokes and let the audiences do the breaking up. This is a habit, though, that Red will never overcome. It's wrapped up with his manner of delivery. He's a happy comedian on stage. He smiles and laughs a lot. He enjoys himself. Once in a while, for all I know, maybe he really does get the giggles.

Some comedians, especially those who have worked in vaudeville, employ the chuckle-device as a cover-up and a come-on. In a big theater it sometimes takes a second or two for an audience to absorb a joke and respond to it. Many comedians fill that empty spot with some sort of nervous mannerism. George Burns and Ken Murray wiggle their cigars, Bob Hope pretends to be sailing right into the next sentence, although he rarely says more at such times than "I-uh," "but I really—", "But I wanna tell ya—". Some comics—Pinky Lee was one—make a sort of grunting or chuckling noise to cover the unbearable silence before the laugh comes. If Red Skelton is to break the habit it will be a struggle, and before he tries I suppose he should take his own survey.

Red frequently employs food or drink as a comedy prop. One of his greatest TV sketches involves his portrayal of a starving tramp—Freddie, the Freeloader—who is mistaken for a film actor *dressed* as a tramp. When the actor doesn't show up Red is shoved into the breach. The first scene is supposed to take place at a restaurant table. The comedy reaches great heights as the desperately hungry Red tries to eat the food on the table, but the director keeps insisting that he forget the food and concentrate on the business at hand, which involves welcoming a girl who plays the role of a starving waif. Red finally goes berserk from hunger and does one of the funniest bits of pantomime I've ever seen when he picks up the girl's hand and mistakes it for a piece of chicken. His business of separating the fingers as if they were chicken bones and, with delicate gusto, picking out the imaginary bits of meat from between them, is a comedy delight.

Unfortunately sketches this strong cannot be written every week; from the first some of Red's television difficulties stemmed from that old bugaboo, a shortage of strong material.

"In my first year on TV," says Red, "I used up a hundred and sixty-five routines. Some of it was stuff I'd spent years putting together."

Another reason Skelton had a tough row to hoe in TV is that he chose to be pretty much the whole show by himself. Jackie Gleason depended on Art Carney and his other supporting players. Sid Caesar needed a comedienne—Imogene Coca or Nanette Fabray—Carl Reiner and Howard Morris. Bob Hope will not do a show at all without an important line-up of guest stars. But Red, although he employed supporting players and guests, never built up a cast of people upon whom he could depend for help as did Jack Benny, Milton Berle, and others. He had a few characters helping him on radio, but they never panned out as pure gold and didn't survive the move to television.

But the important fact still stands out clear; Red Skelton is wonderfully funny. The rehearsals for his TV programs were often so riotous they disrupted the workday schedule at CBS's Hollywood television studios. Executive scoldings finally had to be put up on office bulletin boards forbidding workers to leave their desks during Red's dress rehearsals, between 3:00 and 4:00 P.M.

Red suffered a tragic blow in 1958 when his son Richard, a handsome and appealing child, died of leukemia. I had gotten a phone call from Red in mid-December of 1957. "Steve," he said, "I've noticed that Richard didn't get a Christmas card from you."

I was momentarily at a loss since, while I had been aware of Richard's tragic condition it hadn't occurred to me to send a special card to Red and his family. In the entertainment field the average performer does not send cards to at least 99 percent of his fellow actors.

"Gosh," I said, "I guess you're right, Red. I'm certainly sorry about that, and I'll be glad to get one right out to Richard." I deliberately avoided asking about the child's condition since I knew there could not possibly be any cheerful news to impart. Suddenly inspiration hit me.

"I'll tell you what," I said. "I'll be coming out to the coast in a few days anyway, to visit my own sons for Christmas, and, if you like, I'll be glad to drop by your place and pay Richard a visit and perhaps bring him a little gift of some kind."

"That's a great idea," Red said. "Georgia and I would really appreciate it."

Several days later my sons Brian and Steve and I drove to the Skeltons's house one night and spent about an hour visiting with them, joking with young Richard, of whose fatal condition there was little visual evidence. He was a bright child, good looking, sweet, and remarkably cheerful considering his circumstances. The house was well decorated for Christmas and presents of all kinds—mostly for Richard—were piled here and there. Richard told me that he enjoyed watching the comedy program I was then doing—the one with Louis Nye, Don Knotts, Tom Poston, Bill Dana, Gabe Dell, Dayton Allen, Pat Harrington, and the rest of our wonderful gang. I made small talk, as up-beat as possible, and told Richard I'd be glad to visit with him whenever he was in the mood.

Twenty-five years later, in July of 1982, Brian, his wife, and their three children spent an afternoon and evening with Jayne and me aboard the *Pacific Princess,* when it stopped at Vancouver, British Columbia. Brian told me he had recently seen Red in concert in Seattle, where Brian lives.

"I sent a note to him backstage before the show," Brian said, "mentioning your name and telling him I'd enjoy saying hello to him after the show."

"Did you get to see him?" I asked.

"Yes—and he was very nice—but an odd thing happened. When I went back, we shook hands and I said, 'Did you get my note?'

"'I never read notes like that before a show," he said, "because one time, years ago, somebody handed me a note backstage, just as I was about to go on. It said that my wife had been in a serious car accident and the guy that wrote the note had some important information for me. You can imagine how I felt, having to go out on stage and do a show being afraid that my wife was dying. The terrible thing was that the guy came backstage after the show, laughing his head off. He said to me, 'Well, I guess you fell for my little joke, eh? I just sent you that note so I could get back here to talk to you.'"

On February 16, 1958, we were doing our Sunday night comedy hour from Hollywood, instead of our New York studio. Red appeared as a guest, working in one of our Man-on-the-Street sketches.

STEVE: Now it's time to meet our good friends, the men on the street. And of course, here in Hollywood, you never know exactly who you're going to meet. Tonight's question is one that people often ask about this city. With such stiff competition, how does a person get ahead in Hollywood?

Well, we're going to find out now as we meet our first Man on the Street. Let's see if our cameras can pick him up. Ah, yes, there he is. And may I ask your name, sir?

RED: Clem Cadiddlehopper. I am a movie producer and a car hop.

STEVE: Wait a minute. A movie producer and a car hop. That's a very interesting combination.

RED: Well, don't knock it. Last year I made 2 million, and that's plus tips.

STEVE: Well, what kind of movies do you produce, Clem?

RED: Oh, I do all those teenage pictures. You know, like "I Was a Teenage Gabor Sister."

But next month I'm doing a teenage picture that will end all teenage pictures.

STEVE: That's not a bad idea. What's it called?

RED: It's called, "I Lied About My Age."
So, should we go into that rinky-dink stuff? Or would you like to ask me some questions?

This was a line Red ad-libbed because he had been amused to discover—during the in-studio rehearsals earlier in the afternoon—that Louis Nye, Tom Poston, Don Knotts, and the rest of us never did the actual lines of our sketches, although we had used them during the rehearsal hall run-throughs earlier in the week. The reason we did our entire show-date rehearsals in double-talk was that I had observed, in the early 1950s, that the studio personnel would laugh hysterically the first time they heard the jokes. But then—after hearing them three or four times—they would not laugh at all once the show was on the air.

Rehearsal-time laughter, I realized, didn't mean a damn. The only thing that counted was what happened when you went on the air.

In any event Red, who had never encountered this practice before, had asked questions about it earlier in the afternoon, using the term "rinky-dink," his version of one of our nonsense words.

STEVE: Yeah, we'll play it straight here, Clem. And here's the big question: how does a person get ahead in Hollywood?
RED: That *is* a good question. Now if we can just come up with an answer, we're in.
But I'll tell you how that works. It's all in your attitude. You gotta be determined. You gotta have determination. Like when I left home, you know, you can't worry about what people say about you. When I left home and headed west, I kept goin' and finally I stood on top of a hill and I looked out and I said—after I took a deep breath, see?—I took a deep breath and I shouted, "Hollywood, I will lick you. Hollywood, I will conquer you. I'll do this or my name ain't Clem Cadiddlehopper." And then everybody laughed at me.
STEVE: Why did they laugh, Clem?
RED: I was in Chicago at the time.

The jokes were fine, but it was Red's marvelously comic face, and the Clem Cadiddlehopper voice, that made them seem even funnier. Our audience—and all of us—loved Red.

One of the strangest things about Skelton is that he has often criticized other comedians—although not by name—for doing off-color material. The natural implication is that he himself is above that sort of thing. On August 29, 1981, while working in St. Louis, Red was interviewed by radio personality Jack Carney. At one point he did a little joke and then added, "I think jokes like that are better than sex jokes and off-color things that a lot of the comedians use now—four-letter words and things like that. I don't believe that you should have to pay your money and go—even into a night club—to hear things that you could read on walls in restrooms."

"You've never done blue material, have you?" Carney asked.

"No," Skelton said, "never did. None at all. I don't believe in it."

The truth is, as it happens, quite otherwise. As Arthur Marx observes in his remarkable and touching biography of Red:

> One of the little white lies that Red has always tried to foster throughout his career is that he never had to rely on ribald language or dirty jokes to get a laugh. "Not even when I was playing burlesque," he once told a magazine biographer. "You can always get a big laugh with a dirty joke, but often the people are laughing out of embarrassment."
>
> Red may have been against vulgarity in theory, but evidence indicates he rarely practiced what he preached about ribaldry. Red hadn't been a member of the Metro stock company very long before he had acquired an almost Rabelaisian reputation for his extensive vocabularly of four-letter words and a penchant for entertaining the cast between takes with the filthiest dirty jokes imaginable.
>
> "I think I learned every four-letter word I've ever heard from Red," recalls Esther Williams, who was a young, and presumably virginal, girl of twenty when she made *Bathing Beauty* with him. "He used the filthiest language on the set imaginable. He'd shock me so I'd go back to my dressing room and cry."

I first became aware of this behavior pattern when I made a guest appearance on one of Red's shows in the late 1950s. He did a dress rehearsal of the program in front of a full studio audience—which largely consisted of women and some children. Despite their presence Red did a number of vulgar, raunchy lines.

James Bacon has described a typical Skelton TV rehearsal at the time as "the filthiest hour you can imagine." Bacon has also written of Red's using a powerful film projection machine to project a particularly gamey stag film on a neighbor's white garage door. This was years before the "porno" film had become all-too-characteristic of our culture.

It's a free country, as the saying goes. Today hundreds of comedians work in the same deliberately shocking manner. But the strange thing is that Red still insists that entertainers ought not to do this.

Skelton's irresponsibility with money is legendary. At one time he owned over 200 neckties, all of one color—maroon. Expensive custom-made suits he would sometimes order 25 at a time. Since he had a mental block against wearing relaxing attire or even casual sports clothes—due, perhaps, to the fact that he had never owned a suit until he was 14—Skelton would quickly ruin his expensive, hand-tailored suits while doing laboring work on his house, digging in the garden, or performing in sketches that involved his being sprayed with seltzer, hit with pies, or covered with paint. Many entertainers, after suddenly coming into more money than they know how to spend, indulge themselves to the extent of buying a Rolls Royce. Skelton at one time owned five. His friend, columnist James Bacon, asserts that at another point he owned eight.

One of the odder things about Skelton, Hope, Benny, and other major comedians who had achieved their stature before television is that, judged purely within the television context, they have never been recognized as having made contributions of major importance to the medium. In the case of Fred Allen there was no particular mystery to this; he simply never succeeded in television as he had in radio. But Bob Hope's specials—if not always distinguished in quality—have usually received high ratings. Jack Benny's shows were almost invariably well done. The situation is perhaps the most puzzling in the case of Red Skelton, who was employed in television for some twenty years. George Gobel, by way of contrast, had one season of dazzling TV success; yet it was his picture that appeared on magazine covers of the time. Ernie Kovacs, too, did not have a long career in TV and was popular mainly in New York. Sid Caesar's reign as king of satirical sketch comedy on TV ran an incredible ten years; in other words, not nearly as long as Skelton's tenure of office. But start a casual discussion among people over fifty about important television comedians of the last 35 years and Skelton's name will rarely come up. The conversation will concern Milton Berle, Sid Caesar, Jackie Gleason, Lucille Ball, Carol Burnett, your obedient servant, and perhaps another name or two, but not—as I say—the pre-TV giants. There seems to have been the unspoken sense that because they were already established there was nothing particularly newsworthy about their move into the then-new medium of television. As regards the rest, television audiences were involved with discovering us. The older comedians were simply a given of American society of the early 1950s. The rest of us achieved major success only in television.

As regards three of us—Sid Caesar, Ernie Kovacs, and myself—there was the sense, at least among professional critics and students of the medium, that we were not simply performing on television forms of comedy originally suited to vaudeville or radio, but were incorporating the new technology itself as one of the tools of our trade.

Another part of the mystery is explained by the media's incessant search for new faces. The next time you're at a magazine stand, stop for a moment and study the faces on the covers of fan magazines, *The Enquirer,* and other publications that cater to public fads and fancies. Sex, actual or alleged, and scandal have far more to do with such decisions on the part of editors than does talent. If talent is honored, it will usually be because the performer is relatively new on the entertainment scene.

In Skelton's case perhaps another reason he has been given less media attention than some of his peers, despite the brilliance of his talent, is that he dislikes being interviewed and has often deliberately made himself unavailable to journalists. In contrast to Bob Hope, who seems willing to do almost anything in order to avoid being alone, Skelton is one of the entertainment industry's true loners. He associates with those with whom he is working, with his wife, with his expensive toys—cameras, cars—but is apparently insecure in society. It is hardly surprising that most entertainers prefer the company of fellow professionals. We all feel a certain at-homeness with those who share our professional interests. But Red's case is more extreme. There are very few entertainers who could say of Red that he is a close, personal friend. This is so probably because during his early years fate denied Red anything remotely resembling a normal childhood. He simply had too little opportunity to learn to socialize, to relate to others as human beings. Although he is tall, and was blessed by nature with a strong physique, he has always been, as an adult, partly the child that he was never permitted to be early in his life. Consequently he has felt most at home with strong, dominating women, women who could mother him.

Because Red has long suffered bouts of paranoia, he has a fairly long enemies list. Unfortunately not everyone on the list deserves to be there. Some long-time, loyal coworkers have been simply dismissed, without explanation. But when Skelton felt that someone had purposely wronged him or written something critical, Red performed a strange Oriental ritual, in which he asked his wife, Georgia, and daughter, Valentina, to take part. The three would repair to a small shrine in Skelton's Japanese garden, kneel, bow heads, and try to think of three good things about the individual Red felt had wronged him. At a later point, if Skelton still viewed the offender as an enemy, he, his wife, and daughter would repeat the ceremony but this time visualize the wrongdoer as mentally buried. "If anyone hurts me or my family," he once told his producer, Guy della Cioppa, "I consider them dead and never think of them again."

Even during the various periods of his greatest success—in vaudeville, films, radio, television—Red seemed never to have fit in socially with any particular group. He was not comfortably part of the Beverly Hills-Bel Air milieu. Later, when he moved to the Palm Springs area, he generally stayed aloof from the show biz-politics-rich businessmen circle. Although many of Red's coworkers in the comedy field were Jewish, he never became part of the Jewish show business culture, and was rarely seen at the parties and public functions where one might run into Milton Berle, George Burns, George Jessel, Jack Benny, Red Buttons, Jack Carter, and other prominent Jewish comedians, as well as gentile entertainers. The pattern is reminiscent of that of some children who are afraid to play with strangers. In Red's personal relationships with people he had to work with there was often a childish factor to the communication. On the one hand there was the appealing, funny, anything-to-please side of Red. But when he was displeased—rightly or wrongly—he seemed simply not to know how to express his displeasure in a conventional way. We are all capable, I suppose, of being driven to distraction, but with Red almost any provocation seemed to suffice. Tantrums and running away were a normal method of expressing anger. The repeated emotional explosions showed, at least, that he seriously cared about the issues at hand, but the care was rarely acted out in the form of full, professional dedication. Having done comedy in television for thirty-five years I can report that producing and performing on a weekly series is a demanding, full-time job. One of the reasons the prime-time shows I worked on were so good is that our troupe of comedy professionals rehearsed a full five days in preparation for the telecast. There was nothing special about this; it was the norm, the involvement a network had a right to expect for paying enormous sums of money to the performers involved. But in many instances Red, like Dean Martin, seemed to be refusing to put in the proper number of hours or days, as a way of showing that he simply didn't need to, that long rehearsals were for amateurs, or at least for others. That his shows were often good, nevertheless, that he himself was almost invariably funny, was attributable to his comic gifts. What he never seemed to realize was that his shows would have been immeasurably better if he had cooperated with his producers, directors, and writers to the full, normal extent.

One of the stranger aspects of Skelton's life is that, having heard that some writers tape-record philosophical observations, jokes, sketches, and essays, Red decided to do the same. His observations, he says, are not only transcribed and filed but bound in expensive leather. Nothing wrong with this, except that there has been apparently no other human testimony to authenticate the story. In the same category are the thousands of melodies Red reports having composed. Certain professional song-writers are remarkably prolific, but the odd thing about Red's story is that he knows nothing whatever of either music or the art of composition. He hires a piano player to whom he hums melody lines, naturally unaccompanied by harmonic information.

That Red's childhood afforded him little opportunity for even basic education is, as I have noted, understandable; one would hardly expect him to be an avid reader. But he is said to have a collection of over 22,000 first editions.

Again—more than in the case of any other prominent comedian, Skelton has always had difficulty separating reality from fantasy. After the public embarrassment of the Guzzler's Gin plagiarism, reports Arthur Marx:

> By the time of Fred Allen's death in 1956, Red had convinced himself of a whole new fairy tale regarding the birth of his most famous single piece of material.
>
> As it happened, Allen expired on a Tuesday—the day of Red's television broadcast. But Red, who barely knew Allen, was so "moved" by the comedian's passing that near the end of his broadcast Tuesday night he suddenly turned solemn and spent the next five minutes eulogizing him. The gist of his lachrymose tribute was that not only had the world lost one of its greatest comedians, but he, Red, had lost one of his dearest friends— a friend so dear and generous that he had personally written "Guzzler's

Gin" for Red and started him on the road to his first big success. Moreover, Allen had done it out of the goodness of his heart and not for any financial consideration.

In the radio interview with Jack Carney of St. Louis, Red—in all seriousness—casually mentioned having composed 64 symphonies. It will perhaps bring the claim into sharper focus if I explain here that Mozart wrote forty-one symphonies, Beethoven ten, and Bach and Wagner did not write any. Writing a symphony, even a poor one, is a major musical undertaking and requires a sophisticated grasp of musical theory.

A television producer who does not wish to be identified has an interesting theory about Skelton's telling journalists he has written thousands of songs, countless short stories, philosophical observations, etc. "I have worked with Red," he says, "and I simply don't believe him when he talks about writing 20,000 songs. Irving Berlin is our greatest songwriter and he only wrote a thousand songs. I think Red—who has very little sense of arithmetic, or money—I think he just pulled the number 20,000 out of the air, to impress people. Also, people have got to understand that it is not that big a deal to write a song. In fact, one of the reasons things are so difficult for amateur songwriters is that there are millions of people who try their hand at it. You yourself do a stunt where you get four different people out of your studio audience, have each of them hit a note on the piano at random and then you make up a song based on those four notes. Red probably does hum some little phrases into his tape recorder, or maybe he puts one finger at a time on the keyboard, and then has his piano player take these little bits and pieces and make a song out of them. If he had actually written 20,000 songs, he would be the most prolific composer in the entire history of music. That kind of genius you couldn't keep under a bushel. Another thing is that Red has been a millionaire for the last forty years or so. Jackie Gleason, who also knew nothing about music, used to make beautiful record albums just by hiring good musicians to record some pretty tunes that Gleason liked. If Skelton was a real composer, it would have been the easiest thing in the world for him to commission some albums of his songs. The same thing goes for his short stories. Red is one of the world's greatest comedians. Do you think if he wrote or published some professional short stories that Simon and Schuster wouldn't be after him to bring them out? The one thing people might figure that Red could write would be jokes, but he doesn't. Like Bob Hope, Jack Benny, Jackie Gleason, and a lot of other great comedians, he's not able to. His genius lies in performing, and at that he's one of the best. But he's always hated to give his writers credit. So personally I don't think he has any real track record as a comedy writer, a short story writer or a songwriter. But if that's so, then the fascinating question is—why can't Red be content with being what practically everybody acknowledges him to be, one of the world's great comedians? The reality of the man is really impressive; onstage he's a powerhouse. So why does he have to depend on fantasy? It's sort of the same thing when Red criticizes comedians who use off-color material. Everybody in the business knows that he himself is the King of Filth. His rehearsals at CBS in the old days used to be really hysterical. Red is the funniest really dirty comedian in the business. Okay, great. But then why at the same time does he try to pose as Danny Decent, with all the God Bless and patriotic talk and flag-waving and doing the Republican conservative bit. I'm not knocking him for his politics or for his vulgarity. But why the fantasy? Why the denial of reality?"

Why, indeed? It is easy enough to draw upon Freud and say that Red suffers from such personal and professional insecurity that, like a child, he needs to give his ego extra support by resorting to make-believe, exaggerations, and lies. But such a hypothesis—even if valid—is hardly a full answer to the mystery of Skelton.

Oddly enough, one extracurricular activity of which Red does not boast, because he does not have to, is his painting, for which he has a true talent. His oils of clowns, in particular, are of professional quality and, in fact, highly marketable.

Perhaps Red has always felt inferior to comedians such as Fred Allen or Groucho Marx who were literate enough to write not only comedy material but books. What Red has perhaps not grasped is the measure of his own greatness as a comedian. His own basic act is stronger than that of Fred Allen, and far stronger than Groucho's. Groucho rarely worked as a single and when, in later years, he did he invariably disappointed audiences, with what really came under the heading of "An Evening With Groucho Marx," rather than a performance by Groucho Marx. He would make little jokes, tell autobiographical stories, and sing some of his old songs, the humor of which would have been considerably less apparent if the numbers had been performed by anyone else. Groucho was a great spontaneous wit, but he was incapable of delivering a strong performance on stage alone. Red Skelton is a master of precisely that.

In conclusion, Red is almost a classic case of the tragic clown, able to make audiences laugh, but troubled and insecure in his own life. But despite his imperfections—of which we all have our share—he is one of the world's great comedians. A friend told me recently that he is working on a television special for which Red will tape his basic concert act, which is the best news I've heard in a long time. I advise the reader to see that special when it is aired and—even better—to secure it in permanent video-tape, video-disc or film form. No serious or even casual student of comedy should be in ignorance of the genius of Red Skelton.

On Jack Carney's radio show in St. Louis, Skelton was asked, "If you had the opportunity to write—in a sentence or two—Red Skelton's philosophy of life—what would it be?"

"Don't love anyone," Skelton answered. "Like everybody. Because love can hurt."

Red must have been hurt a great deal, early in life, to entertain such a philosophy.

"... That Old Gang of Mine"

Dayton Allen
Bill Dana
Gabe Dell
Pat Harrington, Jr.
Don Knotts
Steve Lawrence
Louis Nye
Tom Poston

THE MARCH, 1961, EDITION OF *Playboy* carried the transcript of a wonderfully insightful and witty panel discussion in which the participants were Lenny Bruce, Bill Dana, Jules Feiffer, Mike Nichols, Mort Sahl, Jonathan Winters, and myself. During the course of the discussion, Mort was kind enough to say that he thought my Sunday night NBC comedy show had the funniest stock company of all time. He was absolutely right. Our players—Dayton Allen, Bill Dana, Pat Harrington, Jr., Don Knotts, Louis Nye, and Tom Poston—were a truly gifted company.

Consequently, since I am personally fond of the various members of our old troupe—and see them socially fairly often—it seems fitting to express my thanks, for both their friendship and professional support, by writing about them here. (The order is alphabetical.)

Dayton
Allen

THE LAST TIME I SAW JACK KEROUAC was late one night in Hollywood in the winter of 1959. We had just left a recording studio on
Sunset Boulevard near CBS and our farewells, for no particular
reason, had turned to horseplay. Two days earlier, Jack had appeared on
my television show, reading great rolling, period-shy paragraphs from
his novel *On the Road.* Now, in a whimsical mood, slightly intoxicated,
he stood on Sunset Boulevard, shouting mildly obscene pleasantries
after me as I walked down the quiet side street where my car was parked.
I waved good-bye and responded somewhat less raucously—not because
I had any better sense than he but because I was sober.

The reason I bring this up now is that Jack was not speaking to me in
his own voice; he was imitating Dayton Allen. "Steve *Allen*," he was
shouting, at half past midnight, "how's your sister? And Whoy . . . *not?*"

Some may attribute to the power of television the fact that Dayton's
rubbery-mouthed phrase "Why not" became part of the national ver-
nacular. Actually, very little of the torrent of wordage with which TV
daily floods the country ever catches in the memory. The primary reason
we remember and are amused by "Why not" is that we remember and are
amused by Dayton Allen.

Dayton is something of an anomaly in this age of the comedy, a
throwback, the kind of good old-fashioned nut that, as George Gobel
used to say, you can't hardly find no more.

To begin with, he has the *face* of a nut. That's important. Fred Allen,
for all his brilliance, could never have been a clown-comedian. He wasn't
physically the type. But Dayton has a wonderful face for comedy. He is
funny just standing there, as the saying goes.

At our rehearsals we frequently would surround him and begin
plying him with questions, to which he would respond as if he were an
important personage submitting to a press conference. His answers—
wildly inventive, weird, and usually for-adults-only—were invariably

amusing. His range of characters, too, is wider than our television audiences ever knew, for on our show he almost always played the *Why Not Man*—when he was not doing Groucho Marx—but he also does remarkable imitations of Eisenhower, Roosevelt, an evil old nineteenth century cockney innkeeper, a good-natured village dope, and assorted Italians, Jews, Negroes, Scotsmen, Irishmen, and what-have-you.

This versatility served him well for the many years that he contributed off-camera voices to the old "Howdy-Doody" program and children's cartoon shows.

Another thing marking Dayton (who, by the way, is no relation—at least not of mine) from other comedians is that he writes a great deal of his own material. Originally his monologues on our show were produced by our writing staff, but when they saw what Dayton did with the material, often rewriting it almost completely, they at last turned the assignment over to him. Dayton is a true humorist, as well as a comedian. His book *Why Not,* published in 1960, establishes the fact.

And, like all comedians, he has his serious side. He invests judiciously in the gold market and gives sober thought to pressing social questions. It is also possible to carry on a perfectly serious conversation with him, at least for a few minutes at a time. But inevitably his comic gift bubbles up into the dialogue, sometimes obliquely and irrelevantly, sometimes as pertinent punctuation to a point seriously intended.

To fully appreciate the humor of the following monologue you have to visualize Dayton delivering it in his inimitable serious-goof manner.

NATIONAL SURGEON WEEK

Being a very famous surgeon, surgery to me is more than just a way to make a good fast buck.

A patient and a doctor are two separate people. The patient is one and the doctor is the other. This makes two.

The technical advances in operating have been really swell—clean gloves, nice lights and a bunch of other stuff.

There are certain unwritten laws in surgeon work. Like:

1. Don't get cute. Always wait for the patient to get a little dopey, so they don't feel anything.
2. Before operating, always wash your hands, if they're very dirty.
3. The patient requiring immediate surgery should be considered as sick, and the surgeon shouldn't even kid around.

Quite often, as chief surgeon of the hospital, I would even operate on *people*. Many of these people at the time were even sick.

Of course, once in a while, as in any other profession, you would get a kvetch, which means "crank" in Latin. They would insist I operate with medical instruments. To these I answered simply but firmly, "What are you—a religious fanatic?"

I shall always be indebted to Dr. Iva Spasm, who was my instructor in bellies and heads. Dr. Spasm introduced me to my first patient, who was a real good sport. May he rest in peace. The patient, who at the time looked terrible, was actually suffering from a very bad thing.

I am proud to say that, although I never went to a real doctor school, I honestly hung around an actual drugstore a lot.

Several times throughout an operation, I will stop, look around the whole room, wink, laugh and punch the patient a little. This, to let the nurses and other doctors know that the patient is still alive.

To return to a less comical subject, when I first went into business to do doctor things, I turned away two hundred sick people who came to my office. I didn't want to catch anything. Today, these same people still respect me for this and go to other doctors.

A dear friend of mine, who had been a total stranger to me before I knew him, confided in me and told me an important fact.

Another amusing incident happened when I first started operating. A patient called up excitedly and said he had acute appendicitis and wanted me to please operate immediately. I laughed and hung up on him. I just felt like being silly.

A number of doctors, other than myself, wrote to me, by letter, asking what I thought about a very terrible disease. I told them, point blank, I thought it was a rotten thing, and was causing the people who had this disease a lot of sickness. To me such truth in medicine is a beacon to the ill.

Just last week ago, a woman customer of mine asked me what I thought about her losing weight. I told her I thought it seemed like a good way to reduce.

I would like to say in closing to those wishing to become doctors: study medicine and stuff like that, learn about hearts and lungs, and those things. It will come in handy, because education is a good way to learn. Also, take a temperature or two, with some sort of thermometer. Take it from me also, the patient who lives on after the operation is a happier patient, boobie!

Bill Dana

I HAVE SELFISH REASONS TO BE PLEASED at the extent of Bill Dana's gifts, since he served as a member of my television writing staff for several years. He might still be toiling in such relative obscurity, in fact, were it not that I was finally able to induce him to perform some of his own dialect routines publicly, one happy result of which was that his original characterization, Jose Jiminez, became a national favorite almost overnight.

So popular were Bill and his alter-ego that shortly thereafter, in fact, Danny Thomas's production company prepared a situation comedy series for him.

I had decided to hire Bill as a writer after comedian Don Adams had done a brilliant series of guest shots on our show. Don worked partly as an impressionist and one of his best impersonations was of William Powell, speaking as the private detective he played in the Thin Man films. "There's your man, inspector." When I asked who had written Adam's strong material and discovered it was Dana, I suggested we add him to our team.

Dana was not involved with the production of Adam's later TV series "Get Smart," created by Buck Henry and Mel Brooks. "My contribution had come much earlier. Don Adams and I created the character as the star of his night club routines in the 1950s," Bill has recalled. "He would be a defense attorney; a football coach. Writing those routines got me my job with your show. Then when I got my own show as Jose Jimenez, I brought along Don to be the hotel dick, Byron Glick. He played the same type character as he did in his night club routines.

"I wrote the first 'would you believe' joke in 1954."

Andy Kaufman's popular character Foreign Man is much like Bill's Jose Jimenez. It is not possible to say from what geographical or ethnic background Foreign Man comes. With Jose we did know that he was Latin but beyond that there could be no certainty. At first Bill was simply imitating the voice and accent of a man he happened to meet in Puerto Rico, although whether the gentleman himself was Puerto Rican is not clear. He introduced himself to Dana by saying, "I'm the Dutch representative in the islands."

"Oh," Bill said, "you're from the Netherlands?"

"No," the man said "You don't un'erstan' me. I'm the Dutch representative. You know, Chrysler, Plymouth, Dutch—"

Jimenez first appeared on the Allen show in 1959. "We dreamed up this Spanish Santa Claus for a pre-Christmas show," Bill recalled. "Naturally, when a Spanish Santa says, 'Ho, ho ho,' it comes out 'Jo jo jo.' I played it ala Jose Jimenez and the character really took off." Not long after, Bill recorded an album with Pat Harrington, which I describe in a later section of this chapter.

Born fifty-eight years ago in Quincy, Massachusetts, Dana grew up with five siblings in an impoverished household. His father, an immigrant Hungarian Jew—the family name is Szathmary—had been wiped out in the Depression. Following three-and-a-half years in the U.S. Army's occupation forces in Austria and France, Dana attended Emerson College where he majored in English. After college Bill realized he'd never had a vacation.

"I hopped a bus and 150 rest stops later I arrived in California—the smog ridden dismal Los Angeles bus depot—with twelve dollars in my pocket.

Dana landed an interview as an actor.

"They told me to go home and stay by the telephone. I stayed next to it growing thinner and thinner. The part I was supposed to get—and didn't—was the Humphrey Bogart part in *Sirocco*. I realized that acting jobs were scarce so I began looking for other work."

"I was a telephone paint solicitor for a while. Then I got a job as a Good Humor man, sold shoes at an outlet store and worked at the post office during the Christmas rush. The best job of the lot was at Douglas Aircraft. No wonder we didn't get our missiles off the launching pad!"

Bill worked at Douglas as a layout electrician.

"Some guy came up to me and started talking about cathode asithoscopes. I thought he was putting me on. When I found out he was serious I asked to be transferred to the administration section."

Dana faked his job in administration until he got a call one day from Gene Wood, an old friend now heard as the announcer on "Family Feud." Dana and Wood worked as a nightclub comedy team for a couple of years until Bill began writing for me in 1956. He became my head writer by 1961.

In the early '60s, Dana became a partner in a successful management and advertising company. A client was Herb Alpert and the Tijuana Brass.

Gabe Dell

$\mathcal{G}$ABRIEL DELL DEFINES HIMSELF AS an actor. He first came to national attention as a member of the Dead End Kids, in films. Although he is an adept comic performer, comedy seems always to have been a sideline with him. His sense of the ridiculous is sharp, however, and he was wonderfully effective in countless sketches on our shows. He is also a good dialectician; his Dracula is still the definitive one. Indeed, most comedians and actors who do the Bela Lugosi voice are really doing Gabe's version of it, rather than conforming to the original. The peak moment of hysteria when Gabe did Dracula as one of our Men-on-the-Street, or in the context of a "Where Are They Now?" sketch, came after I would say to him, "Well, Count, I know your many admirers have always been astounded and impressed by the remarkable physical transformation you undergo when you change yourself from a genial, sophisticated member of the aristocracy into a fiendish monster. I wonder if you would *show* us that transformation." Gabe would say, "Certainly, Steef. I'll be glad to," at which he would begin to mix various brightly colored, foaming, smokey liquids on a laboratory table before him, drink the apparently odoriferous mixture and then, to the accompaniment of spooky music, flashing lights and distant thunder, throw himself into some sort of a fit from which he would emerge, a few seconds later, with his face hideously contorted and his eyes wild.

"My goodness, Count," I would say. "How did you do that?"

"Do what, Steef?" he would say, his face suddenly calm, and his tone very matter-of-fact.

Gabe's performances as Dracula always had a particularly nutty element. Frequently he would burst out of the confines of the sketch and stage-scenery in which he had been working, and apparently decide that his very physical survival depended on drinking my blood. I would see him rushing, or creeping, toward me across the stage, and—throwing myself into the nuttiness of the moment—feel unmistakable fear as the

★ 295

arch-fiend advanced upon me, his artificially reddened mouth wide open, teeth glistening, cape raised in a batlike position.

"Ah, Steef," he would say, threateningly, "how handsome you look. What a fine figure of a man you are, Steef! I want to talk to you. I want to be very *close* to you. . . ." And at that he would fling himself at me and I would try to fight him off. Sometimes he would wrestle me out of my chair, if I were behind the desk in a talk-show setting. In other cases he would have to chase me about the stage before catching me, after which we would bump into scenery and fall to the floor. It was always pure, comic mayhem and seemed to delight the members of our crew and staff even more than it did the sometimes puzzled studio audience. I think that at such moments, some part of Gabe actually believed he was Count Dracula, for Gabe—like many comedy performers—has always been something of what is usually called "a character." He does not drive a car, for example, as do the rest of us, but gets about on a very old motorcycle. One time when I played Vegas and we had put a "Bride of Dracula" sketch into the act (which included a black-wigged Jayne in the title role), Gabe put his motorcycle in an old milk-delivery truck we had borrowed, piled in a couple of wooden coffins, and took off. And what a wild two weeks at the Flamingo that was. The audience would shriek with delight every night as his onstage, up-ended wooden coffin would open to reveal an apparently sleeping human vampire within. The wildest night of all happened one time when Jayne was ill. Since we did not want to lose the whole sketch, I played both Jayne's part and my own. My regular role on the sketch was essentially the straight one of the leading man who, having been forced to delay his passage through Transylvania because his car could not pass a bridge which had been downed by heavy flooding, had to put up for the night at Count Dracula's castle. We were doing a musical version of the classic story—*Dracula* as it might have been produced by Rodgers and Hammerstein. I appeared at the castle door, with an attractive young woman, and asked for lodging for the night. Count Dracula welcomed us. A few minutes later, Jayne was supposed to make an entrance, which was signaled by the knocking on a door.

I remember that when the door-knock sounded, Gabe read his usual line, "Who's that?" to which, in this instance, I responded by saying, "I think it's me."

From that point on I did a series of quick changes, somewhat in the manner of the old vaudeville master of quick-change, Owen McGivney. But, of course, none of Jayne's clothes fit me, so the changes were ridiculous. Gabe had no trouble doing all the ad-libbing that was necessary to keep the sketch moving.

In recent years he has appeared on and off Broadway and made occasional television appearances. He was always a million laughs.

*B*RING UP THE SUBJECT OF PRACTICAL jokes and you'll usually discover two violently opposed attitudes. Some regard the practical joke as the highest, most satisfying form of humor. Others insist it is a sadistic, or at least juvenile, type of comedy. In any case, the practical joke was responsible for bringing Pat Harrington, a brilliant funnyman, to humor-hungry American TV audiences. Discovered at the bar of Toots Shor's restaurant by Jonathan Winters one winter afternoon in 1958, Pat (as Guido Panzini, Italian golf pro) was introduced to television night owls. He fooled them completely, and, in fact, did such a remarkable job with his fascinating brand of sleight-of-tongue Italian dialect-and-doubletalk that within a few weeks NBC received a telephone call from a representative of the United States Immigration Service. "Where can we find this guy Panzini?" the official said. "We've got no record of his port of entry."

That Pat could so completely trick millions of people (including myself, by the way) is doubly remarkable when you realize that he does not speak one word of Italian and has never been closer to Italy than Manhattan's West Side, where he spent most of his childhood.

The gag that started him on a show business career came about as a spur-of-the-moment bit of tomfoolery at Toots Shor's, back in 1956, one day when Pat and good friend Lynn Phillips were taking a breather from their jobs as commercial time-salesmen for NBC television.

The *Andrea Doria* collision was the big news of the day and, spying a CBS man at the bar, Phillips decided to put Pat's talent for mimicry to work. "This is Guido Panzini," Phillips said, manufacturing the name on the spot. "He's a survivor of the *Andrea Doria*. He was on the bridge when it happened."

"What was it like up there?" the CBS man asked, all ears.

Guido had great difficulty in explaining, but at last managed to blurt out, "Well, it was a-dark. Verra dark. But we knew we were-a close when-a Captain Calamai ask a question an' somebody answer in Swidish."

In a few minutes the funny little Italian was the center of attention as intrigued barflies clustered around, peppering him with questions. The stunt was such a success that it was taken on the road, to another bar down the street, where some Italian waiters got into a vehement argument with Guido about rumors that the *Andrea Doria* crew had headed for the lifeboats well ahead of some of the passengers.

When Pat realized that Guido could even fool Italians he knew he was home. He and Lynn expanded the routine in the course of time and gradually Guido became a golf pro. The rest, as the saying goes, is history. But this practical joke, momentous as it was, is not Pat's sole experiment with the form. He personally is prouder of another stunt.

"This friend of mine and I were in a bistro one day when we happened to see a little guy who looked exactly like General Sarnoff, the boss of RCA and NBC. We gave him twenty bucks and told him to show up at our office the next morning right after our weekly sales meeting. Well, he did, and by golly he looked more like the General than Sarnoff himself. I had cued him to walk up to me and ask my name. He did. I told him and then, as rehearsed, he asked me what I did in the department. Everybody just stood around with their mouths hanging open. "I'm a time salesman," I said, "and why don't you just get back upstairs and tend to your electrons. I'll take care of the sales if it's all the same to you."

"Well, my fellow workers practically fell through the floor, but my friend, the General, stuck out his hand and shook mine. He said, "Good for you, young man. That's the spirit." And then he walked out. I walked over to the head of our department and said, "Look, I'll be out for the rest of the day, okay?" Before he could think of an answer I walked out, too.

The young Harrington never actually had his sights set on show business. Even after he was working regularly in television he looked upon acting as a sideline. "Some guys play golf as a hobby," he said. "Me, I do the 'Steve Allen Show' for a hobby." It was only in 1960 when our show moved to Hollywood and Pat received a call from Danny Thomas to do a series of guest appearances on his program that he began to realize he might never again sell a piece of TV or radio time.

On our program he was invaluable. Oddly enough his talent at submerging himself into a role was so great that frequently he did not get the credit he deserved simply because, although people would enjoy his characterizations (a famous jockey, a former boxing champ, an Italian busboy, a Scottish laird, etc.) they often didn't realize it was the same man playing all those parts.

On a comedy album recorded in 1961, Pat worked with one of our writer-performers, Bill Dana. Bill was on my writing staff for about five years. Like Pat he is a gifted dialectician and, again like Pat, he has a lightning-quick mind and a superbly delicate sense of the ridiculous.

Probably the most amazing thing about their album is that it was partly ad-libbed. The Guido Panzini golf routine and *Andrea Doria* routines had been done, in essence, before, but oddly enough Pat had never written them down and consequently they tended to vary with each performance.

The other sketches were suggested by those of us present at the recording session and were entirely spontaneous. Elaine May and Mike Nichols blazed this particular trail, the ad-lib comedy-sketch, but Harrington and Dana followed it to new and whacky lengths. So polished and funny were the takes that no routine was even tried a second time in hopes of getting a better version, nor was there more than a slight bit of tape-editing done.

Actually routines of this type were more or less part of the general office and rehearsal-hall routine around our show. Our writers and actors had a wonderful rapport, engaged in a never-ending exchange of nonsense and, to a degree, the album therefore sounded like one of our rehearsals tape-recorded.

Pat is perhaps the only one of our group—the possible exception being Tom Poston—who can play serious roles convincingly. The others all have a certain silly glint in their eye that would render them less than believable if they took on such assignments. But Pat can do it. This, in fact, is one reason why his character of Schneider on "One Day at a Time" is so successful. The jokes, the comic cocky attitude, are all second nature to Pat. And I would imagine that his performance doesn't differ a great deal from the first day of rehearsal read-through to final performance, so well-suited is he to the role of the blarney-talking New York Irish character who—for reasons known only to the producers—has a non-Irish name.

Harrington comes by his talent naturally, in that his father was an entertainer. In the 1920s a comedian named Jack White was one of the best of the small club MC's. He was a witty ad-libber, knew a million old jokes and had a peppy, wake-'em-up delivery. One night he muffed one of his lines and, since ad-libbing was permitted, wasn't too surprised to be heckled by a young Irishman who had just come in from Cincinatti after being fired as a singer at a local radio station. The heckler was Pat Harrington, Sr. After the show White talked to the young man and decided to make him a permanent part of his act. In those days, hecklers—who pretended not to be connected with the show—were a staple of vaudeville entertainment. Gradually Harrington came to play a more important role. One of the group's routines involved White doing Edgar Bergen and Harrington playing Charlie McCarthy. At one point, White would clear his throat, as if to spit, but the dummy—Harrington —would do the *ptooie*. Naturally, the business got a big laugh. This led to the following exchange:

> WHITE: Charlie, if you're not a good boy, I'll put you back in the trunk.
> HARRINGTON: Oh, please don't put me back in the trunk.
> WHITE: Why not? Are you going to behave?
> HARRINGTON: No, the trunk stinks.

Later Frankie Hyers, a spontaneously witty fellow and good tap-dancer, joined the team. They worked at the famous 18 Club, on New York's 52nd Street, for a good many years. For a time Jackie Gleason was part of the troupe. Needless to say, working so loose, and being so naturally witty, they had no trouble topping even more famous ad-libbers who came in to see them, partly because the others were at tables and they had control of the microphones. Reportedly, the only one who ever stumped them was the charming Marie Wilson, one of the early "dumb blonde" comedy actresses. She happened to come in to see them one night and, spying her pretty face, the boys descended on her table and said, "It's great to have you here with us tonight, Marie. Would you like to say a few words?"

Marie's companion frowned and shook his head as if to say, "Don't do it; they'll murder you." Marie nevertheless smiled in a ladylike way, took the microphone, and quietly said, "Don't drink your bathwater."

Three of the best ad-libbers in show business history simply looked at each other and broke up. Not one of them could think of anything to even add, much less to top Ms. Wilson with.

Pat, Jr. would have made a great member of his father's troupe, as he was of mine.

Don
Knotts

ON KNOTTS, NOW 57, IS THE YOUNGEST of four brothers. He grew up in Morgantown, West Virginia, where, he recalls, "I was bullied a lot as a kid. So I told jokes in self-defense." At the age of 13 he took up ventriloquism, borrowing material from Edgar Bergen. Many famous entertainers got their start on the old Major Bowes Amateur Hour. Don auditioned for it and was turned down.

His education at West Virginia University was interrupted by World War II. Drafted into the Army he performed in the service show *Stars And Gripes,* which proved to be a turning point for him. When the show's producer refused to let him work as a comic, Don threw his dummy overboard in the South Pacific and got his first exposure doing stand-up comedy.

After the war Don returned to West Virginia University, got his degree, married, and headed for New York, where he spent five years on a radio kiddie show, "Bobby Benson and His B-Bar-B Riders," playing the part of Windy Wales. Next came two years on Broadway in the cast of *No Time For Sergeants* and three years on "Search for Tomorrow," an early soap opera. He joined our comedy troupe in 1956 and was brilliantly funny from the first.

Don's early monologue, "The Weatherman," which he wrote himself, is, in my opinion, equal to the best of Benchley's spoken essays, to which it bears some slight resemblance in style. Don, like Benchley, is a good natural actor, and each man was superbly realistic in portraying the essentially reasonable, serious individual lost in a crazy world, or at least in an insane predicament of the moment.

He got the idea for his well-known nervous, shaky character early. "I was attending a dinner in Morgantown and the speaker was shaking and spilling water. So one night I dreamed this monologue. Then I got up and wrote it."

THE MEDICAL CONVENTION

Ladies and gentlemen, if I may set a little scene for you, picture a medical convention. The hall is packed with doctors, and a famous Dr. Hillary, from the Acme Drug Company, was supposed to speak and announce a new discovery—but he couldn't make it, and at the last minute the company sent a little man to fill in, a man who hadn't made a speech since high school. And he's been told to "*sell* the new product." He has just been introduced.

Thank you, Mr. Chairman . . . er, Mr. President . . . and good evening. Now I'm not a speaker, but as you know, Dr. Hilly Harrily, er, Hirry Hellery, Harry Hillary was *supposed* to speak, but he couldn't make it. And believe me, taking his place is having to fill a couple of awfully big shoes.

Well, I don't mean to imply that Dr. Hillary has big feet. Just big shoes.

Well, anyway, gentlemen, my laboratory has finally done it. We have come up with the perfect tranquilizing pill. And there it is *(Holds it up)*. It's just a small thing. But believe me, we've had wonderful results with it. Its tranquilizing effect is just remarkable.

(Takes one with a quick, desperate gulp.) And it's different from the other tranquilizers on the market. A real departure. It's neither reserpine, meprobamate, nor chloropromozine.

We call ours simply (stuttering nervously) B--B--Be Calm. Be calm with Be Calm. Say, there's a slogan for you!

In fact, with these pills you can have *(counting on fingers)* calmness, confidence, happiness . . . and the fourth thing is . . . and the fourth thing you can have with these pills is . . . *(sneaks a look at his notes)* . . . a good memory.

Being calm, of course, has many advantages. Makes you steady of hand. This gives you a better penmanship, helps you to write better. In fact, to prove the confidence they give you, we tried them out up at state prison. And just let me read a paragraph from the letter the warden wrote to us. *(The letter shakes so much he can't read it)*

Well, I think I can remember it. *(gulps another pill)* No, I can't. *(reads)*

After taking one of your pills, I let our worst men up out of solitary and permitted them to throw a party among themselves. Head guard Jenkins, who had put these men in solitary, took three of your pills and attended the party unarmed.

He will be buried on Wednesday.

Well, of course, the important thing is that he enjoyed the party.

But the most amazing thing about these pills is that there are no side effects. As you know, some of the other pills do produce various side effects, but so far in ours *(He yawns heavily)* they have found no side effects . . . *(He sneezes hard!)*

Oh, I seem to be catching a cold. Is there a doctor in the house? A little humor there.

Anyway, no side effects with these. We don't have to worry about putting labels on the bottles saying "Causes drowsiness, do not take while driving." *(His eyes are drooping)* Anyway, I wish Dr. Hillary could have been here . . . since he steered the experiments . . . on this pill . . . but he couldn't make it.

He's up at Smileview Sanitarium. He flipped his lid.

They've got him on phenobarbitol. They've got him on phenobarbitol. *(Repeats the phrase like a broken record.)*

But I . . .

(He falls fast asleep, snoring heavily.)

In the other early routine Don did for us, the premise, which he sets up himself, is equally hilarious.

THE WEATHERMAN

I don't know about you people, but I never turn my TV set off until after I've watched the late news and weather report, and I never cease to marvel at the poise and assurance of the weatherman. But, of course, there's absolutely *no* pressure on him. The actual weather forecast is compiled by a competent meteorologist and passed to him to relate to the viewers, so even if the forecast is wrong he can never be blamed, you see. So naturally he's quite at ease before the cameras.

However, I wonder just how calm and poised he would be if the weather report didn't show up in time. Let's look at this man under these circumstances.

You still haven't gotten through to the weather bureau? But, Herb, I've *got* to get through. What am I going to do? I can't stand out there and stall for five minutes! This is a *weather* forecast—I'm not an entertainer!

Please, I've only got five seconds! Can you please get through—can you—*(Sudden smile)* GOOD EVENING!

Hello, everyone, and welcome to your 11:10 ... ah ... weather forecast, as it's brought to you every evening at 11:10 ... at this same time.

The ... ah ... present ... ah ... temperature ... *(Drops a piece of chalk and mumbles as he stoops to retrieve it.)* in degrees.

And the wind is coming from the ... well, the wind is coming from ... well, the wind is coming from the ... and the wind is coming from the window, isn't it?

Close that window back there!

See, it's *heated* here in the studio, so we have no way of telling actually what the weather is outside. Well, we *have* ways! You don't have to ... well ...

Let's just take a little look here at the map. *(No map)*

Well, there she is—the good old USA! This, of course, is Maine.

And this is Florida.

And way over here in the west, of course, is California.

Let's just pencil that in, California there.

And, of course, you do get varying degrees and temperatures in those ... er ... different areas!

I was *born* right in here!

That's ... that's West Virginia there, and I'll bet it's really cold down there now, Herb. Really cold in West Virginia about now, huh?

He doesn't know.

Anyway, I think we are expecting a front in ... backed up by *another* front ... in the *back* there.

Well, actually *this* is the front here, and the back is ... uh ... in the *back*.

That reminds me of a little story about this fella who said to his friend, "I understand you're doing very well by your gambling casino" and his friend said, "No, the gambling casino is just a front. In the *back* is a candy store."

Of course, I mean ... I'm not a comedian or anything ... but I do like to get my licks in.

The *least* you can do is laugh it up, Herb.

Anyway, speaking of weather ... as we are here tonight ... the other day my little boy was asked by his teacher to spell "weather" and he spelled it w-a-n-t-h-e-r ... and that's just about the worst *spell* of weather we've had in a long time ... *(ha .. ha)*

(Dying) Oh, boy!

Can you get me an *old* report, Herb? Give me an *old* one! Another *day*. *Any* day .. QUICK!

Oh, here's a *bulletin,* folks! Just came in. Heavy snowfalls are predicted in the Valley Forge area. Troop movements have been halted by General Washington—That's not funny, Herb. That's not funny!

Are you leaving? Are you *leaving*, Herb? Don't leave.

Would you check and see if it's raining? Oh, never mind. Fred is still here. Good old Fred, he'll stay with me, won't you, Fred?

Anyway, folks, we'll be right back after this message from our sponsor. What? No?

Well, then, we seem to no longer *have* a sponsor.

All-in-all, two of the funniest monologues in comedy history.

Although Don played in all sorts of sketches during the four years he was with us, he is best remembered for his work in the Man on the Street routines. We simply took the character he had created for himself in his two early monologues, and our great writers—Stan Burns and Herb Sargent, later Don Hinkley, Bill Dana, Leonard Stern, Arne Sultan, and Marvin Worth—created routines on the simple theme of Don's nervousness. One joke was so strong that it has subsequently been "borrowed" by any number of other performers and shows. Don claimed to be a football coach—a funny idea in itself, given Knotts's physical reality—who had just seen his team win an important Thanksgiving Holiday game. "Two of the biggest players on the team," he said, "lifted me up to their shoulders—and then one of them said something that made me very nervous."

"What was that?" I asked.

"'Make a wish,'" he said.

Another joke lifted by less imaginative comics was the formula involving various switches on the names Don used in the Man on the Street sketches. Louis Nye's character was always known as Gordon Hathaway, but with Don we deliberately gave him different initials every time, although using the surname Morrison. One exchange went as follows.

STEVE: Good evening, sir. What is your name?

DON: *(Trembling violently)* My name is K. B. Morrison.

STEVE: And what do you do for a living, Mr. Morrison?

DON: I'm a munitions and bomb-disposal expert.

STEVE: I see. By the way, what do the initials K. B. stand for?

DON: Ka-boom!

In another sketch:

> STEVE: Ah, here's an interesting-looking man on the street. And what is your name, sir?
> DON: My name is D. B. Morrison.
> STEVE: Nice to meet you, Mr. Morrison. What do you do for a living?
> DON: I'm an animal trainer. I work in a cage with lions and tigers.
> STEVE: I see. By the way, what do the initials D. B. stand for?
> DON: Down, boy!

After our program Don went on to five years on "The Andy Griffith Show," then did several films. Most recently he's been featured on the ABC network's popular situation comedy, "Three's Company."

Steve Lawrence

*P*ERHAPS THE WITTIEST OF THE OLD gang, the reader may be surprised to learn, was Steve Lawrence, the young singer who was part of the "Tonight" show from the first moment it went on the air as a local production of NBC's New York station in late 1953. Steve auditioned wearing the same white sailor suit he had worn a few nights earlier when he had won a prize on the "Arthur Godfrey Talent Scouts" program. He looked about 16 at the time and at the moment of this writing—mid-1982—did not look a great deal older.

We hired Steve because of his beautiful baritone crooner's voice. Eventually, after three years of experience on the "Tonight" show, as well as countless performances in night clubs, concerts, and television guest appearances, Steve developed the polish to perform in light sketches, although such duty has been more or less par-for-the-course for singers in the field of television variety. But as effective as Steve is in such relatively formal settings, his true comic gift flourishes—alas for the general public—in purely ad-lib social situations. One night recently, for example, I attended a surprise birthday party for a dear friend, comedy writer Saul Turtletaub, given by his wife, Shirley. A number of the men in attendance were long-time professional jokesmiths. Each spoke and was richly funny. Humorous remarks were also delivered by Mary Ann Mobley and her husband, Gary Collins, ventriloquist Shari Lewis, Alan Alda and his wife, Arlene, actress Janet Leigh, Eydie Gorme, and myself. It was one of those warm, magic evenings when a group of close friends could be assured of being understood by others who spoke the same language, a situation in which humor seems invariably to flourish.

To give you an idea what sort of repartee characterized the evening, a comedy writer named Sam Denoff spoke first, made just a few brief remarks and unexpectedly concluded by saying, "And now, ladies and gentlemen, I give you Steve Allen."

I had prepared absolutely nothing to say and was totally blank-minded as I rose.

"To tell you the truth," I said, "I stand before you without a single thought in my head."

"That never stopped you before," Shari Lewis said.

Again, every one of us who spoke was greeted with the heartiest laughter from all present. But far and away the funniest speaker of the evening was Steve Lawrence.

Near the end of the evening, sensing that if someone did not move toward a conclusion the banter might go on forever—or at least too long—I rose and said, "Saul, if someone doesn't soon say, 'And in conclusion—' we may be here long enough for my jacket to go out of style."

"That happened some time ago," Steve called out.

Louis Nye

*A*LTHOUGH I AM FREQUENTLY CREDITED with having introduced Louis Nye to television, I did not. I discovered him working on a more-or-less dreadful late night local show in New York, a program on which he was the one bright note. It was not that all the other participants in the program were untalented—though some of them, I suppose, were—but even the ones with ability seemed adrift in a sea of production-confusion. It is a rare performer who can look good with everything collapsing around him. But Louis made me laugh every time I saw him on this other show.

Shortly thereafter, I happened to see Louis getting off an elevator in the NBC section of the RCA building.

Introducing myself I said "Louie, I've seen you on that show you've been doing and I think you're terrific. I'll be starting a new program soon and if you'd like to be part of it, from time to time, it would be my pleasure to have you join us." The only regular members of the program's family, when it started, were orchestra leader Bobby Byrne, announcer Gene Rayburn, and a boy-singer and girl-singer. The boy was Steve Lawrence, who a few nights earlier had won a prize on an "Arthur Godfrey Talent Scouts" show. The young woman was Helene Dixon. But I told our production people—and our two writers, Stan Burns and Herb Sargent—that I wanted to use Louis frequently and so it turned out.

One of the reasons I had enjoyed Nye's work from the first is that he is one of that small group of comedians who have what I call a Silly Center. I do not mean to suggest that comedians without such a quality are inferior. Some of the most successful comedians of our time, in fact, do not have the quality of silliness: Bob Hope, Danny Thomas, and Jack Benny, for example. Even so great and respected a humorist as Will Rogers—whose work I loved—did not have a Silly Center. Some who do are Tim Conway, John Byner, Dom deLuise, Mel Brooks, Jonathan

Winters, and Sid Caesar. In any event, Louis has it. Consequently he always amuses me, even when he is working with less-than-brilliant material.

When performing, Lou contributes a good deal more than is on the paper. There is a sense in which every comedian—even every actor—does this, so I stress that I am not talking about that always-to-be expected something that a performer adds to the written word. In Louis's case—as in Sid Caesar's—not only do you get a funniness of performance, you actually get more words than those the writers provided. In most cases writers are not entirely happy about this. But in the case of performers such as Louis, Sid Caesar, Jonathan Winters, Robin Williams and some others the writers rarely complain, because they are aware that the comedian is adding rather than detracting.

Another interesting point about Nye's style of comedy is that it has very little relation to reality. Like Jonathan and Sid his characterizations are wild, impressionistic, exaggerated cartoons. Comedians like Bob Newhart, Bill Daily—even Tim Conway, to some extent—are close to reality. Louis, never.

Born in Hartford, Connecticut, the son of a grocery store owner, Louis as a boy in his father's store watched and listened to people from different ethnic backgrounds. In time he began to imitate them. He realized while still young that he wanted to be an actor, but didn't know quite how to become one. His high school guidance counselor couldn't help, and when he tried to join the dramatic club he found he was ineligible because he had not been able to pass algebra.

Nye took a part-time job at a local radio station, doing assorted characters, until he finished high school. After knocking about in summer stock, he headed for New York where he did radio work until he got his first small Broadway part. He was in three Broadway musicals before landing his first television job. He received important early TV exposure on Jack Paar's old morning show.

After our chance meeting at NBC, Nye hasn't stopped working since. He has appeared on television with Jack Benny, Bob Hope, Jonathan Winters, Jimmy Durante, Ed Sullivan, Jackie Gleason, and Steve Martin, and was a semi-regular on "The Beverly Hillbillies." He has also made several films and continues to perform in nightclubs and theaters all over the country.

Unlike the routines of Don Knotts, which read almost as funny as they play, most of Nye's humor does not successfully make the transition to paper, because it is not primarily verbal. The faces of a great many successful comedians do not mirror a large range of emotions. Nothing especially funny ever happened on the faces of Bob Hope, George Burns, Fred Allen, Bob Newhart—or myself, for that matter. But Louis makes incredible use of his face for comic effect, somewhat in the way that the great Harry Ritz did. When Louis, for example, does a dialect, he not only *sounds* Italian, Greek, Jewish, German, or whatever; he somehow magically makes himself *look* Italian, Greek, Jewish, German, and what-have-you. He does not simply do a voice transformation as do Rich Little and most impressionists. With Louis a mysterious total transformation takes place.

In contrast to the other members of our gang, Louis always worked with a hint of the naughty. I do not refer to the sort of Teamster-gutter language now common among even young woman entertainers. Nor do I refer to Louis' sexual innuendos critically. Somehow from him they have never seemed objectionable. This is partly, I think, because the actual Louis Nye always seems somehow invisible. He seems to slide—as does Jonathan Winters—from one characterization to another. And even when he seems to be working as himself, he often does not speak in a truly natural manner, but puts things into invisible quotation marks, disguising his true self—wherever that lies—and donning a series of comic masks. One of his older routines, for example, involves an outline for the protocol for showering with a member of the opposite sex. Even back in the late 1950s and early 1960s, this routine—which, in the hands of some, could be offensive—never really seemed so. Nor were there ever any complaints when Louis raised the question of why all television newscasters must be straight-arrow Anglo types, which led him into a rendition of the nightly news as read by a thickly accented, middle-aged Jewish newsman who insisted on adding little warm, human touches to the news items he related. In Louis's lampoons of Japanese films such as *Rashomon* or *Shogun,* I do not think even the most humorless Japanese have ever objected to his hilarious characterizations of various Japanese men and women in the story, and his references to certain parts of the body.

Nye's occasional sexual innuendos seem never to offend even conservative audiences. In the same way Gay Liberationists seem not to take any exception to the homosexual component in some of his characterizations. The question first came up in the mid-1950s, when Louis did his famous Gordon Hathaway character as one of the Men-on-the-Street.

There were never, needless to say, any jokes even remotely suggesting that Gordon was homosexual. It *was* clear, from the beginning, that he lived with his mother. But Gordon always spoke in a somewhat effeminate manner. It was never at any time the broad, vaudeville or burlesque lisping and mincing that most older comedians do when they portray effeminacy. There was in Gordon Hathaway, as someone once put it, just a hint of mint. I've seen my share of critical mail about my television comedy programs over the last three decades but never saw a single letter—from either straights or gays—even mentioning this aspect of Louis's characterization, much less complaining about it. I think it is Louis's air of carefree, airy innocence and basic niceness that explains this, since the same material in the hands of other performers would, by some, be considered objectionable.

Louis's army routine is, beyond question, one of the single most effective comedy monologues of all time. How it would play today to an audience of young people, few of whom have ever served in the army, navy, or marines, I do not know, although I'm sure it would get laughs even from them. But to a slightly older generation it is as sure-fire a comic exercise as the art has ever known. The primary speaker is a lower-middle class white army sergeant who is welcoming new recruits into the army. The lines would be amusing even if delivered by a relatively inept performer. The sergeant from Brooklyn is assisted in his effort by a corporal from a southern state whose accent is so thick that it is impossible to understand much of what he is saying. Some audiences interpret the character as black, but it doesn't matter whether he is perceived as black or white. The important thing is that his backwoods southern accent is almost incomprehensible to northern urban ears. Each man, attempting to enlighten new arrivals—*enrivees,* Louis calls them—reveals himself to be incredibly ignorant. The sergeant refers to the United States as being a "democratical way of life." But somehow one comes away with the feeling that Nye is not really putting down such characters, but simply having good-natured, even affectionate fun with them.

One of Louis's occasional vehicles is "Charley's Aunt," but unlike some comic performers Nye has never settled into one basic role or character. A perfectionist, he never stops adding to his seemingly inexhaustible family of comic characters.

"I'm a people-watcher," he says. "I enjoy eavesdropping on the sounds, the looks, the gestures, and the mannerisms. And not just people: animals, too—" whereupon he miraculously does his favorite parlor or talk-show impression of a dog howling in the distance.

Although, like all comedians, Louis has certain standard bits and routines, he does not perform them the same night after night as do less-imaginative performers. There is always, with Lou, an element of spontaneity and expansion of territory previously explored and conquered.

*I*N THE MID-FIFTIES TOM POSTON HAD had more experience as an actor, in both comic and serious roles, than any other member of our team, so he would be given certain kinds of assignments that might not go to the others. Tom's first appearance on television was in 1947—when the medium itself was merely a technological wonder and few people had sets in their homes—in a production of *Cyrano de Bergerac,* starring Jose Ferrer. The two had earlier performed the same production on Broadway. Poston also worked in early television productions of *Macbeth,* starring Charlton Heston, and *The Tempest,* with Richard Burton.

With this sort of background, Tom was occasionally given the assignment of playing straight for me, since our other cuckoos had such an innately comic image that they were not believable in a supposedly realistic setting. It was Tom, then, who worked with me in "The Question Man" sketches, in which he would give me an answer and I would produce a question to fit it. The routine is familiar to a younger generation of television viewers as "The Great Carnak" of "The Tonight Show."

Another delightful comic character that Tom did for us from time to time was Francis X. Tishman, a former silent screen idol whose name, of course, was a switch on the actual film star of the 1920s, Francis X. Bushman. Tom wore a sort of high, Shakespearian wig and exaggeratedly heavy eye makeup, and all-in-all looked remarkably handsome indeed, as he answered my questions in a voice that, because it would crack like a teenager's every few seconds, had obviously contributed to Tishman's failure to repeat his silent film success once talking pictures had been invented.

Tom is also in that category of long-faced, blue-eyed comedians who have been influenced by the great Stan Laurel. Because of his slight resemblance to Laurel he was able to do a marvelously realistic impersonation of him, sometimes working with the clever Chuck McCann—the John Candy of the 1950s—as Oliver Hardy. Stan Laurel, parenthetically, was a fan of our show and we naturally let him know that we were doing the sketch, which he later told us he had enjoyed enormously.

But the characterization with which Tom made the most lasting impression was that of the dopey Man-on-the-Street who was so out of it that he had trouble remembering his name. It is one of the best-remembered routines from the old show. This characterization, too, was influenced by Stan Laurel, although essentially it emerged out of Tom's own creativity. The character grew out of conversations with Tom that took place in our offices. We had an open-door policy in those days whereby almost any funny performer could wander in, sit down with our staff, and kick around ideas for sketches and characters. The writers began to ad-lib questions to Tom, just sitting around in the office, and he improvised some responses. He remembers that I was present at the meeting, putting questions to him, although I'm sorry to say I can't recall the incident. In any event, the gimmick of extreme forgetfulness came out of the office improvizations and "The-Man-Who-Can't-Remember-His-Name" was introduced at once, sandwiched between Louis Nye's Gordon Hathaway and Don Knott's Nervous Little Man.

Tom had prepared for the legitimate theater in the early phase of his career by studying at the American Academy of Dramatic Arts in New York. He still laughs recalling how his acting instructor, an old gentleman named Charles Jehlinger, used to get his name wrong, calling him Mr. Piston. Eventually, Tom realized that Jehlinger had been addressing him by the wrong name on purpose, as a way of making him laugh and hence relax.

Although Tom is often referred to as one of the performers I introduced to television, he had, in fact, worked in television before I did. He had also—at the same time that I was hosting the original "Tonight Show"—been the host of a daily two-and-one-half hour program seen from 12:30 to 3:00 P.M. on WABC-TV in New York, working with two friends of mine, a singer named Marian Colby and another vocalist who would years later star in companies of *Fiddler On The Roof,* Bob Carroll. Comedian-straight man Gene Wood, who later did a two-man act with Bill Dana, was also a member of the WABC show's cast. Called "Entertainment," the program permitted Tom and the writers to be as creative as they wished. On one show he was discovered lying face down on the floor, from which position he looked up into the camera and said,

"This is for all the people who have been saying, 'You just watch—that kid is gonna fall flat on his face.'" Another funny routine from the show involved Tom supposedly talking to his mother on the telephone. She asked if he would wave to her, which he did, but she reported that she couldn't get the TV set adjusted properly—a common problem in the 1950s. At this point the sketch became slightly unrealistic in that Tom was telling his mother that she was turning the wrong knob on the set. The program's other viewers saw Tom fading from view and going in and out of focus, appearing in negative image, etc. *New York Telegraph* critic Leo Mishkin, reviewing "Entertainment" at the time said, "One day this week Mr. Poston went down into the audience, just like Steve Allen, and persuaded some of the customers down there to come on up to the stage and dance around a while with the other members of the cast. I also have some recollection of Mr. Poston being given advice on how to behave like a really big-time master of ceremonies—you know, the surprise like when he finds the camera peeping over his shoulder. Or the friendly, smiling look when he fades off on the introduction of another singer. Or the startled expression when he comes up on this TV audience without ever guessing that they were there. You've seen 'em, I'm sure."

Like the other members of our comedy family, Tom continued to be active after we all went our separate ways early in the 1960s. For several years thereafter he was a regular panelist on the popular "To Tell the Truth." Oddly enough, he eventually concluded—as have other entertainer-panelists—that being so closely identified with a game show became, in time, a mixed blessing. "A lot of people began to think of me as just a panelist," he has said, "not even that my participation was to the extent of being the host."

My wife, Jayne, among others, has experienced the same problem. After having distinguished herself on Broadway and in films, she accepted an assignment as panelist on CBS's "I've Got a Secret" and remained with the series for seven years. This was at the time when game shows of that sort were enormously popular and both "I've Got a Secret" and "What's My Line" were often in the Top Ten. At first the results were beneficial in that when Jayne was in plays—*Tea and Sympathy,* for example—she would often set box office records because she had become nationally known as a panelist. But after a few years the strong identification as TV game-player somewhat obscured her talent as both a serious actress and a comedienne, particularly the former.

In time Tom had similar misgivings about his long tour of duty on "To

Tell the Truth." "People not only thought of me as a panelist," he has said, "but because I was always seated people thought I was short."

During the 1960s and '70s Tom was in frequent demand as an actor in plays and also made a number of film appearances. More recently he played a regular character, "Mr. Bickly," on the popular "Mork and Mindy" show, which he greatly enjoyed. "When I see Robin or Johnny (Winters) working or improvising in front of me or anybody else who will stand and watch—oh, God, it's hysterical. My jaw just sags." In September 1982, he was a regular on Bob Newhart's new series.

Tom was always gracious enough to acknowledge the talent of others. I am pleased to acknowledge his.

Conclusion

N O SPECIAL SIGNIFICANCE SHOULD be attached to the inclusion or exclusion of one comedian or another from either *Funny People* or *More Funny People*. There is room for less than twenty analytical essays per book. There are major comedians galore about whom I have not yet written—Chaplin, W. C. Fields, Robert Benchley, Will Rogers—and there are some I have written about who I would not list among the funniest performers of the century. In any event, work has already begun on *Funny People, Volume III*. What has emerged so far—and what, oddly, I did not anticipate at the outset—is a portrait of the typical American comedian as personally a tortured soul, thus authenticating the stereotype of the Pagliacci who makes others laugh though his own heart is breaking. The stereotype, of course, does not apply to all cases. And even as regards those comedians who are most clearly the victims of unstable childhoods and who seem the least able to sustain mature adult relationships, it is only rarely the case that while a performer is actually on stage he is, in his secret heart, in a state of misery because of the torment of his personal life. It is truer to say that the moments of greatest contentment, happiness, and elation for many comedians comes while they are on stage, even at times in their lives when they are most unhappy. A comedian may be temporarily crushed by personal tragedy, by the failure of his show—a cancelled television series, an out-of-town closing of a theatrical production, negative reaction to his work in a film—but if he can just manage to get on stage in front of a thousand people who find him amusing, his back will stiffen, his eyes shine, and his blood race. At such times he may be likened to a great athlete. Those who depend on the strength or agility of their bodies, too, may know collapsed marriages, divorces, angers, hatreds, paranoia, drug or alcohol abuse. But while they are in the ring or on the playing field, while they are winning, performing gracefully, with the cheers of thousands ringing in their ears—at those times they are happy, not secretly miserable.

The misery returns only when the crowds have gone home. When the theater is darkened and the parking lot is empty, the performer must then face the painful reality of his offstage life. It is then that the clown may weep or rage.

CREDITS